PRAISE FOR *MARKETING METRICS*

D1091923

The days of fuzzy math and pure right-brained creativity in marketing are over. To build a career in marketing requires data literacy, but the metrics used are often superficial and too narrow to build a successful strategy. Christina Inge shows how to harness the power of big data analytics to drive better decisions; but beyond that, she addresses the needed mindset, teamwork and soft skills to humanize data and build successful marketing programs rooted in customer empathy. A must-read for the modern marketer.
Lauren Turner, Director, Global Customer Marketing, Qlik

Christina Inge dives deep into building a data-driven culture to catalyze business growth. She goes beyond best practices and details techniques that any business can deploy to make better decisions based on data.
Dale Bertrand, Founder, Fire&Spark marketing agency

This is a book for anyone who is interested in learning about the numbers and data behind successful marketing campaigns. From direct mail to email, social and mobile, whatever channel is being used to market products and services, you'll learn what it takes to set goals with confidence, gather the data and analyze the results. It's a book for anybody who wants to ace the subject of marketing analytics.
Bob Cargill, former President of the New England Direct Marketing Association and American Marketing Association Boston

Whether you're justifying your marketing spend or trying to predict future market conditions, measurement skills are key to a successful marketing career. This book insightfully weaves practical measurement tips and techniques into a series of strategic frameworks that will help marketers make the right choices no matter what the challenge may be.
Todd Van Hoosear, Senior Lecturer, Mass Communication, Advertising and Public Relations, College of Communication, Boston University

For years I've turned to my friend and colleague Christina Inge for any and all questions related to marketing metrics. Not only does she know the subject inside and out, she explains it in simple and clear ways for those of us who are novices. Now that I have my copy of *Marketing Metrics*, I may not need to bug Christina quite so much!

Ed Powers, Faculty Lead, MS in Corporate and Organizational Communication, Northeastern University

Marketing Metrics

*Leverage Analytics and Data to
Optimize Marketing Strategies*

Christina Inge

KoganPage

Publisher's note

Every possible effort has been made to ensure that the information contained in this book is accurate at the time of going to press, and the publishers and authors cannot accept responsibility for any errors or omissions, however caused. No responsibility for loss or damage occasioned to any person acting, or refraining from action, as a result of the material in this publication can be accepted by the editor, the publisher or the author.

First published in Great Britain and the United States in 2022 by Kogan Page Limited

2nd Floor, 45 Gee Street
London
EC1V 3RS
United Kingdom
www.koganpage.com

8 W 38th Street, Suite 902
New York, NY 10018
USA

4737/23 Ansari Road
Daryaganj
New Delhi 110002
India

Kogan Page books are printed on paper from sustainable forests.

ISBNs

Hardback   978 1 3986 0661 6
Paperback   978 1 3986 0659 3
Ebook   978 1 3986 0660 9

British Library Cataloguing-in-Publication Data
A CIP record for this book is available from the British Library.

Library of Congress Cataloging-in-Publication Data
Names: Inge, Christina, author.
Title: Marketing metrics : leverage analytics and data to optimize
    marketing strategies / Christina Inge.
Description: London, United Kingdom ; New York, NY : KoganPage, 2022. |
    Includes bibliographical references and index.
Identifiers: LCCN 2022026862 (print) | LCCN 2022026863 (ebook) | ISBN
    9781398606593 (paperback) | ISBN 9781398606616 (hardback) | ISBN
    9781398606609 (ebook)
Subjects: LCSH: Marketing–Management–Data processing. |
    Marketing–Technological innovations.
Classification: LCC HF5415.125 .I54 2022 (print) | LCC HF5415.125 (ebook)
    | DDC 658.8–dc23/eng/20220615
LC record available at https://lccn.loc.gov/2022026862
LC ebook record available at https://lccn.loc.gov/2022026863

Typeset by Hong Kong FIVE Workshop
Print production managed by Jellyfish
Printed and bound by CPI Group (UK) Ltd, Croydon CR0 4YY

CONTENTS

13   What are the skills of a metrics-driven marketer? 270

14   Marketing metrics resources 286

PREFACE

This book started one cold day in the mid-2000s when I learned about this new tool called Google Analytics that could tell you what people were looking at on your website, how long they were staying, even where they were located. It was the data tool I had needed all my career as a content creator, ad copywriter, and digital media developer, but had not even imagined existed.

At the time, I was working in market research for a publishing company and as a marketing copywriter. As someone who loves data and has always been interested in understanding how people interact with web content, Google Analytics was like a dream come true. For the first time ever, I could see what people were looking at on my clients' websites and how long they were staying. Armed with this knowledge, I could begin to understand what people found interesting and make better decisions about the content I created.

Fast-forward a few years, and Google Analytics has become an essential tool for anyone with a website—including you, whether you're an online business owner, marketer, or just someone with a blog. In this book, I'll show you how to use marketing metrics to create more strategic marketing across a range of programs and channels.

Marketing long struggled with being seen as essential to a business. Challenging to measure for decades, it was seen as a cost centre. No matter how many leads you generated, how much traffic and conversions you drove, you could never prove that sales growth was due to marketing efforts, and not random chance or the product's attractiveness alone. Marketing was often not part of the C suite, and it was often the first to be cut in a downturn. Metrics offered the promise of a better way of understanding and structuring marketing. Marketing measurement grew from a few simple tools to the robust ecosystem we have today, and with it, a new awareness of marketing's centrality to business was born.

This book was also born on the Longfellow Bridge in Boston, MA in the spring of 2014. I had been laid off on a Monday afternoon from a startup that had run out of capital. I headed out into the April sunshine at 1 pm, parted with my intern, who had left rather than do the work of two for low wages, walked around Boston Common, and began to stroll and think. The world needed a new kind of marketing agency, one that was metrics-first, that used a collaborative, educational model. I was tired of working 70-hour weeks while my real dreams back-burnered. My mother, aged 67, had terminal cancer. I felt life was short. I began to walk the city, planning my company, where I could start to create a new vision of how marketing works. By the time I reached the bridge, I was calling an attorney friend, Rob, to help me incorporate my business. "Finally!" he said. "I was wondering when you were going to start your own firm. When did you get laid off?" "About an hour ago," I replied. He laughed and gently suggested that I spend two weeks creating a business plan, then he'd help me file the paperwork to form the company.

I reached the bottom of the bridge, and bumped into an entrepreneur friend, Byron. He asked how I was doing, and I told him the whole thing. He congratulated me and said he'd like to work with me.

The next day, I created a simple logo using PowerPoint—I was launching an agency. The phone rang hours later. It was my first customer, a connection I had made years before. In 25 hours, I had gone from laid off to a company with customers. Shortly thereafter, my mother found an online posting for Impact Hub, a new community for socially minded entrepreneurs launching in Boston. In exchange for a few hours' help running the community, they were offering free office space in downtown Boston. When I arrived to interview for the opportunity, the building was being gutted, and only the freight elevator worked, which you reached by walking over plywood. I got the role, which entailed eight hours a week of everything from loading dishwashers to organizing events. The building slowly transformed into one of the most beautiful in the city, and the community grew from 20 to over 200. It became my work family, the home for my business that every entrepreneur should have. Thoughtlight, my boutique agency born on a walk through Boston, has flourished for the better part of a decade, and I owe it all to embracing marketing metrics.

We have served everyone from Fortune 500 companies to small startups with our brand of data-driven marketing. We have been able to show the value of marketing through tangible results, and our clients continue to see remarkable growth as a result. We have created brand strategies, supported digital transformation, and brought marketing back to the heart of a business by aligning it with customer-centricity. Through it all, we have been blessed with an amazing team of talented individuals who share our vision and values.

The Covid years brought personal loss: of my mother, of the Hub community, of a sense of certainty. But it has also brought a sense that the things that once felt so sure have crumbled, often for the better. Marketing is no longer a vague, unmeasurable cost centre. We are rebuilding, reinventing, and reimagining what it means to be a marketer. We are also rebuilding ourselves.

This book is dedicated to my team, especially James and Anil, my students, my Fellows Matt Cole and Ram Raju, my Impact Hub family: Hilary, Alisha, and Geoff, and many marketers out there looking for a compass to navigate the world to come. It's time to build.

01

Data-driven strategy

Many brands talk about creating a data-driven strategy. Yet, for most companies, the use of data is still focused more on validating whether what has happened in the past or what's happening now is working. Few companies take the time to ask what they should do differently or better in the future. Yet, it is this long-term strategy that drives real results. You can optimize channels and campaigns using limited amounts of data, often with strong impact on the business. That impact is short-term, however, and also limited to the teams that are doing the testing. When one person moves on or gets too busy with other work, the use of metrics tends to deteriorate. That is the problem with informal use of marketing metrics across the organization. Solutions using data tend to be spot solutions, inconsistently applied, and relevant to only part of the firm's marketing. There needs to be a more systematic approach. In this chapter, we will learn how important metrics today are to the average marketer, and the many different ways you can use data to improve your marketing, based on real-life stories.

The marketing metrics revolution

Marketing metrics are critical to the success of any organization. They provide a way to measure and understand what is working and what is not in your marketing efforts. However, as with any tool, if they are not used correctly, they can do more harm than good.

In the past, marketing metrics were often confined to simple measurements such as website visits, click-through rates, and email open rates. While these measurements are still important, they no longer provide a complete view of how well your marketing is performing.

With the advent of big data, new marketing metrics are now available that can help you understand how customers are interacting with your brand. These metrics can help you determine such things as where customers are coming from, what they are looking for on your website, and how likely they are to purchase from you.

Big data has also allowed for the development of predictive analytics, which can help you determine what customers are likely to do in the future. This information can help you better target your marketing efforts and increase your chances of success.

In order to take advantage of all that big data has to offer, brands are struggling to keep up with the range of metrics they have on hand. Seeing the complete picture, across channels, customer segments, and metrics points, is still a critical challenge for many organizations. Here are some statistics on how marketers are making sense—or not—of their metrics today:

1 Consumers say that they are 80 percent more likely to purchase from a brand that uses their data to personalize offers, messaging, and other aspects of marketing.[1]

2 Nearly two-thirds (64 percent) of executives feel that data-driven marketing is critical to competitive advantage.[2]

3 The CMO Council finds that marketing funnels are "no longer linear," which makes customer journeys more complex to understand than ever.[3]

4 Forty percent of marketers are increasing their investments in data-driven marketing.[4]

5 When it comes to what data organizations are using to get results, 63 percent of companies that have increased their conversion rates using data have used customer journey metrics, while 83 percent have used consumer data for personalization.[5]

6 Overall, 67 percent of companies surveyed in a Merkle study are using at least some personalization across several channels, yet they struggle with the quality of that data.[6]

7 Over 90 percent of all display advertising is being bought programmatically—that is, based on extensive data on consumer behavior and ad inventories.[7]

8 US firms spend $30.6 billion on marketing data annually, according to a Statista dossier.[8]

9 Of companies surveyed for the Crayon State of Competitive Intelligence report 98 percent say that data about their competitive landscape is mission-critical.

10 One-quarter of marketers look to their metrics every time they make decisions, as found by the firm Ascend in a recent study.[9]

Yet, marketers are still seeing challenges. These center on the effective use of data, the need to find new ways to collect it after the end of third-party cookies, and the ability to act on data in near-real-time, according to *AdWeek*, the advertising industry's leading publication.[10]

Brands also struggle to personalize consumer messaging in ways that help consumers by providing relevant content, products, and offers, while still respecting their privacy. All told, marketers face more challenges in collecting accurate metrics and getting their organizations to act on them. They also struggle to use them to satisfy consumer needs and optimize marketing key performance indicators such as ad clicks and impressions.

- According to a recent Merkle report, 90 percent of surveyed brands say they need to consolidate consumer profile data.[11]

- Eighty-seven percent of marketers say that their organization's data is under-utilized.[12]

- Consumers are worried about how companies handle their data: 79 percent say they are at least somewhat concerned about how responsible companies are with their data, and 66 percent will stop buying from a company that they feel misused their data, according to the Adobe Trust Report.[13]

- Metrics solutions that will help them address the post-cookie world are a top priority for 57 percent of marketing professionals, according to eMarketer.[14]

- In 2021, social media clicks and impressions grew by a mere 13 percent, roughly half to one-third the growth rates of 2020 and 2019, according to Kenshoo.[15]

- Only 37.7 percent of marketing projects used metrics in decision making, according to Statista.[16]

- The average data breach—when a firm's consumers' data gets compromised by hackers—costs a company over US $8 million, notes Statista.[17]

- Fifty-seven percent of marketers say their efforts to track competitors are ad hoc or just coming together, according to the Crayon State of Competitive Intelligence Report.[18]

- Fifty percent of marketers surveyed for Marketing Charts said their data is poorly organized.[19]
- Another 38 percent say that metrics-gathering processes are too slow, according to the same study.

With all of this data available, why is it harder than ever to use it strategically across the whole organization?

One reason is that data is becoming more complex and harder to manage. With the advent of big data, artificial intelligence (AI), and machine learning, data is now being generated in ways that it never was before. Also, with the General Data Protection Regulation (GDPR) going into effect in the European Union in May 2018, data privacy is now a critical issue for companies.

Furthermore, data is often siloed in different parts of the organization, making it difficult to get a comprehensive view. As marketing increasingly uses first-party data (information collected directly from customers), it becomes more important to have good internal data practices in place.

In addition, brands are challenged to keep up with the latest martech advances. While most marketers feel good about their understanding of current marketing technologies, they are uncertain about their ability to use AI and machine learning for marketing purposes. According to Gartner, for instance, just 17 percent of marketing leaders use AI to personalize the customer experience, even though they see personalization as a key priority.[20]

Finally, marketing still needs to become more agile in order to take advantage of the latest opportunities. Too often, companies don't act on data because doing so means changing processes that took years to build and will take months or more to replace with more responsive, real-time ways of doing things.

All of this makes it hard to use data to inform marketing decisions. We're doing a decent job, often, of making spot decisions based on data. An email subject line tested here, an ad click-through rate improved there, and we're happy to be using metrics effectively. We have the power to do so much more with the right investment in metrics.

Building a metrics-driven culture

In order to use data effectively, companies need to develop a metrics-driven culture. This involves creating a metrics-driven mindset within the company and then empowering people across the organization with the ability to make decisions using data. The goal should be for everyone in the company to be looking at data and asking themselves how they can use it in their work to drive better results. But if you want to innovate and leap ahead of the competition, you need to use data in a much more fundamental way—by looking at how it can shape your overall strategy.

In order to create a metrics-driven strategy, you need to start by looking at your data in new ways. You need to ask yourself questions that you haven't asked before. You also need to build structures that span marketing channels. For instance, you might want to create a centralized data warehouse or use marketing technology that can help you track customer behavior across channels.

Once you have the data, you need to find the right people to analyze it and make decisions based on it. This is where the data-driven mindset comes in. You need to be comfortable with ambiguity and uncertainty. That probably sounds a bit surprising. After all, isn't the use of data about removing uncertainty? Numbers are supposed to be cold, hard facts; they are not supposed to be ambiguous. But they are.

This is because data is only one piece of the puzzle. You also need to understand your business and how it works. You need to have a good understanding of the customer and what they want. And you need to have a clear idea of where you want to go. Only then can you use data to help you get there. Metrics, in brief, are all about context. Take, for instance, pricing data. What is the ideal price of something?

You're about to say "It depends." The ideal price of a Rolex is different from the ideal price of, say, a box of tissues. But what if you are a mid-range watch company that wants to increase market share? You might lower the price of your watches based on what the full range of watches in the market cost, from Rolexes to cheap kids' watches. Context is everything. Interpreting data depends on context, which by its very nature contains a whole lot of ambiguity. For instance, what does "increased market share" mean? Is it relative to the competition, or is it an absolute increase? That is a value call, one that depends on your company's goals, its risk tolerance, and what you think the global future holds. So, although numbers can give us answers, they also raise a lot of questions, and those answers they prov   ˜
always clear or easy ones. That means that smart metrics-drive
learn to navigate uncertainty using data as a compass, not alw;
let alone turn-by-turn directions.

Systems thinking: the next level of metrics-driven marketing

Once you have the data and the ability to make decisions based on it, you need to start thinking in terms of systems. What does that mean? Systems thinking is the process of looking at problems and opportunities as part of a larger whole.

You start to identify patterns and insights in the data that can help you make better decisions. Remember, metrics are your compass, not the GPS telling you exactly where to turn left and how many feet to the next corner. How do you look for patterns?

First, as a systems-thinking marketer, understand how all the different parts of your marketing work together. You also need to be able to see how changes in one area will impact other areas. For example, if you decide to increase your spending on online advertising, what impact will that have on your other marketing channels? If you change your branding to appeal to a younger audience, will that impact sales to your core, older audience? Systems thinkers use paradigms to create structures that help them see the big picture. A paradigm is a mental model, a way of looking at things. It is a way of organizing your thoughts so you can see the world in a more insightful way. In marketing, a paradigm can be a model of how markets work, of effective branding strategies, or of consumer behaviors. For instance, the models of market segmentation and targeting are paradigms. We also have a ton of paradigms that we learned in school, at work, through experience, and through our own learning.

Once you have a paradigm, you can start looking for patterns in the data that support it or challenge it. You can also start to identify opportunities and challenges that you might not have seen before. But you need a reference point, a set of theories, to make sense of the metrics you're seeing. So, to start using metrics more strategically, you have to first articulate your paradigms of how marketing works. That way, you not only have a set of explanations for what you are measuring, but you have also articulated the biases that might impact your interpretations of data. For instance, let's say you were taught that direct marketing is always more effective than untargeted advertising. If you start measuring the value of a campaign by how much money is spent on direct mail, you are likely to be biased in favor of that campaign, even if the results are terrible. You need to be aware of your biases and how they might be impacting your decision making, while at the same time still using paradigms as a starting point to organize, interpret, and act on data. It is a delicate balance. You want to use what you know to understand the unknown, while still keeping your mind open to the fact that you are very likely sometimes biased.

Once you have the data and you have a systems thinker on your team, you also need to be comfortable with experimentation. You need to be able to try new things, even if you are not sure they will work—and you need to be prepared to fail.

Marketers need to be willing to experiment. At Thoughtlight we are always trying new things, testing new channels, and tweaking our campaigns. Let's take an example. A couple of years ago, we decided to try Facebook advertising. We were not sure how well it would work, but we were willing to experiment. We were looking to grow our market share with local small to midsize businesses (SMBs). A locally popular web platform for SMBs, Drupal Gardens, was closing down, so we decided to focus our efforts on their customers. We created a series of ad campaigns and targeted them to small-business people who lived near our office. The ads directed people to a landing page and had similar keywords as our existing Google Ads. We also created a Facebook pixel and tracked people who clicked on the ads.

After running the campaigns for a few weeks, we found that Facebook was not driving conversions. In fact, it was costing us more money to get people to our landing page than we were making from the ads. We stopped the campaigns and decided to focus on Google Ads. Those had a very respectable 8 percent click-through rate (CTR).

What went wrong with the Facebook campaign? Well, there are a few things we could have done better. We could have A/B tested more, investing the ad spend upfront to test different calls to action, pain points, and offers. We could have targeted a different audience, such as people who had visited our website in the past. And we could have used better creative, which again would have meant spending more.

Even though the Facebook campaign didn't work, it was still a valuable learning experience. We learned what channels worked for us. But that wasn't the real learning in this experiment. Remember that the Google Ads did deliver strong return on investment (ROI) in the form of leads. When we followed up with those leads, though, we found a surprise. They had tiny budgets. Serving them would put us below the hourly rate that is minimum wage in our community. While serving SMBs was realistic for some business models, our bespoke, high-touch, one-on-one service just didn't make sense for businesses with such small budgets.

This experience taught us that, while we want to serve SMBs, we also need to be realistic about the services we offer and the budget that those businesses have. It's something we have kept in mind as we have developed our business model and continue to experiment with new channels and strategies.

Systems thinking is a valuable tool for any marketer, but it is especially important when you are dealing with data. Data can be overwhelming, and it is easy to get lost in the numbers. With paradigms in place, you can extract more meaning, more quickly, because you already see the big picture into which your metrics fit. It can also help you to ask the right questions of your data.

Testing and experimentation: the other side of the metrics

We need to be willing to experiment with data. We need to be able to try new ways of looking at things, new ways of combining different types of metrics to see a complete picture. For example, at Thoughtlight, we often use website data to understand how people are interacting with our existing content. We also use keyword search volume metrics to identify trending topics relevant to our audience. Next, we conduct social listening to see how content on those new, keyword-linked topics is performing. We then use that data to create new content and test it to see if it performs better.

Another way to find patterns is by using data mining techniques. This involves digging into the data to see what relationships or trends exist. You might, for instance, look at how different customer behaviors are related.

Once you have found patterns, you need to use them to make decisions. But, even then, it is not always clear what is the best decision. This is why even the most advanced developments in AI don't replace marketers' know-how. In the end, it is still up to us to interpret the data and make decisions about what to do with it, based on nuanced understanding of metrics. There is no replacement for understanding the data yourself.

But making decisions based on data is only part of the equation. You also need to be able to act on those decisions. This means that you need to have a structure in place that allows you to quickly implement changes based on the data. And you need to have the ability to track the results of those changes so that you can learn and improve over time.

In the end, understanding and using data is a skill that takes practice. It's not something you can learn overnight or from one book. But, if you are willing to put in the time and effort, you can use data to make your marketing more effective.

This is a lot of work, but it's worth it. A data-driven strategy can help you leap ahead of your competition and achieve real results for your business. To see how, let's take a look at one case study.

Metrics-driven strategies in real life: Coca-Cola case study

The first step is to understand your metrics, and the second step is to use that data to make better decisions.

The best way to do this is by using data-driven decision-making tools, which will help you to make decisions based on your data instead of on gut feel or assumptions. These tools include things like business intelligence (BI) software, as well as the tools built in to virtually every marketing tool, from free social media platforms to marketing automation tools with six-figure subscriptions.

However, marketing metrics are not about tools. They are about understanding your customers and prospects so you can develop the right marketing strategy and tactics.

To get started, you need to identify your customer's buying process and map it to your products, service, and digital footprint. You also need to identify all of the different channels that your customers use to interact with you, as well as the engagement points within those channels.

We are also seeing a shift from descriptive analytics, which seeks to diagnose and monitor, to prescriptive analytics, which shapes brands and builds strategy. Prescriptive analytics moves beyond understanding what has happened in the past and provides insights that allow you to make predictions about the future.

To get started with data-driven marketing, you need to understand your customer, their buying process, and how they interact with you. At the heart of all marketing metrics are customers: their needs, their actions, their attitudes, and their whims. This understanding depends on something that no AI-based metrics platform has: empathy. We need to remember that all this data is meaningless without a human connection. Machines can give us data and insights, but it is up to us to use that data to create a connection with our customers. In order to use data effectively, we need to have empathy for our customers. What does that look like? Let's see an example.

Coca-Cola is a brand that has experienced a range of relationships with consumers. When the brand launched in 1886, it was marketed as a medicine. It was also positioned as an alternative to alcoholic beverages, meant to reduce alcohol misuse in the community. It also contained cocaine. It saw different incarnations of its positioning throughout the 1800s, including the sale of syrup used in making the drink as a digestive.

By the 1900s, the beverage formula had changed. Medicinal uses were still a feature of some ads, but the focus of the brand was as a fun beverage. The brand continued to be marketed with "feel-good" marketing, so much so that one classic ad becomes a plot point in the advertising drama *Mad Men*. By the 21st century, health-conscious consumers and governments worldwide began to question the health impact of sweetened beverages. Coca-Cola faced new brand image challenges.

Through three centuries of branding, what has remained constant is consistent use of the brand logo and design, creating a stable visual image of the product even as its role in consumers' lives changed repeatedly.

Today, Coca-Cola is pioneering the use of big data to optimize its brand positioning. While the look and feel of Coca-Cola's branding is consistent, it is a bit deceptive. Underneath that steady commitment to visual design is a continually responsive, AI-driven process of adjusting to ongoing consumer needs across cultures. To accomplish this, the brand uses every data source it can, from listening to consumer conversations on social media to monitoring drink dispensers to tracking e-commerce transactions. The results are impressive. Coca-Cola manages to keep a global image while adjusting its branding for different local markets.

The brand's use of data analytics has evolved to using data to launch new products. In the United States it launched Cherry Sprite, after data from soda fountains that allow restaurant consumers to mix their own soda flavors indicated that it might be a welcomed flavor.

They also engage in social media listening to track mentions of their products in context, measuring time of day, sentiment, location, and other data to optimize targeted promotions and understand customer needs.

Social listening also helps determine promotional placements. The brand has gone so far as to invest in AI that scans social media for users' photos that include any of the company's logos or packaging. Post a selfie to Instagram with a bottle of Cherry Coke in your hand? The Coca-Cola Company is watching. Gathering this data helps optimize promotional spending, which is why it is so important. For example, knowing what proportion of Coca-Cola drinkers are sports fans or outdoors enthusiasts helps the brand pinpoint their sponsorships and ad spending to where it will have the most impact. If social media metrics show that Coca-Cola drinks often feature in photo posts from sports stadiums, the brand can then invest more in sponsorships with that stadium, reaching more fans.

With all this data, Coca-Cola is continually monitoring, evaluating, and acting on data. It is not afraid to make significant decisions, such as launching a new flavor, based on metrics. In fact, metrics are at the heart of the creative marketing that Coca-Cola does. Brands that want to remain responsive to today's increasingly sophisticated consumers must stay on top of their metrics.

Empathy-driven marketing metrics

If using AI to watch all the selfies in the world, looking for photos of your product, feels a little bit mechanized, rest assured that the process is about more than just robots crunching data. Indeed, gathering data means nothing unless it is applied to knowing what real consumers want. Those selfies at ball parks on a hot day, with a cold soda in a mother's hand as she takes her child to their first game? An AI might be finding them, but it takes knowing the deeper meaning of that family moment to draw useful marketing conclusions.

That is why, though numbers may seem cold, metrics are at heart about creating greater empathy from brands towards their customers. Empathy is the secret sauce that makes data useful, and it is what sets Coca-Cola apart from other brands when it comes to marketing. It's the understanding of *why* people buy a product—not just what they buy.

Start by looking at your customers with empathy, and you will be on your way to a data-driven marketing strategy.

Data as the differentiator

Think with Google tells us that the most successful marketers are over 70 percent more likely than average to invest in collecting first-party data—that is, their own data that they collect, control, and use.

Most of the focus on data these days is on collecting and understanding as much customer data as possible. But what most companies do not realize is that they already have a ton of data at their disposal that they can use to create a data-driven marketing strategy—if they know where to look.

This includes things like website analytics, social media analytics, email marketing analytics, and even call center data. Some of this data is unstructured, which means it is not in a format that can be easily reduced to numbers. Machine learning techniques such as Natural Language Processing can parse unstructured text data and extract insights from it. But at its core, it must be analyzed and interpreted by humans. This is where data-driven marketing leaders become the differentiator. They have the ability to take all of this data and turn it into insights that can help them make better decisions about their marketing strategy. That is what you can become.

What this book is about

This book is about how to lead digital transformation with metrics. Think of it as your guide to managing with metrics:

- How to understand your customers.
- How to build a more robust product pipeline.
- How to develop a data-driven culture.
- How to use metrics to manage your team.
- What are the essential KPIs you need to track.
- How to use data to drive marketing decisions.
- And more!

This book also introduces three frameworks for managing marketing: the ICED model for using data, content mapping for data-driven content marketing strategy, and the content value score for optimizing the impact of inbound marketing across every kind of content. I hope these frameworks will be of use to you as you strive to make your marketing more data driven.

If you are looking for a book that will help you understand how to make your business more data driven, this is the one for you. This book shows you how to apply the latest analytics to all aspects of marketing management. It is filled with real-world examples and case studies, and it provides step-by-step instructions on how to create a data-driven marketing strategy. Throughout the book, real marketers like you share their triumphs with marketing metrics, how they use them, and what they want other marketers to know about leading with data.

Marketing metrics are an adventure. They are not just about understanding what happened in the past, but also about using that information to shape what will happen in the future. That's why it is so important to have a data-driven marketing strategy. Whether you are a veteran with metrics or just coming to the discipline, welcome to the journey. Let's get started!

Endnotes

[1] Anon (2018) New Epsilon research indicates 80% of consumers are more likely to make a purchase when brands offer personalized experiences, *Epsilon.com*, https://www.epsilon.com/us/about-us/pressroom/new-epsilon-research-indicates-80-of-consumers-are-more-likely-to-make-a-purchase-when-brands-offer-personalized-experiences (archived at https://perma.cc/BD48-46L6)

[2] Anon (2015) New Report shows data-driven marketing crucial for success in hyper-competitive global economy, *Forbes*, https://www.forbes.com/sites/forbespr/2015/11/03/new-report-shows-data-driven-marketing-crucial-for-success-in-hyper-competitive-global-economy/?sh=2a7cac2065dd (archived at https://perma.cc/86NZ-JWGL))

[3] Anon (n.d.) Why customer service is the new marketing, *Cmocouncil.org*, https://www.cmocouncil.org/thought-leadership/reports/why-customer-service-is-the-new-marketing (archived at https://perma.cc/TV76-4VQG)

[4] Shukairy, A (2016) The importance of data driven marketing—statistics and trends, *Invesp*, https://www.invespcro.com/blog/data-driven-marketing/ (archived at https://perma.cc/4LHX-X9ZV)

[5] Ibid

[6] Anon (n.d.) The state of customer experience transformation, *Merkle*, https://www.merkleinc.com/emea/thought-leadership/white-papers/state-customer-experience-transformation (archived at https://perma.cc/ZP4R-FW76)

[7] Verra, P (2022) Identity resolution 2022, *Insider Intelligence*, https://www.emarketer.com/content/identity-resolution-2022 (archived at https://perma.cc/2ZFD-8CQF)

[8] Guttmann, A (2021) Topic: data usage in marketing and advertising, *Statista*, https://www.statista.com/topics/4654/data-usage-in-marketing-and-advertising/#dossierKeyfigures (archived at https://perma.cc/Q2XP-JHS6)

[9] Anon (2020) 1 in 4 marketers say they always use data as part of their decision-making process, *Marketing Charts*, https://www.marketingcharts.com/customer-centric/datadriven-113273 (archived at https://perma.cc/C9WH-WZQ2)

[10] Anon (2022) Challenges marketers face with data, *Adweek.com*, https://www.adweek.com/digital/7-challenges-marketers-face-with-data/ (archived at https://perma.cc/K6SZ-5MM7))

[11] Anon (n.d.) The state of customer experience transformation, *Merkle*, https://www.merkleinc.com/emea/thought-leadership/white-papers/state-customer-experience-transformation (archived at https://perma.cc/ZP4R-FW76)

[12] Shukairy, A (2016) The importance of data driven marketing—statistics and trends, *Invesp*, https://www.invespcro.com/blog/data-driven-marketing/ (archived at https://perma.cc/4LHX-X9ZV)

[13] Anon (2022) In better customer experiences we trust, *Adobe*, https://business.adobe.com/resources/reports/adobe-trust-report.html (archived at https://perma.cc/U4B7-76PL)

[14] Goldman, J (2022) Google's decade-old analytics platform is going away as the company embraces the post-cookie, cross-channel future of measurement, *Insider Intelligence*, https://www.emarketer.com/content/google-announces-deprecation-of-universal-analytics-move-toward-google-analytics-4 (archived at https://perma.cc/74J4-HWCX)

[15] Anon (2022) Forecasts: insider intelligence estimates and historical data, *eMarketer*, https://www.emarketer.com/forecasts/58fe4ebad2670009840a9edf/58e401313ff5e905a0f34c93 (archived at https://perma.cc/H2WK-72KH)

[16] Anon (n.d.) Marketing analytics usage in the U.S. 2020, *Statista*, https://www.statista.com/statistics/453658/marketing-analytics-use-usa/ (archived at https://perma.cc/7WUU-UNLQ)

[17] Anon (n.d.) Data breach: average U.S. organizational cost 2020, *Statista*, https://www.statista.com/statistics/273575/average-organizational-cost-incurred-by-a-data-breach/ (archived at https://perma.cc/53GR-GXV9)

[18] Anon (n.d.) 2022 State of Competitive Intelligence Report, *Crayon.co*, https://www.crayon.co/state-of-competitive-intelligence (archived at https://perma.cc/FPD9-G68A)

[19] Anon (2021) Gaining meaningful insights from data is still hard. Why?, *Marketing Charts*, https://www.marketingcharts.com/customer-centric/datadriven-116403 (archived at https://perma.cc/7H8T-3GZS)

[20] Anon (2021) Gartner says 63% of digital marketing leaders still struggle with personalization, yet only 17% use AI and machine learning across the function, *Gartner*, https://www.gartner.com/en/newsroom/press-releases/-gartner-says-63--of-digital-marketing-leaders-still-struggle-wi (archived at https://perma.cc/SSU7-ZDJM)

02

Customer data: the core four

As marketers one of our biggest responsibilities is understanding our customers. We spend billions of dollars every year understanding every nuance of our customers' attitudes, demographics, shifting needs, and behaviors. Doing it right can mean the difference between lackluster performance and a blockbuster year. In this chapter, we talk about the different kinds of customer metrics and how they work together to build that 360-degree view of the customer that we all seek.

The shifting sources of customer data

We have a wide range of data available about our customers. From the emails they open to how they engage with our websites, we can track their needs, actions, and tastes. The data we gather about our own customers is becoming all the more important with the end of third-party cookies, which have for years allowed ad networks to gather individual data about consumers. This global tracking has faced consumer resistance as well as legal restriction. Thus, it has become more challenging to get data about individual customers from outside sources. This is a call to action to marketers to improve the ways we gather data to understand our own consumers. No longer can we rely on easy options such as retargeting our website visitors by demographics or buying from third parties a web-wide audience, based on their interests. We must strive to build our own internal data sources.

For the purposes of this discussion, customer data is information on specific customers of an organization. It is the metrics that allow us to assess each customer as an individual, delivering a customized experience, while also understanding customers as segments. It is specific and identifiable. We use customer metrics in a range of ways to optimize our campaigns:

1 Delivering personalized content, offers, and experiences. According to Blake Morgan, writing in *Forbes*, 70 percent of consumers expect brands to provide them with a tailored experience, taking their business elsewhere if they are treated as part of a crowd. Even as consumers worry about their privacy, they want the brands they do business with to understand them.[1]

2 Assessing individual customers' potential for your brand. This includes predicting customer lifetime value, identifying customers likely to churn, and determining which customers are worth retaining.

3 Understanding customer segmentation. For generations, marketers relied on generic assumptions about different demographics to segment their audiences. Customer data allows us to segment based on real-time consumer actions, not assumptions.

4 Building data-based personas to guide all aspects of our marketing and better target campaigns.

In brief, just as customers are the heart of a business, customer data is the heart of marketing metrics.

Multiple sources provide the metrics we need to understand customers both individually and at scale. In this chapter we cover the key ones, including customer relationship management (CRM)/marketing automation data, search, and more. Most critically, though, we go beyond the tools to look at how to relate to our customers by using data. Customer metrics consist of four basic types:

- revenue
- conversion
- communications
- customer loyalty, value, and retention

We will examine how you can use each of these types of data to create closer customer relationships, engage your audience, and plan optimized campaigns.

CRM data: the core of your customer metrics

Before we dive into the data, let's look at your core data source: your CRM/marketing automation system. The first place many of us look for data is our customer relationship management or CRM system. After all, these systems are sold as the platforms for gathering unprecedented amounts of data on our customers, from the last email they opened and the precise second they opened it, to what they hovered over on our website. Your CRM, properly configured, is working in the background to gather all this data 24 hours a day. Provided it is part of or integrated with marketing automation tools, such as email and ad targeting, it is also the means of making customer data actionable.

Today, you can obtain basic customer data from virtually any digital marketing platform. Most social media channels will provide the age, gender, and location information of your audience. You can also check metrics for the times of day your consumers are most engaged on different channels. A CRM with marketing automation brings all of these disparate sources into a single platform, where you can analyze and act on it with confidence.

A note on terminology: in this chapter, we use CRM data to include email, customer service, and most importantly, e-commerce data. A decent CRM should be capturing all e-commerce metrics relevant to individual customers and segments. If it isn't, rush immediately to the CRM configuration quick start guide, *Nuts and Bots*, in the next chapter.

You don't need to be overwhelmed by your CRM data. Like any data source, it has valuable information mixed in with information that can often be ignored, or at least made lower priority. In the next section we cover the metrics that matter. If you don't have a CRM, skip ahead to *CRM Nuts and Bots*, where we will get into how to turn your CRM into a customer data optimization machine. You will need a working CRM in order to use the insights in this chapter most effectively.

Basic customer metrics: the core four

To manage customer metrics, focus on those that help you to:

- target individual customers with messaging, offers, and products most relevant to them
- build customer segments that allow you to understand you markets better
- pinpoint those customers and segments that contribute the most revenue

What are some key metrics that help us achieve those goals? I call them the core four:

- revenue-based metrics
- conversion metrics
- communications data
- customer loyalty, value, and retention data

These four lenses through which you can view consumer data transform an overwhelming set of numbers into clear customer insights. These are by no means the only ways of looking at metrics; they are, though, a framework that helps you focus your analysis based on results. That can help you decide which metrics to focus on at specific times; for instance, if you are looking to accelerate revenue, you can zero in on the revenue metrics. If conversions are not where you want them, you can look to conversion metrics. These frameworks are there to help you find the numbers you need, when you need them.

Revenue-based customer metrics

Metrics that help identify which customers and segments drive the most revenue are critical. They are also plentiful within your CRM. Let's explore some of the top ones that a good CRM will provide for each individual customer. You can use this data to understand how valuable a specific customer is to your business. As we learn in the interview in the next chapter with Hope Neiman of Tillster, some customers contribute disproportionately to your bottom line. It is important to identify these customers—it helps you give them VIP treatment, such as exclusive offers, a higher tier of service, and other perks. However, there is also a bigger-picture reason why you need to learn about your most profitable customers. Odds are, they are not random clients, but they instead show specific patterns. For instance, Hope Neiman finds that there is a significantly higher customer lifetime value (CLV) of customers acquired through certain digital media channels. High LTV customers in her industry—restaurants—also tend to be those who dine at a venue a specific number of times per month. Knowing this helps her pinpoint those customers whose needs and preferences should be given priority in product decisions, user interface (UI) design, and price points. In addition, identifying the top channels for acquiring high-CLV customers means brands can invest in those channels, achieving higher marketing ROI. Thus, customer metrics tied to revenue have a strong impact across organizations, and should be made a priority in any CRM metrics program.

Individual customer revenue metrics

Let's start our customer revenue metrics analysis on the individual customer level. This is where you can use data to achieve a better customer experience for your best customers. It is also where we start to identify those customers who might make up an especially profitable segment. When looking at individual data, try to wear two hats. Think about how you can use the data to please your customer. Also, however, start to think about what patterns you see in the data. Are your most profitable customers arriving at your site from a specific acquisition channel? Do they spend a certain amount? Do they prefer a given product type? Look for hints, however small, of a bigger picture. That will get you ready to start using customer metrics for segmentation.

When looking at individual customer revenue metrics, here are the top ones, in approximate order of importance:

- Most recent purchase date: when was the last time this customer bought from you?
- Purchase frequency: how often does the customer make a purchase? How does this compare to the average purchase rate overall? How does it compare for customers in the same segment?
- Number of purchases by month, quarter, and year.
- Customer lifetime value (CLV): is this number trending up or down? Remember, it's not a fixed number. Recalculate CLV periodically to ensure it is still accurate.
- Shopping basket size: also known as average order size—this is the average size of a customer's purchases.
- Last purchase: what product did they last purchase? How typical is this product of their usual buying behavior?
- Most frequent purchase: what is the product they purchase most often? What product or service categories do they purchase?
- Frequency of customer service contact: customers who request service more often than average may be costing a firm money. Look at the amount of revenue that you can attribute to this customer over the past year. Examine their CLV as well. Does the amount of revenue this customer gives you pay for the additional hours of service they require? If not, they are costing your firm, and you are actually in the red by keeping them.

- Types of customer service contacts: this can also give you valuable product data. What if your top CLV segment is requesting a feature? You may want to build it so your product meets the needs of your most attractive segment.

Tracking revenue on the customer level is important, because it can help you identify your most profitable customers. It can also identify opportunities to upsell and cross-sell. You can never gather too much customer revenue data.

Customer conversion metrics

You can learn a wealth of information from your CRM data about what is driving conversions. Now that you have a sense of who your most profitable segments are, it's time to retrace their customer journey from awareness to conversion. It is helpful to work backwards. This lets you understand the critical steps in the customer journey. So, let's start with acquisition and conversion metrics. These are the metrics that tell you how customers initially found you and what drove their conversions. Here are the top CRM data sources to help you understand your acquisition and conversions:

- **Acquisition channel**: what channel did the customer originate from? Using multi-touch attribution, what other channels did you engage them on before they converted?
- **Acquisition message**: what specific messages led to their conversion?
- **Number of touches**: how many touches did it take before the customer converted?
- **Conversion path:** what specific path did the customer take to conversion? For example, did they start out with organic search, return a month later through a social media link, and ultimately convert in response to an email pop-up offer?

These metrics will tell you two important things: on the individual consumer level, they will help you understand what converted a specific customer, helping you better understand what drives them; in aggregate, they tell you what is getting consumers to convert. Taken together, this data can help you increase customer satisfaction, grow your customer base, improve marketing ROI, and improve customer lifetime value.

Let's take an example: Jeffrey Wu has been shopping at Moonstone Gardens for two years. A new homeowner, he originally found the brand through social media, via their Instagram posts. He was drawn to their simple perennial border designs—they looked easy for a beginner gardener. The posts' message, that anyone can create a classic English garden, interested him, so he visited the center's website. There, he browsed the plants over a 10-minute session. He didn't visit the center until two weeks later, when he and his partner were driving back from the supermarket. Jeffrey purchased some plants and chatted with the knowledgeable staff. He didn't give his email address at the checkout, concerned for his data privacy. Pleased, however, with his initial visit, he returned a week later for more plants. This time, he provided his email address to receive notifications of upcoming promotions.

From this information, the Moonstone team can understand Jeffrey as a customer. From his acquisition channel, they know he is an Instagram user, so they now know how to engage him in the future. From his acquisition campaign messaging, they understand he is a novice gardener: he initially responded to a social media ad that read: "New Gardener? Get Started the Right Way." From the small number of touches required for his initial conversion (three: Instagram post, site visit, and seeing road signage), they deduce his strong interest in their offerings. Putting all of this data together, they identify Jeffrey as a potential high-CLV customer. Now that they have his email address, they send him offers for their loyalty program, as well as gardening tips tailored to new gardeners. Their messaging content and cadence are personalized to his specific needs, thereby increasing the likelihood that he will remain loyal. No matter what your marketing efforts, you can gather more data on your customers than large enterprises could in years past.

Note that here we are discussing personalization by using individual customer data. Later on in this chapter we talk about how to use aggregate data to build more accurate customer personas. Both personalization, which involves using specific data about individual customers to deliver their preferred experience, and persona building, which requires creating aggregate profiles of representative customers, are important uses of customer data.

Customer communications data

Once customers have converted it is time to kick into high gear in communicating with them to ensure high CLV. Optimization remains a critical goal, so let's take a look at the data you can gather from your CRM on how well you are communicating with your current or prospective customers. Here are some of the top metrics to look at when measuring your communications efficacy:

- **Email open rate**: how often do they open your emails? Has the frequency recently changed? In what direction? What events preceded a sudden increase or decrease in open rates? For instance, could they have had a customer service call that may have alienated them, reducing their open rates? Or was a recent purchase especially satisfactory, leading to greater affinity with your brand?

- **Email click to open rate (CTOR)**: how often do they click on any link in emails they open? How many links per email, on average, do they click? Has this number changed recently? One sign of a customer about to churn (marketing-speak for abandoning the firm, and no longer doing business with it) is less engagement with emails. By the same token, customers who are suddenly engaging more with your emails may be ready to make a purchase.

- **Top email topics**: well it's great to know that your emails are popular, but it's more important to know what is making them popular. One of the top metrics in digital communications is the popularity of different email topics. For example, let's say you are a dress shoes company who make trendy knit shoes from recycled materials. Every month you send out a newsletter in addition to the usual offers. You have articles featuring professionals in a variety of fields, average people who wear your styles. You also include on-brand topics: tips on better posture, staying healthy at work, and nutrition. To build a better profile of your audience you want to know what aspects of your brand appeal to consumers: is it the stylishness of your shoes? Is it the fact that they promote healthy posture? Is it that they are eco-friendly? By looking at the top email topics by click rate in your past 52 emails, by customer segment, you learn that amongst your high-CLV customers, eco-consciousness is twice as interesting, as measured by email clicks, as healthy posture. This is valuable data in building a profile of your top customer persona. We will talk more about personas later on in this chapter, but for now start thinking about how metrics from CRM can help you ground your personas in more realistic data.

- **Social media engagement**: does the customer follow you on any social media? Are they engaged with you, or are they a passive follower? Do they like, comment on, and share your content? If so, how often do they do it?

- **Reviews**: customers who leave reviews are rare; you should always pay attention to those who do. What ratings are they giving your products? Frequent reviewers who have positive things to say should be considered for special promotions, personal outreach from your leadership team, or other relationship building, to improve word of mouth. Don't lose sight of negative reviewers whose comments seem reasonable, especially if there is a pattern to who they are, behaviorally. They are giving valuable feedback on what customer segments may not be the right ones for your business. Your reviewers are your most engaged consumers, providing incredibly valuable data on which you can act.

Optimizing communications today means customizing communications. Use comms metrics to understand consumers' preferred cadence, formats, media, and messaging.

Customer loyalty, value, and retention metrics

When it comes to marketing ROI, customer retention is the gold standard. In almost every industry, retaining existing business costs less than half what it costs to acquire a new customer. Not to mention that loyal customers are a sign of quality products, responsible company values, and good service. Thus, you want to keep a close eye on customer loyalty, value, and retention.

Customer loyalty must be understood in context. A convenience store near a college campus will have much higher turnover than a small-town supermarket. For some businesses, such as driver education schools or criminal defense firms, success means never seeing a client again! Thus, when measuring individual customer loyalty, you first need to establish benchmarks for typical loyalty for your brand. Looking at your data, ask questions:

- How long do you retain customers on average? Does this vary by segment? If so, what is the average tenure of each segment?
- How often do they purchase?
- What are the indicators that a customer is about to churn—that is, leave? Do they tend to abandon their carts more often, purchase certain products, or call customer service with a specific complaint?
- What are the indicators that a customer is about to increase their loyalty—for instance, switching to an annual subscription or upgrading their services? What actions do they take before doing so?

Aggregate retention data tells you on average how long customers stay. Industry benchmarks can tell you retention data for your sector, so that you can compare your success at keeping customers with that of your competitors.

Once you have this data in aggregate, you can then start to identify your most loyal customers. You can also flag those who are likely to churn or are open to an upsell, targeting them for specific interventions. For instance, let's say you're a graphic design platform with a freemium model; you find in your data that 80 percent of customers who downgrade their subscriptions cancel their service entirely the next month. When asked why they cancel, consumers typically cite price. With this customer data, you can create a new tier of subscription that is more affordable, offering it to consumers when they downgrade. By providing this more cost-effective option, you cut customer churn by 40 percent.

Another loyalty metric is customer lifetime value (CLV). This metric tells us the total income a customer will bring to a firm over the course of their time as a client. Typically, this metric is calculated as:

$$(\text{annual profit or revenue generated by customer} \times \\ \text{customer relationship in years}) - \text{acquisition cost}$$

CLV is focused on the value you get from specific customers. While it can help you understand a customer, it is important to remember that the revenue a customer brings to you matters more to you than to them. We will look at CLV from the company's perspective, including as a metric of channel, product, and campaign performance, as appropriate throughout this book. In this chapter, we talk only about CLV for delivering customer value.

CLV can be an indicator of customer loyalty. High CLV is either an indicator of high spending with your firm or long customer tenure—maybe both. Thus, it is a proxy for loyalty. Look at CLV as a way to determine how happy a customer is with your brand. When CLV increases, look to see what may have sparked the change, and track interventions that grow CLV. For instance, if you find that offering a middle tier of subscription service grows CLV by reducing churn, you now have another tool in your arsenal to keep customers happy. Segmenting customers by CLV can also identify:

- **Potential advocates:** high-CLV customers might be possible ambassadors for your brand, power users, or potential influencers.
- **Loyalty program success stories:** growing CLV can be a sign that loyalty programs, which typically aim to increase both spending and longevity, are working.

- **Sources of vital feedback**: your most loyal customers know you. Recruit them for customer panels, focus groups, and customer communities. Longtime or large-scale users' feedback provides critical insights you can use to improve your offerings for all.
- **Less valuable users**: the other side of high-CLV power customers are low-CLV customers who don't bring value to the business. Tracking CLV for all customers can help identify customers whom you might be losing money on.

Keep track of CLV for each customer, and develop a workflow to assess relationships with those whose CLV suddenly grows or drops.

Managing customer loyalty in a competitive environment is more challenging than ever. Use CLV, loyalty, and retention data to address problems before they start. Be proactive in retaining customers, rewarding your most loyal shoppers, and engaging those who might churn. Your bottom line will improve with even a small investment in customer loyalty metrics.

Beyond the individual: other consumer metrics that help you win the war for customers

We've talked a lot about CRMs, but they are not the only tool that helps you gather customer metrics. We've also explored in depth those metrics that start with individual consumers, and can be used to profile customers and better understand our audiences. However, we can also gather insights from outside our companies. Data on consumers in our target markets can provide insights beyond what we can glean from internal sources. We also need to understand larger consumer trends happening outside our companies. Fortunately, even in a post-cookie world, there are many sources of aggregate data that can help us understand emerging consumer trends. In this section, we explore some of the most popular, universally legal, and cost-effective methods.

Keyword volume

Search marketing data is an underrated source of information about our customers. We often approach search engine optimization (SEO) from the opposite end. We try to optimize our search marketing efforts based on what we already understand about our customers. We perfect our keywords based on what we think our customers are searching for; we develop landing pages catering to their needs, as we understand them from other data sources. However, what if I told you that you can use search data to better understand your customers? It's actually quite simple. Keyword data is a rich source of what our customers are thinking at the moment that they decide that they are ready to learn more about potential products or make a purchase.

The important thing is that you start gathering data about what people on the web are habitually searching for within your industry. Let's take an example. Business is booming at TeaTop, a healthy tea company, and the customer segment of health-conscious, frugal shoppers are driving the growth. Customer insights manager Andrew Cho is looking to find out precisely what these health-conscious consumers look for when they shop for tea. He turns to a keyword tool to analyze current keyword data to understand current searches for tea. He finds that monthly searches for one of his target keywords, "healthy tea," hovered at 2,000—that is a good number. However, it is the other keyword data that helps Andrew develop a fuller idea of his customers. According to the keyword tool, people who searched for "healthy tea" also searched for the following:

- Mediterranean diet
- jackfruit (a type of fruit thought to have health benefits)
- benefits of green tea
- turmeric (an antioxidant spice)
- chia seeds
- pomegranate

This data tells Andrew several things about his customers. One is that they have a general interest in health, going beyond tea consumption. Second, they have an interest in specific ingredients that can be part of teas, such as turmeric and pomegranate. Third, their interest in health includes interest in specific plant-based diets. This is a rich vein of customer data, allowing Andrew deep insights into the role TeaTop products play in customers' lives, their perceptions of health, and even their flavor preferences. Knowing this can help tailor future product offerings to their collective needs, improve branding, even indicate the channels on which outreach should occur. Keyword data can also indicate shifting consumer trends long before they can be surfaced through more direct methods, such as surveys. It is a great way to explore consumer motivations without surveys or focus groups.

To gather keyword data, invest in a keyword tool. They provide eye-opening data. Some favorites include:

- **SpyFu**: this tool started with competitive paid keyword analysis; it still gives you the keywords your competitors are using in pay per click (PPC). It also has extensive data on question-based keywords.
- **Semrush**: an all-in-one search, social, and content marketing tool, Semrush puts your keyword data into context with rich competitive insights; rather higher-cost than competing tools.
- **Ubersuggest**: this freemium tool gives keyword volume data, suggestions (as the name implies), and competitive data.
- **AnswerThePublic**: billing itself as a "search listening tool," this tool is like Google Trends with more detail. Visual maps show you search trends on thousands of topics. This solution is a must for understanding deeper consumer psychology around search.

Alternatively, Google Ads also offers its own free keyword tool. The important thing is to do your research regularly on keywords; at least once a quarter, though weekly is best when exploring new markets, audiences, messaging, or creative. At Thoughtlight, we use keyword tools at the start of every campaign, even those without a search component. They provide topic-level consumer interest data.

Social media for customer insights

We tend to look to social media for channel or campaign metrics, rather than customer insights. This makes sense, as growing concerns over privacy have made consumer data from social media limited. That said, it is still a data source we cannot ignore. While each social media channel handles customer data differently, a common rule is that you can obtain aggregate, account-level data about your audience for all of your organic content. To see customer data on the post level, you will need to invest in paid posts using advertising.

Let's take Facebook for an example. In their Insights tab for a brand page, you can see the following data for the consumers who like your page:

- demographics limited to age, location, and gender identity
- psychographics based on Facebook Interests targeting, limited to groups of consumers over 1,000 in number

- device data
- language information
- times most active in engaging with your page
- comparisons of the above data to average Facebook users

Though it won't tell us who is interacting with our specific posts, this is still a wealth of data. It can help us make decisions such as what types of consumers to target on a given social channel. The comparison charts can help us to see how well we're engaging specific demographics and psychographics in comparison to platform-wide benchmarks.

The Interests data is especially helpful when trying to transition from demographic to psychographic targeting. It can also flesh out fragmented psychographic information. We saw this at Thoughtlight when we started to target demographics on behalf of our client, a dinnerware company. Their goal was to start selling their beautiful sets of dishes directly to consumers. In addition to building a mobile-friendly e-commerce platform for them, we were also tasked with helping them identify their ideal segments. Analysis of a sample of prior direct customers from a pilot showed that the average age was 50. We decided to use a Facebook ad campaign to reach this audience. Using Insights metrics, we were able to identify the interests of women over 50 who were interested in home entertaining. They also were interested in travel, cooking, and crafts. Using this interest data, we created a campaign targeting users by both demographics and psychographics, reaching nearly 14,000 users with a budget of US $4,000. The strong response validated this data. Thus, we used it to build more precise personas, which we then used across all marketing channels, from email to native to influencer marketing, in order to improve CTRs.

A/B testing further allowed us to hone the message, which is an important thing to remember: social media data can tell you whom to target, and what their interests are. You still need to use channel metrics, as covered in Chapter 4, to ensure that your message resonates with the audience. Every type of marketing metric works hand-in-hand with every other one.

By using aggregate social media consumer data, we were able to quickly identify audience needs in rich detail, when all we started with was one obvious piece of psychographic information—interest in entertaining—and two bits of demographic information—age and gender. You can use these insights to point the way to better targeting, round out customer profiles, and generate data-driven personas. For every social channel you use, you should be checking audience data monthly, using it to drive targeting, creative, and messaging decisions.

Ad metrics and customer insights

We learned in the previous section that we can get aggregate data if we're using organic social. To get post-level data, we need post-based advertising. When you "boost" a post on Facebook or promote content on any social platform using the channel's advertising features, it unlocks gigabytes of useful data. Let's take a look at LinkedIn for an example. If you run an ad, you will see the job functions of all users who saw the ad, as well as of those who clicked on it:

FIGURE 2.1   Ad metrics, LinkedIn

View: Demographics ▼   Display: Job function ▼   Time range: 12/5/2021 - 1/3/2022 ▼   Demographics metrics are approximate to protect member privacy Learn More

Name ⬍	Impresssions ⬍	Clicks ⬍	Average CTR ⬍
Operations	286 (34.32%)	21 (52.5%)	7.34%
Community and Social Services	151 (38.12%)	8 (20%)	5.3%
Education	142 (17.05%)	7 (12.5%)	4.93%
Information Technology	128 (15.37%)	Below reporting minimum	-
Program and Project Management	54 (6.42%)	Below reporting minimum	-
Finance	51 (6.12%)	Below reporting minimum	-
Administrative	42 (6.64%)	Below reporting minimum	-

In addition, placing an ad reveals a range of demographics and psychographics when you create a targeting audience. Audience selectors allow you to choose users who belong to specific interest-based groups, hold a given job title, attended certain schools, and speak specific languages. This targeting can help you estimate how large an audience is. Then by running an ad targeting that audience, you can learn how well your message resonates with that audience. Let's return to TeaTop for an example. They are looking to hire a Human Resources (HR) specialist, and prefer someone with beverage industry experience, and who supports sustainability. They go on LinkedIn to find over 5,000 professionals who fit into all three segments. Using ads to gather precise segmentation data is increasingly useful. It can give you a sense of what consumers in your audience are like, but without a lot of ad spend. Indeed, it is completely free to build an audience; you don't need to actually run the ads to do so. However, it is often worth doing an ad that targets a segment, in order to measure what makes them click. To test out the appeal of their HR specialist role, TeaTop runs an ad targeting the eco-conscious HR specialists they found. The ad gets a lot of clicks, but not many conversions. This helps TeaTop understand that they need to make changes before their ideal candidates find them appealing. They improve their landing page to showcase training benefits, flexible work hours and location, as well as travel opportunities. Applications increase 300 percent. Combining ad audience targeting data with A/B testing, the brand now has much stronger insights into this segment.

Paid search is another channel that provides rich data, including the exact keywords driving traffic to your site, the demographics and psychographics using those keywords, and their conversion, shopping, and other behaviors once on your website. When you integrate Google Ads with Google Analytics and run ads, you can discover:

- what exact keywords drive consumers to your website
- which keywords have the highest conversion rates
- how different keywords work to convert different in-market, affinity, and demographic segments
- when consumers tend to use different keywords, depending on seasonality, time of day, and position in the conversion path

Many brands run ads just to gather data. That is a reasonable approach. If that is your current advertising goal, start small. Think about a hypothesis that you can best test through advertising, such as what ages use what keywords. Run ads for long enough, with sufficient budget, to achieve statistical significance. Monthly small tests of a few hundred dollars can gather consumer insights that pay you back with highly relevant observational data.

Surveys and focus groups

Tried and true, focus groups have fallen out of favor in recent years at many organizations. They are expensive, time-consuming, and why not just conduct a survey? Yet, brands that conduct focus groups find they gain baseline information vital to gathering more precise metrics in other ways.

The purpose of a focus group is to help you learn what you don't know that you don't know. Surveys, keyword data, and CRM metrics are ideal when you have specific questions. Keyword data can help you, for instance, learn the language that consumers use when searching for your product. It can't, however, help you learn about marketing channels your customers use at the information-gathering stage that you have not considered. The weakness of many metrics is that they can only measure what is known. Focus groups offer the serendipity of identifying facts about your consumers that you don't know.

For example, when my company Thoughtlight worked with a dinnerware manufacturer that wanted to learn what motivated consumers to buy new dishes, logic dictated that life transitions, such as moving to one's first apartment, led to most such purchases. Yet, a focus group found quite the opposite, at least when it came to highly patterned dishware such as the company offered. Focus group participants surprised us by noting that they purchased special dishes for special occasions: new salad plates for a family gathering, special teacups for Christmas. Far from purchasing entire sets for daily use, they instead viewed dinnerware as seasonal decor. This insight led to new promotional efforts. This included social media ads targeting women aged 35–70 with holiday messages, seasonal recipes, and special-occasion table design inspiration. The results were a 100X increase in web traffic, as well as sales that doubled month over month. Focus groups give you new directions for branding, messaging, product lines, and targeting.

When you have questions in mind to which you need definitive answers, on the other hand, surveys are most effective. Surveying your customers can give you aggregate information from either your entire customer base, or a segment of interest. Surveys have to be written carefully to obtain unbiased answers; in addition, brands need to consider whether a focus group would not provide broader information. A survey can only give you answers to the questions it asks. Use surveys when you have clear, unambiguous questions that you can only get answers to by asking customers directly, such as their feelings about the service in your stores. If, on the other hand, you want to know what type of layout your customers would prefer, a survey is the least likely to get you useful information. The reason is that you would have to already know the exact possible layouts that could interest all of your customers, in order to include each one on your survey questionnaire. A focus group, in this case, would be a more open-ended way to get fresh ideas that you may not have considered for your store layout.

One other drawback to surveys is their low response rate. Respondents can also ignore surveys if you constantly ask them to take a new one. For example, those stores that put a survey on every receipt—how often have you taken one, even if promised a coupon for your response? Exactly! This doesn't mean that surveys are not useful. For getting quick, direct answers, they are the only option, and can be effective when used for their original purpose. They are a vital piece of your arsenal. Include surveys one to ten times a year, depending on your audience size, in order to add direct feedback to your customer metrics.

Web analytics data

You might think your web analytics tool is mostly for channel and campaign metrics. After all, it tells you how users are interacting with your website. Increasingly, our web analytics data gives us aggregate customer insights. Again, consumer privacy limits the individual data we can gather, but as a source of audience insights, it is vital.

Logged-in, opted-in data

If your website requires consumer logins, such as an e-commerce site, your web analytics data should be feeding rich insights to your CRM. For a logged-in session, you should be able to see each consumer's online behavior, including:

- **Visit acquisition channel**: whether this customer came to your site from a link in an email, by typing in your URL, social media links, or some other way.
- **Pages viewed**: what precise pages the customer viewed.
- **Time on each page**: how long they spent on each page.
- **Total time on site**: how long they visited the site today.
- **Navigation path through site**: how they moved through your site—what order they viewed the pages, whether they backtracked, stayed on a page for a long time, or searched.
- **Shopping cart actions**: whether they put products in their cart and how far they went in the checkout process.
- **Reviews and comments**: any ratings, reviews or comments they created.
- **Site searches**: what terms they searched for, if they used your site search.

All of this data becomes part of a customer's record in your CRM, so you can use it to customize their service. For example, let's say Jeff returns to your site after his fourth in-store visit. He receives your weekly email, clicking on a link to your new blog post about summer annuals. Starting with your blog, he spends 20 minutes on your site, looking at annuals. He searches for shovels, viewing three but not putting any in his cart. He puts a bag of topsoil in his cart, but abandons his cart after getting to the shipping cost. Later that week, he comes to your center, buying the topsoil in person, which you were able to track since he used his loyalty card at the checkout. You now know a lot more about Jeff's gardening interests, as well as how he feels about shipping costs. You can now send him an email coupon for free shipping, as well as notices when gardening implements such as shovels are on sale.

Tracking such as this depends on first-party cookies. These are cookies that site owners use to track and personalize the web experiences of opted-in visitors. You cannot collect data about individual users in the way outlined above unless they are logged into your site, having registered in order to use parts of your site, such as the ability to place an order, or read gated content. This is not data you will collect about every user to your site—only those who have a relationship with you.

Logged-in consumer website data is legal to collect under privacy laws, as of this writing, provided you disclose that you are doing it. Consult Chapter 11 on data ethics and governance for details on tracking users. In general, consumers expect a personalized service, so some data collection may be welcomed by users. Be sure to be completely transparent with customers that you are tracking all their actions on your website. Always use the data you collect to improve the customer experience, as seen in the above example with Jeff. Customers who receive value from tracking are more likely to accept your first-party cookies.

Aggregate data

We can collect an infinite amount of web data about our logged-in customers. But those customers represent a fraction of our website visitors. Most of our visitors are not logged in—and it is imperative we understand those anonymous visitors, because they are the prospects we hope to convert to the next customer. Luckily, web analytics tools provide rich anonymous data on all of our website visitors.

Demographics and psychographics

Google Analytics will tell you the ages of your website visitors, whether they are male or female, their geographic locations, and many of their consumer attitudes or behaviors. Let's start with demographic data. Your analytics reports will tell you visitors' ages, allowing you to segment that information further by behaviors such as visitors to a certain page. Most vitally, we can analyze the demographics of those who converted, right down to giving us the age breakdowns of those who bought a specific product or category of products.

Even more delightfully for marketers, Google tells us the in-market and affinity segments of all our website visitors. To clarify, in-market and affinity segments are both psychographic data. The difference is what it tells us. Affinity segments are general interests of consumers, often held for a long time. In-market segments represent groups of consumers, on the other hand, who appear ready to buy a specific type of product. There is a temptation to focus on in-market segments, because they are flagged by Google as more likely to be on the point of converting to buyers. However, both types of data can be equally important for marketers looking to understand their consumers. Indeed, affinity data can be more important, as it represents a strong interest or attitude of a consumer that can form the basis of strong CLV.

Diving deeper into affinity and in-market data

Correlate in-market and affinity segments with specific website behaviors for richer insights. You want to look at:

- **Conversions**: which in-market segments are most likely to convert? You may be surprised that they are not those who are "in market" for your specific product type. The reason is that in-market data lags. It draws from searches consumers conduct, ads on which they click, websites they visit, and other online behaviors. A consumer thus may have already made the purchase for which they are labeled as being "in market" long ago. This makes affinity data the more reliable information for understanding your consumers' true needs. This data is also drawn from searches, clicks, and site visits—however, the actions are of a longer duration. Affinity segment data is based on months of consistent actions. It's really like conducting a survey of what your consumers like to engage with online, so use this data.

- **Conversion paths**: do people interested in cars, for instance, take longer to convert than those interested in travel?

- **Content consumption**: do particular segments consume particular kinds of content? For instance, do visitors who are in-market for travel tend to read blog posts about easy-care plants? Do consumers with an affinity for luxury cars read about exotic plants?

- **Site visit patterns**: how often do attractive segments visit your site? What times of day seem to be more popular with segments you wish to attract?

- **Acquisition channels**: how are you acquiring your most desirable segments? How do their acquisition channels compare to your average? For instance, are luxury consumers more likely than average to arrive at your site from social media? Are customers who are in-market for your type of product more likely than average to arrive via your advertising?

- **New vs returning visitors**: do visitors who are on repeat visits to your site do anything different from those seeing your site for the first time?

- **Depth and length of visit**: do some in-market or affinity segments tend to view more pages than average? Fewer?

- **Pages viewed**: do specific pages appeal to specific affinity groups? Do customers who are in-market for a particular product view pages related to that product type on your site?

- **Number of touches**: does it take a specific number of touches to convert a given in-market or affinity segment?

This data can profile your website visitors in ways that you otherwise would need to use surveys to accomplish, if you could get this depth of data at all. It is a valuable resource that too few marketers use.

You may not get that clear a signal if you have modest traffic—under 5,000 unique visitors per month. If that is the case, select a longer timeframe for looking at your data. That should help you reach the 5,000 user threshold and gather relevant data. For instance, if you have 2,000 visitors per month, you will need to look at 2.5 months of data to have enough traffic to assess these customer insights. If seasonality is important to your business, select the smallest timeframe necessary to get data. If seasonality is less important, select a long timeframe to have more confidence in your in-market and affinity data; the larger the sample size, the more trustworthy.

We cover other web analytics data in the chapters on channel and campaign metrics.

Customer data in a privacy-driven world

As tracking across the web becomes increasingly limited, data about consumers is locked increasingly into "walled gardens" of social media platforms, Google, and publisher networks. It has always been important to gather your own insights about your customers. However, many of us grew to rely on the supplementary data from third-party sources, letting our internal customer insights languish. Now is the time to set up your CRM to be a data powerhouse. Start collecting every bit of data you can from customers. You cannot rely on audience buying to target customers that you understand only in part. Instead, you need to use real-time, internal data to build better personas, understand your segments, and see a nuanced view of your customers. We'll dig into the details of using customer data while respecting privacy in a later chapter.

In the meantime, here are a few general tips:

- Make sure you have a clear understanding of data privacy regulations in your country or region, such as GDPR in the European Union.
- Get explicit consent from customers before collecting data about them. This may seem like an obvious one, but it is easy to get complacent about collecting data when everyone is doing it.
- Keep data only as long as you need it and delete it when you don't. This will help to keep your data sets small, which makes them easier to manage.
- Be clear and transparent with customers about what data you are collecting and why.
- Give customers the ability to see, change, or delete their data.
- Have a plan for what you will do if there is a data breach.

By following these tips, you can ensure that you are collecting and using customer data in a responsible way.

It is important to remember that, when targeted appropriately, consumers prefer to receive offers based on their consumer profiles. According to a 2016 study by Adlucent, 71 percent of consumers would rather receive targeted ads,[2] while more recent research from Visible Objects found that 59 percent of consumers pay attention to retargeted ads for products they have searched (check out the research at https://visualobjects.com/digital-marketing/blog/search-retargeting). Thus, although being respectful of consumer privacy is critical, so is using the data you have collected to improve the customer experience.

Creating a comprehensive customer view

Once you have data coming in from multiple sources, you will want to start thinking about how to create a comprehensive view of your customer. This view will include data from your CRM as well as data from other sources, such as social media, website visits, and purchase history. The more data you have, the more accurate your insights will be.

There are a few ways to go about creating this comprehensive view:

- Use data matching to combine data from different sources. This can be done manually or through automated processes.

- Integrate your CRM with other systems, such as your e-commerce platform, social media platform, and email marketing system. This will allow the data to flow seamlessly between systems.

- Use customer data to build custom audience segments. This will allow you to target specific customers with laser precision.

- Use analytics to track customer behavior over time. This will help you to understand how customers are interacting with your brand and how they are changing over time.

The key is to use the data you have to create a complete and accurate view of your customers. With this view, you will be able to target them with relevant offers, improve the customer experience, and increase loyalty and retention.

CRM data is only as good as the people who use it

Once you have your customer data in a CRM, it is important to make sure that it is used effectively. This means not just dumping all the data into a spreadsheet and calling it a day. The data needs to be analyzed and used to inform decisions about marketing, sales, and customer service.

This is where having a good CRM team comes in. The team should be composed of people who are data-savvy and can use the data to make decisions about how to improve the customer experience. They should also be able to track customer behavior over time and identify trends. Training is vital to using your CRM effectively. Make sure that your team is properly trained on how to use the system and how to interpret the data. Too many companies purchase an expensive CRM, then never realize its full ROI because no one knows how to use it. Make training a priority, and you will be able to get the most out of your data. Have multiple people trained on the CRM, and do regular checkins to ensure that the tools are being used.

Conclusion

CRMs are the key to unlocking the value of your customer data. Without a CRM, your customer data is scattered across multiple platforms, making it difficult to get a clear picture of your customers. A CRM gives you a centralized view of your customer data, making it easy to segment, understand, and take action on your data.

There are many CRMs on the market, so it is important to choose one that fits the needs of your business. If you're not sure where to start, look at your goals, data volume, and organizational analytical capacity to help you make a decision. Implementing a centralized consumer data platform can be time-consuming. Unless you are already using a full marketing automation suite, it means transitioning to one, or creating a complex web of data integrations. However, the rewards are rich customer insights independent of industry shifts in third-party data collection. More importantly, it will reward you with a closer understanding of the heart of your business, which is your customers.

Endnotes

[1]   Morgan, B (2020) 50 stats showing the power of personalization, *Forbes*, https://www.forbes.com/sites/blakemorgan/2020/02/18/50-stats-showing-the-power-of-personalization/?sh=6dcf68b12a94 (archived at https://perma.cc/LQJ9-6FKN)

[2]   Pauzer, H (2022) 71 percent of consumers prefer personalized ads, *Adlucent*, https://www.adlucent.com/resources/blog/71-of-consumers-prefer-personalized-ads/ (archived at https://perma.cc/A8BL-CJ66)

03

Metrics-driven customer journeys and personas

It's a group project: turning consumer metrics into large-scale strategic insights

Up until now we've talked about the role of metrics in understanding the individual customer. We can use this data to target Jim with the right offer, keep Sally from going to our competition, and make sure Jeff spreads the word about us. We've also taken a tour of metrics that give us broader insights into what our audience needs as a group. The same two sets of metrics can also be used for broad strategic insights about your audience in general. Let's take a look at how we can use them to build a data-driven profile of our audiences.

Customer data plays a vital role in campaign planning through:

- segmentation
- persona development
- customer journey mapping

All of these core marketing activities depend on solid customer-level information. In this segment we will learn how to optimize these functions with customer metrics.

Customer segmentation

Customer segments are groups of individuals. Thus, once we understand our individual clients we can group them into segments. Now that we understand our individual customers and have started to look for patterns, it's time to get serious about building realistic customer segments.

Many companies don't use their CRM data for segmentation. They start out with assumptions based on demographics or external data. They often then try to make the data fit the preconceived segments rather than the other way around. It's better to start with your CRM data on the individual customer level and then use that real customer data to build realistic segments grounded in your actual customers.

Let's look at an example. Segmentation can be based on behavior, demographics, psychographics, acquisition channels, and other key factors. For example, Moonstone can build a segment of "New Gardeners," a psychographic segment; "Retirees," a demographic segment; and "Social Media Followers," an acquisition channel segment. However, without data, these segments just assume that new gardeners, retirees, and social media connections have different needs, shop differently, or respond to different messages. Thus, these segments may be meaningless. Start instead with the data, analyze it, and build segments accordingly. We start by looking at demographics. Where age is known, we separate customers into age groups, then look at their buying habits, favorite marketing channels, CLV, and loyalty. We don't see a pattern. Age, for Moonstone, is not a segmentation factor that impacts marketing.

Now, let's examine "New Gardeners" vs "Experienced Gardeners." We look again at the same factors, and find that, indeed, these segments do make sense. New gardeners tend to shop less often, buying more on each trip. Experienced gardeners are at the garden center more often, but they tend to buy fewer items on each trip. These two segments do have different buying habits. Thus, it makes sense to use them for planning our marketing campaigns. When it comes to segments, use only those that make a difference in your marketing. Segments that tell us what a customer will likely buy, click on, spend, or otherwise do are the only segments you need. The way to find those segments is with metrics. Take all of your existing segments and examine them using your real customer data. Do they all truly predict consumer actions? Eliminate any segments that the data does not show as having differences that impact your marketing.

Next, start finding segments you didn't know you had. The individual customer metrics we reviewed in Chapter 2 are all jumping-off points for finding new segments. For instance, we looked at how we can personalize messaging to individual customers based on their email clicks. We can also easily build segments in our email or marketing automation platform based on customers who have similar click patterns. For instance, we can create a segment of customers who read blog posts about perennials. We can segment customers by acquisition time or channel, CLV, and more. Look for patterns in customer data that can indicate a segment; not all patterns are worth turning into formal segments. For a pattern to be a segment, it should be:

- **Large enough**: say you have a small group of customers who love gerbera daisies only—if they are less than 5 percent of your customers, they are likely not a big enough group to make a segment. How large should a segment be? Typically, unless it is a very profitable group, a segment should include 10 percent or more of your customers. Very large companies may do enough volume that they can afford to have 50 or more segments, but rarely should most firms divide their customers into so many groups and then try to market to each in different ways. It will spread your efforts too thin.

- **Profitable**: a group of customers may be large, but the factor they have in common may not make them profitable. Customers who only come into your store during your 75 percent off clearance are certainly a segment; however, it may not be worth focusing efforts on them.

- **Relevant**: is the segment one that your company can reasonably service with its existing products, infrastructure, and business model? For instance, let's say you are a chocolate shop with locations in Boston and New York City. Looking at your CRM, you see 10 percent of your visitors come from Los Angeles. Are you going to open a shop in LA? Maybe. But that is a business decision you shouldn't make simply based on having a potential audience. Sometimes, if we see an attractive, large segment in our data, it makes sense to adjust our overall strategy to reach them. However, it is fully possible you will have segments that don't make sense to serve. Look at your business goals, resources, and long-range plans when assessing your segments.

Building segments based on data can be exciting. It means you finally understand your customers better than ever before. However, it means challenging some long-held assumptions. You may prove that what you thought were your segments are not really relevant. You may end up rethinking your customers entirely. That can result in pushback. Product teams, the C suite, even the marketing team may have spent years focusing on segments with little data to support them. Identifying data-driven segments means shifting the way you work. Proceed thoughtfully. It's time to use your persuasive skills to listen, convince, and build consensus. It's worth the effort.

Putting it all together with metrics-driven personas

Once you have rich data on your customers your personas can be built on real facts, rather than suppositions. Too many brands create personas based on untested assumptions. For example, a garden center may create several personas aged 35–54, based on stereotypes such as "homeowners are usually older, but not retirees." However, the real data may show that gardeners are all ages. Using metrics, you can see the ages of your website visitors. You can dig deeper to compare the ages of those who converted with the average age of visitors.

The advantage of data-driven personas is that they are more accurate than those built on gut instincts. The disadvantage is that these personas, once built on data, need to be updated as reality changes. Let's say over 2020, while most of the world was in lockdown, your garden center's demographics grew much broader, as consumers around the world turned to home-based hobbies. Then, in 2021, during the housing price rise, demographics skewed older again, as many younger consumers lost interest in gardening as home ownership felt out of reach. But then in early 2022, a top lifestyle influencer popular with consumers aged 21–34 began a TikTok series on container gardening, mentioning your center. Touching off interest in small-scale urban patio growing, this mention also drove traffic to you. Now, your demographics shifted not only to younger consumers, but more urban ones as well. If you relied on static personas, you would have missed those trends. But, if you used data-driven ones, you would have noticed shifting demographics in your website visitors, email respondents, and social media followers. Accordingly, you could adapt your marketing in an agile manner: shift ad spending to TikTok one year, Facebook to reach more mature consumers the other. You could change messaging, creative, and offers to have maximum appeal to your current target audience. By identifying your audience through highly accurate, timely personas based on near-real-time data, you can address market trends. This is more work of course than using the same static personas for years. However, the ROI can be significant.

Marketers sometimes ask how many personas a brand needs. A persona also needs to be useful across marketing functions, including branding and product. Having hundreds of personas at one extreme defeats this purpose, by fragmenting your efforts. You generally need enough personas such that each persona represents at least 10 percent but no more than 50 percent of your audience.

Putting it all together with customer journey mapping

Customer journey mapping is the secret sauce of the most effective metrics-driven marketing teams. In this section, we learn how to use our customer data to improve our journey maps.

What is customer journey mapping? It's creating a pictorial outline of your customer's entire set of activities in a specific situation. You might map the process a customer goes through from the moment they start searching for your type of product to the moment they buy from you. You could map the way they use a product, their engagement with customer service, or their entire customer lifecycle.

Take, for instance, our garden center marketing team at Moonstone. They want to understand how gardeners typically find them, as well as what it takes to convert new customers. The team currently has data on search, including keywords, as well as social media, CRM, marketing automation, ad, and email data. Along with their web analytics metrics, they have the information available to create a range of customer journey maps.

Metrics-based customer journey maps start with data, rather than assumptions about how consumers behave. For instance, your company may be convinced that TV ads are customers' first touchpoint with the brand, or that coupons are the driver of loyalty. However, without data, these are assumptions that can get in the way of seeing data patterns clearly. Discard your prior ideas; start fresh.

Select relevant data for each step in the journey, then include those points at the appropriate steps. For instance, let's say our garden center team wants to start with a journey map for your consumers' path from awareness to purchase. Using customer data, they know what keywords consumers are likely to search when they first seek garden products, what acquisition channels bring them to the center's website, and the number of touches that it takes to make them convert. The team can thus outline, with fairly good accuracy, several steps in the journey:

1 A new gardener searches for a basic term such as "easy border plants" in a search engine. We know this from search data, specifically the keyword research discussed earlier in the chapter.

2 They see the site in the search engine results page (SERP).

3 They click through to the website, looking at the homepage, the perennials page, and perhaps a blog post about perennial borders and their design. We know all of this from CRM and web analytics metrics.

4   Next, they leave the site, not to return for a few weeks. This data, too, comes from web analytics data.

5   Eventually, they see a retargeting ad, clicking on it to return to the site. Seeing a popup for a 30 percent discount in exchange for entering their email address, they provide their email. This is tracked with CRM and marketing automation metrics.

6   They redeem the 30 percent off coupon in-store.

7   They return to the website for information on plant care.

8   After a week, they return to the store for additional gardening supplies.

9   Over the growing season, they return to the store five times. Three of those visits follow an email, and include redemption of the offer in the email. The other two are not connected to specific marketing efforts. Instead, they are likely prompted by consumer need.

10 Next growing season, 70 percent of customers who complete at least five store visits after their initial visit return as customers.

Note that this process goes into detail about consumer actions, marketing outreach, and potential customer motivations. That makes for the most effective kind of map. The detailed map shown in Figure 3.1 allows us to plan touchpoints for maximum conversions. For example, let's look at Step 5, the retargeting ad. Initially, the company used retargeting ads that directed consumers directly to the homepage, with no offers appearing once they landed. The conversion rates were impossible to track, as the company could only speculate on how many customers returned to the store on the basis of the ad. They could use statistical analysis to find a correlation between retargeting ads' reach and store visits. However, there was no direct link between the ads and visits. Yet, they could see in their ad and web analytics data that the retargeting ads were driving hundreds of visits to the site. They decided to add a micro-conversion to the retargeting campaign, in order to both increase sales and be able to track them better. The result was immediate insight into the number of times a retargeting ad brought a customer into the store. It also helped them prove retargeting's ROI, by tracing specific sales to the ads, and to better understand their customers' interests.

Another optimization made possible by journey mapping occurred at Step 3. We see from web analytics data that many visitors who originate via organic search look for basic gardening information, rather than a garden center. Knowing this helped the team pinpoint the need for content marketing. Now, they create weekly blog posts to capture search traffic.

FIGURE 3.1   Customer journey map

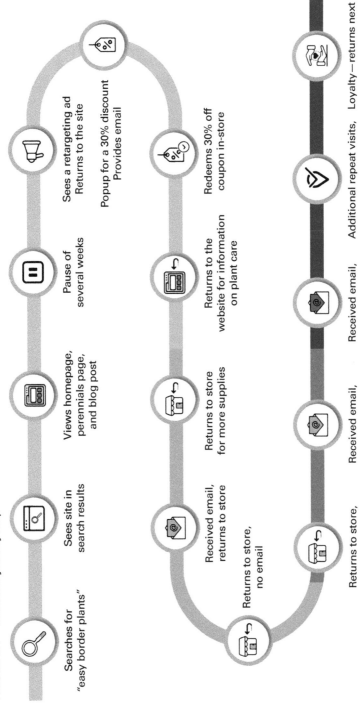

Through customer journey mapping, we can find areas in our customers' interactions that can be optimized for higher conversions, greater customer satisfaction, higher customer lifetime value, or greater marketing ROI.

How do you get started with journey maps? Start by identifying what you most need to know about your consumers: are you puzzled by how they find your site? Interested in what makes them convert? Concerned about why they go to your competitors? If you answered "all of the above," that's normal. Select one journey, though, to start. You want to focus. Think about what your data can tell you about a single small journey. For instance, if you want to know why consumers convert, what data will tell you that? It's your search data, web analytics, CRM, survey data, and ad metrics. Gather those metrics together and ask yourself questions: what do our top search terms tell us about what our consumers are thinking? How do the pages they visit show us their most important topics? Dig deep into the details—that is where the metrics gold is hiding.

Next, start sketching the journey. It is helpful to use sticky notes, or a tool that simulates them when working virtually, such as Miro. Map out several possible journeys, based on what the data tells you. For each step, create several variations. For instance, the first touch for many of your customers may be organic search, but some may originate from social media, outdoor advertising with QR codes, or podcasts. Include each of these initial touches as variations for your journey map's Step 1. If most customers shop primarily in-store, but some order via your app, include both as options for the journey's final conversion step. The key is to capture every major variant of the customer journey. In this way, you will have a pool of documented steps.

Next, put the variations together into complete customer journeys. This is where you will need to bridge data with some common sense.

This may feel like an oversimplification. It's a simplification for certain, but one that will serve you well. Mixing different variables can quickly create a dizzying number of variations. Capturing hundreds of journeys is seldom the best use of time. If you have the resources to map even rare journeys, it can be helpful. However, with a realistic time budget, it is best to prioritize the more typical ones. Create a set of journey maps that represent the typical experience. Focus on specific segments, channels, or products— any journeys that are distinct enough to require a different approach on the part of the brand. Map only the journeys that are unique in some way from the others. For example, you may only need two journey maps: one for your in-store shopping experience and one for the online one. If all of your segments have a common experience that is differentiated only by difference between online and brick-and-mortar, then those two maps are all you need. Tailor your journey maps to those aspects of your marketing that need mapping in order to create effective marketing approaches.

A range of tools, many of them free, make it easier to visualize this journey. In addition, these tools offer specialized journey map templates to detail particular types of journeys. Some useful tools are:

- **Mural**: this rich library of free templates includes a range of different journey maps, from a customer experience (CX) map to a user journey ideal for technology products: https://mural.co.

- **LucidChart**: this charting tool allows you to draw maps free-form using predesigned shapes, or start from a template. For teams that want to create from scratch or develop custom maps, this can be a good option: https://www.lucidchart.com.

- **Miro**: primarily a project management tool, this platform offers journey map templates especially useful for software products, web platforms, and apps. It has a simple, intuitive interface and integrates with user experience (UX) and developer tools: https://miro.com.

- **Edit.org**: a large set of journey maps in different visual styles makes this tool different. For teams with visual thinkers, this library of journey maps is especially appealing: https://edit.org/blog/free-customer-journey-map-templates#ini.

- **Flowmap**: offering both persona templates and journey mapping, this interactive tool lets you build any map from a single interface, and connect it automatically to any persona you create using the tool: https://www.flowmapp.com.

- **Smaply**: if you are the whiteboard type, this tool lets your team take a photo of a map drawn on any surface and turn it into a digital journey map. In addition, it offers standard online journey mapping and persona creation tools: https://www.smaply.com.

Experiment with different templates, since the visualizations themselves often inspire valuable insights. The important thing is that you start being disciplined about your journey mapping.

CRM nuts and bots: making customer data live

We are familiar now with the myriad types of customer data that we can use both to optimize our individual client relationships and better understand our market. We've consolidated data through personas and journey maps, making data actionable in the process. Now, we're ready to get to the heart of our customer data: our customer relationship management (CRM) systems. Your CRM should be the clearinghouse for the majority of your customer data. It is also the platform that allows you to turn customer metrics into the great marketing we've discussed, from instant personalization to continuously updated personas. So why aren't more of us doing this?

The majority of organizations don't know how to leverage their CRM to gather this data properly. Many use it as a glorified address book, perhaps with some notes integrated. So let's take a step back. Let's take a look at how you configure your CRM to make it the data powerhouse it can be.

The biggest barrier we see at Thoughtlight in consolidating consumer data is that organizations cling to the silos they had before CRM implementation. To give you comprehensive metrics, a CRM's usage must also be comprehensive. That means you need to use it with every customer touchpoint. We often hear from clients that they use their CRM to track sales, but that email and advertising are run using platforms that don't integrate with the CRM. What does this mean for your organization? Imagine an organic coffee company, SnowBound Coffee. They sell coffee beans through their e-commerce platform. They also maintain a strong Instagram presence, run social media ads, and send out a weekly email newsletter.

Sales are growing. They are up 40 percent since last year. "What's driving these sales?" asks general manager Julianne Nguyen. "We've been doing great on Instagram, but the opens are also up for the email newsletter. What's behind this growth?" The team has no idea, because they are not tracking it. Within the email platform, they can track opens and clicks, but they need to manually check whether any subscribers who opened subsequently bought—something no one has time to do! They can see clicks on their Instagram ads, but again, they don't know who is clicking and if they bought. And the situation with organic Instagram? The best they can do is track individual sales to a recent Instagram click. They have a CRM, but they are not using it to understand their customer beyond that rudimentary sales data. Sound familiar?

The reality is that many companies are at this stage with their CRMs. The first step to changing is deciding to change. Think about the gaps in your data. Where are you missing information? (It's probably a lot of places.)

Let's see how gathering metrics via a CRM changes the landscape of consumer data. Up the street from SnowBound is TeaTop, a tea company. They, too, sell their products via an e-commerce platform. They also track customer sales through a dedicated CRM. However, they have this e-commerce data integrated with every marketing activity. This allows them to understand every touchpoint their customers have—and, in turn, learn much more about their customers.

Here's an example: June Mayfield is one of TeaTop's newest customers. She placed an order for a tea assortment on February 2, using a promotional code that was only shared via email. Looking at her CRM record, marketing analyst Amanda Nlongo sees that June is not on TeaTop's email list. Thanks to fully integrated customer touchpoints in her CRM, however, she is able to trace June's use of the coupon code to an email forwarded by another user. This marks June as a customer acquired through a current customer referral. Amanda sees that June visited the company's e-commerce site several times before making a purchase. June visited several individual tea product pages before apparently deciding on the assortment pack. Most of the individual teas she viewed, moreover, were herbal infusions, none with caffeine. So, now June's customer record shows her as a referral customer, in the herbal and caffeine-free customer segments.

In the coming weeks, Amanda gathers even more data on June thanks to the CRM. She sees that June clicks often on social media posts on health and wellness. She also views individual teas on the site, but then always purchases assortments that include those teas along with others.

Some of the data helps Amanda categorize June into existing consumer segments. For instance, the segment of customers interested in herbal teas is large, and June fits into that category, enabling Amanda to customize messaging to this particular customer. However, June's behavior also helps Amanda build new customer segments. It had not occurred to the TeaTop marketing team that some customers may view multiple products, then purchase them in an assortment. The assortment packs, they reasoned, were for customers who knew little about the products and wanted to sample them. Seeing June's online behavior helps the team understand more about potential customer behaviors.

Okay, so now you are convinced that a fully functioning CRM is essential to your customer data. How do you set up your CRM to do all this? The good news is that it is built to do so. You just need to take it step by step. Let's learn how.

Integrated vs standalone

The first step to CRM success is to know whether your CRM is part of a single platform with your marketing technology stack, or whether you will continue to use a range of tools to manage your marketing that are separate from your CRM. While the basic steps for CRM implementation are consistent for both situations, they each have their own process.

IS YOUR CRM INTEGRATED WITH YOUR MARKETING TOOLS?

This is the ideal scenario. A full suite of CRM and marketing tools, such as HubSpot or Adobe, allows teams to deploy marketing and gather customer data in one place. The main barrier in such a case is often current systems. For instance, a social media team may have been managing their content using a dedicated social media tool for years, making them reluctant to switch to the new, integrated tool. Other times, teams have tried to use a full marketing platform, but struggled with complexity. The important thing is not how you are using a full-suite tool right now; it is the fact that you are committed to using that full suite. If that's the case, you will gather, process, analyze, and leverage your data all within a single platform. This gives you maximum data quality, makes it the easiest to use your data for personalization, and reduces the time spent on basic data tasks.

IS YOUR CRM SEPARATE FROM YOUR MARKETING TOOLS?

Often, we are not using an all-in-one solution for our marketing automation. We may have a CRM as well as a host of other tools that we use to manage different marketing channels. Dedicated marketing tools often have more features than a single all-in-one. You have an email platform for direct consumer messaging, collecting data on opens and email clicks. Your social media tools are collecting social media metrics, while different ad platforms are collecting vital customer data in a fractured landscape of datasets. Your e-commerce platform, one of the richest sources of data, is generating insights that do not translate anywhere else. In this case, you will need to pursue an integration strategy to ensure proper data collection.

Whether you use an all-in-one tool or integrate your CRM with your marketing tools, it is time to ensure your CRM is set up for customer metrics collection.

- **Channel inventory**: list all of the marketing channels you use, have used, or plan to use. This includes your e-commerce platform, website, customer community, forums, as well as all offline marketing that might generate customer data, such as QR codes in outdoor advertising.

- **Tech stack inventory**: now, list all the tools you use. List your social media tools, content management system (CMS), even the native tools, such as using Facebook Ad Manager.

- **Integrate or shift decision**: having multiple tools really can be a barrier to CRM metrics implementation. However, teams often need the robust features dedicated tools offer. The social media management tool that your team currently uses, for example, might have a more intuitive UI, or more creative options. In this case, something is lost if you transition to the all-in-one tool. This means you must compromise. Fortunately, you can also fully integrate your CRM with your marketing even if you use multiple tools. Be aware it will take a lot more work.

- **Tagging implementation**: whether you decide to migrate to an all-in-one or keep your existing stack, you will need to use a tag manager to add tracking URLs to your marketing. This tag manager must send data to your CRM. Fortunately, many CRMs, such as HubSpot, offer their own tag managers. Google Tag Manager also works with any CRM. Ensure your team is trained on how to use tags to send data about the campaign, messaging, creative, offers, and channels that brought a customer to your website.

- **Data migration**: move your existing customer data into your CRM. Most CRMs allow you to tag individual customer records with what persona best describes them, as well as the segment(s) to which they belong. Start with segment and persona data, so that you can tag individual customers with relevant segmentation and persona information from the moment they are added. Then, import your customer contact information. Tagging usually can be done as part of the import, but check that tags were properly applied after each import.

- **Toolset migration or API connection and workflow development:**
Toolset migration: if you are moving to your all-in-one solution, start using the built-in tools and sunsetting the dedicated old ones. Start

sending all email promotions from your new tool; archive old emails if needed and stop using your email tool. Within 30 days, all of your marketing should be deployed from your new all-in-one tools. If you are retaining your current toolset, now you need to ensure data keeps flowing into a single location. You will need to integrate all your tools with your CRM via APIs or use a dashboarding tool. An API, which stands for application programming interface, is a feature that connects one software platform to another. If you use MailChimp to communicate with customers based on data from Shopify, that connection between the two tools is an API.

Unless you implement APIs, your data will be siloed and relatively useless for personalization and customer insights. For instance, if you keep your email and e-commerce tools separate, you will not be able automatically to send customized emails to shoppers based on their purchases from your email tool. In this situation, you are either manually moving data from one tool to the other using CSV files, connecting tools with multiple clunky APIs, or going without full knowledge of your customers. So, you need to address these gaps. Not all tools offer APIs; this means that some tools cannot be configured to connect seamlessly to one another. However, if you are using popular standards, such as MailChimp, you should find APIs you need. Standalone tools such as Zapier and IFTTT can also connect tools by automatically performing actions that would otherwise be manual, such as adding a customer to your email list if an API can't. The key is to use your CRM as the "single source of truth" in a complex tech stack. Data added to the CRM must be the freshest, most accurate, and clean. If your social media tool is not getting data from your ad manager because you lack an API, your marketing will still work. If, on the other hand, your CRM has missing data, you cannot adequately service your customers. In addition, in a complex tech stack, there will be overlapping data. For example, you may have metrics on what products a customer recently bought in both your e-commerce platform and your email segmentation lists. For example, you might have someone tagged as a "coffee drinker" in your email solution, but your e-commerce will show them as buying tea on their last three visits. Questions will come up about which data is the newest: the email data or the e-commerce? Use your CRM as the single source of the most reliable data. Set up workflows for your team. Have someone responsible for uploading data if it must be done manually. If you are lucky enough to use an API, still have manual checks.

For data insights, you will need a dashboarding tool, such as Google's Data Studio. That will allow you to view data in one place, as you would if you were using an all-in-one tool. These dashboards can be challenging, but you can learn the basics in a few days. For Data Studio, paid tools called "connectors" can automatically feed data, live, into your dashboard, so that it's as real-time as data in an all-in-one tool.

If all of this sounds like a lot of work, it is. While no one can make the decision for you to use a single marketing platform or integrate a complex tech stack, consider seriously whether having your current favorite tools is worth the cost of managing multiple, often costly, data integrations.

Now that you have your CRM up and running, you will begin to enjoy richly integrated data that gives you customer insights. It will help you understand your customers both individually and in aggregate.

Conclusion

Segmentation is one way to drill down into your customer data to understand it more deeply. By creating metrics-driven segments, you can track and analyze the behavior of your segments over time. This will help you to understand what works (and what doesn't) for each segment, so that you can fine-tune your marketing efforts.

Personas are another way to go deep with your customer data. Creating personas helps you to understand your customers as individuals, rather than as faceless segments. This understanding can inform your marketing efforts in a way that segmentation cannot.

In order to get the most out of your customer data, you need to be sure that you are collecting all of the relevant data points about each customer. By building your segments and personas on a sound foundation of data, while also leveraging a CRM fully to target customers based on both individual data, along with segmentation and personas, you can create a customer-centric marketing strategy that will help you to keep your customers engaged and coming back for more.

FROM THE FIELD: HOPE NEIMAN OF TILLSTER ON HOW TO FIND YOUR BEST CUSTOMERS

In Chapter 2 we met Hope Neiman. She has led marketing efforts for legendary brands, ranging from Disney Interactive, where she served as Vice President of Marketing, to ShoeDazzle, where she led as Chief Marketing Officer (CMO). Hope's current work at the startup Tillster focuses on the restaurant industry, a sector in which consumers are famously selective. We continued our conversation with her, asking what metrics matter most to her when it comes to understanding customers. Indeed, it's customer metrics that have helped her clients the most.

But those vital customer metrics are not what one might think. Hope goes beyond a single set of metrics to look at a range of cross-functional data, to know what customers really want.

DO YOU HAVE A FAVORITE EXAMPLE OF A TIME THAT METRICS REALLY IMPACTED A CLIENT'S RESULTS?

"One example that stands out is the many times we have used lifetime customer value to determine the real impact of churn. The longevity of a guest paired with the lifetime value of that guest allowed us to decide that some forms of churn are not concerning. If a guest is using the lowest-cost services, and hence has low LTV, they can churn without much revenue impact. By the same token, the customers with higher LTV, they're spending more money, and yet they are harder to get. But they are extraordinarily loyal once their business is won. Many brands, looking at their marketing metrics, want to point to acquisition, e.g. look at how many new people we acquired. But that really isn't the important metric. The important metric is how many people are you acquiring who are loyal? Focus on not just acquisition, but acquisition of loyal customers."

Tillster's clients are often global organizations. When it comes to offering dining that appeals to consumers around the world, metrics are vital to understanding local tastes. Surprisingly, those metrics are not just about menu items, as we learned when we chatted with Hope about how she uses metrics to understand global consumers.

WHEN IT COMES TO INTERNATIONAL MARKETING, ON THE LEVEL OF LOCALIZATION, HOW MUCH CAN YOU REALLY GRASP THAT MARKET? BECAUSE SPEAKING OF A DIFFERENT COUNTRY, NOT JUST THE UNITED STATES, LIKE YOU MENTIONED, PHILIPPINES OR GUATEMALA, HOW DIFFICULT IS IT TO UNDERSTAND THEIR MARKETING STRATEGY COMPARED TO THE UNITED STATES? DO YOU FOCUS ON UNDERSTANDING CULTURAL DIFFERENCES? OR DO YOU LOOK AT DIFFERENCES IN TECHNOLOGY? BOTH?

"I'll give you some great examples. In the Philippines, except for Manila, many consumers are on 3G. On some islands in the nation, WiFi may not be strong. So, when you're doing things that are having to communicate with a point-of-sale system, very immediately, you have to do it differently. Because you have very low bandwidth options, you must rethink how something appears in a mobile app. This is especially critical because, in this market, ordering is even more heavily a mobile experience.

"You must be flexible and understand how consumers globally think about your digital offerings. That also includes the look and feel of an experience. For instance, what our aesthetic is in the United States is different from the aesthetic in New Zealand or Asia or South America."

Hope goes beyond the conventional metrics to fully understand client customers. She even uses user experience data to pinpoint consumer needs.

"Metrics tell us that if a guest has too many choices on a page, they don't know what the right choice is; they abandon the ordering process because they don't want to feel stupid. So we have to provide just enough information to make it easy for them without taking their eye away from what they should be doing—ordering food. We're tracking what that perfect amount of information is. We are enormous believers in A/B testing. We start first with usability testing, with a very limited number of people in our target audience, to test our basic ordering experience. But then when we introduce a new concept, we almost always A/B test."

In this way, Hope's team compares new app experiences with their baseline experience. They can thus quickly determine whether a new app experience is driving more sales. By knowing her consumers' tastes, Hope can guide menu decisions. However, she takes consumer metrics much further to deliver her results. She uses LTV to understand what customers to single out for retention efforts. She gathers data on technology usage, user experience, and more to build a complete view of the customer. She then creates a fuller picture of a restaurant's clientele, for a true 360-degree view of the customer. Melding UX data, A/B testing, qualitative cultural and localization data, and, most importantly, LTV, Hope Neiman is turbocharging her clients' results.

04

Channel metrics

Channel metrics to know

This is not meant to be a comprehensive look at all metrics relevant to every marketing channel. Instead, it is a management guide to those select big-picture metrics you need to know as a leader to determine whether your team is doing a great job. They are the metrics to watch to be able to optimize your performance, not get into the weeds.

Big-picture metrics

Of course, the real test of marketing efficacy, regardless of channel, is ROI. Whether it is measured in leads, sales, revenue, or conversions, any channel needs to be bringing you customers. For more on those metrics, turn to Chapter 10 on campaign metrics, where we look at the big picture of how marketing campaigns deliver results.

On the way to those results, though, you typically need to do a lot of fine tuning. Before the sale there's a click. Before the click, consumers see an ad, walk past a poster, hear a podcast spot, or interact on social media. It is these metrics that become the leading indicators that a piece of content on a channel is delivering results—tracking these metrics is the way you optimize for success. This is what we're going to cover in this chapter—those nitty-gritty channel measurements that you track daily in a dashboard to monitor the health of your channel.

The first step is to make sure you are monitoring the right channels. Not all channels are created equal, and not every business should be investing in all channels. So, as we learned in the case study in Chapter 2, part of channel metrics is to determine what channels are helping you reach your target audience and deliver ROI. For this reason, we also look at how to test and measure channels over time, to deliver ROI.

Setting channel goals

In order to track the success of your marketing efforts, you need to set some goals first. What do you want your customers to do when they see or interact with your marketing? Do you want them to buy something, download a white paper, or visit your website? Once you know what you want your customers to do, you can set goals for each channel.

For example, if you want people to visit your website, your goal for paid search might be to have a certain percentage of people clicking through to your website from the ad. Or maybe you want more leads from LinkedIn, so your goal for that channel would be to generate a certain number of leads per month.

Once you set these goals, it is important to track how well each channel is performing in reaching them. That's where the nitty-gritty metrics come in.

You are probably familiar with the PESO model of Paid, Earned, Shared, and Owned media working together. As a refresher, the main types of channels are:

- **Paid media**: includes any type of advertising you do, such as TV, radio, print, and online ads.
- **Earned media**: this is any kind of unpaid media coverage or word-of-mouth marketing. For example, PR efforts or reviews on third-party sites.
- **Shared media**: these are channels such as social media, which are owned by another organization, but where you have an online presence that you control to a large extent, such as your profile.
- **Owned media**: this is your owned and operated content, such as your website, blog, social media accounts, and email list.

If you manage a lot of channels, using the PESO model can help you organize them better. As you can see in the model, each type of channel falls into one of the four quadrants.

Paid media metrics

When it comes to paid media, you can more directly measure ROI, since paid channels typically include extensive ROI tracking, such as Facebook business manager. In addition to the usual leads and sales metrics, you can also track clicks, impressions, and cost per click (CPC) on paid media.

For example, if your goal is to get more website visitors from your paid search campaigns, you would track how many people click through to your website from the ad. You can then track how many of those people convert to customers, and calculate the cost per conversion.

You should also track other paid media metrics such as cost per thousand (CPM) impressions, click-through rates (CTRs), and conversion rates (CRs). These will help you determine whether your ad is being seen by the right people, how well it is resonating with them, and whether they are converting to customers.

Owned media metrics

Owned media is a little harder to track ROI on, since you cannot always track how many leads or sales came from a particular piece of content. In addition, owned media is a kind of fixed cost that cannot necessarily be scaled up and down depending on sales. You will not erase web pages, for instance, when sales are down.

However, you can still track website visits, downloads, and engagement with the content. You can also track how well your website is performing from an SEO perspective, and whether people are sharing your content on social media.

For example, you might track how many website visits each blog post gets, how long people stay on the page, and what kind of engagement (likes, shares, comments) the post receives. This will give you an idea of which topics are resonating with your audience and which ones you might want to focus on more. You can also track how well your website is performing from an SEO perspective, and whether people are sharing your content on social media.

Earned media metrics

Earned media is the most difficult to track ROI on, since you cannot always control where the coverage comes from or how long it lasts. However, you can track things like the number of leads or sales generated, and the ROI on those leads and sales.

In addition, you can track mentions of your company or product on social media, as well as sentiment around your brand. This will give you an idea of how well your PR efforts are working and whether you are getting good or bad press.

For example, you might track the number of leads or sales generated from a particular earned media mention. You can then calculate the ROI on those leads and sales. You can also track sentiment around your brand on social media, to see if people are generally positive or negative about your company.

Marketing research-derived metrics, such as lift, brand awareness, and purchase likelihood are also common measures of earned media effectiveness, as we will explore in this chapter.

Shared media metrics

Shared media is another easier channel to track ROI on, since you can directly measure how many leads or sales came from a particular channel. In addition, shared media is the kind of fixed cost that can be scaled up and down depending on sales.

For example, you can track how many leads or sales came from a particular tweet, and adjust your activity on Twitter accordingly. You can also track the number of retweets and clicks a tweet receives, as well as the sentiment around it. This will give you an idea of which tweets are resonating with your audience and which ones you might want to focus on more.

Now that we've gone over the different types of media you should track ROI on, let's take a look at some of the metrics you should use to measure channel effectiveness:

COST PER CONVERSION
This is the most common metric for paid media, and is fairly self-explanatory. It measures how much money you are spending to get a lead or sale.

COST PER THOUSAND (CPM) IMPRESSIONS
This metric measures how much money you are spending to reach 1,000 people. It is often used for paid media, since you can control how many impressions your ad receives.

CLICK-THROUGH RATE (CTR)

This metric measures how many people click on your ad after seeing it. It is often used for paid media, since you want as many people to click on your ad as possible.

CONVERSION RATE

This metric measures how many people who see your ad end up converting (either by clicking through or by filling out a form). It is often used for paid media, since you want as many people to convert as possible, but it can apply to any channel type. It gets hard to measure for earned media, since you often can't track a web lead back to a specific media mention, but lift in conversion rates gives you an approximation.

BRAND AWARENESS

This metric measures how well your brand is known. It can be measured through surveys, focus groups, or by tracking mentions of your company or product on social media.

SENTIMENT

Sentiment measures the overall feeling people have about your company or product. You can track it through surveys, focus groups, or by tracking mentions of your company or product on social media.

PURCHASE LIKELIHOOD

This metric measures how likely people are to buy your product. It can be measured through surveys, focus groups, or by tracking mentions of your company or product on social media.

LIFT

Lift is a marketing research-derived metric that measures how much your brand or product has increased in awareness, consideration, or purchase intent. It can be measured through surveys, focus groups, or by tracking mentions of your company or product on social media.

LEAD GENERATION RATE

This metric measures how many leads you are generating from a particular channel. It is often used for paid media, since you want to maximize the number of leads you are getting from your investment.

SALES CONVERSION RATE

This metric measures how many sales you are making from a particular channel. It is often used for paid media, since you want to make sure you are getting a good return on your investment.

REVENUE GENERATED

This metric measures how much money you have generated from a particular channel. It is often used for paid media, since you want to make sure you are making a profit from your investment.

ROI

ROI is the most important metric of all, and it measures how effective your channel is in generating leads and sales. It takes into account how much money you have spent on the channel and how much revenue it has generated.

Now that we've gone over the different types of channel metrics you should track ROI on, we'll explore the metrics you should use to measure overall channel effectiveness. We'll focus on the most common ones: cost per conversion, cost per thousand impressions, click-through rate, conversion rate, brand awareness, sentiment, purchase likelihood, and lift. Keep in mind that these metrics vary depending on the channel type. For example, you cannot measure click-through rate for earned media, and lead generation rate is not as important for shared media.

Digital advertising metrics

Digital advertising is measurable in ways that traditional advertising is not. This is because digital ads are connected to user actions, such as clicking on a link or visiting a website. By understanding and measuring digital advertising metrics, you can gain insights into how well your ad campaigns are performing:

- **Cost-per-acquisition** (CPA): this is the cost of acquiring one customer through a particular advertising channel. It is calculated by dividing the total cost of advertising by the number of new customers acquired as a result of that advertising. Ideally, you want this number to be lower over time, as your team becomes more efficient in targeting qualified leads.

- **Cost-per-click (CPC):** this is the cost of each click on an advertisement. It is calculated by dividing the total cost of advertising by the number of clicks on the ad. This metric can help you determine how efficiently your team is spending your advertising budget.

- **Click-through rate (CTR):** this metric is calculated by dividing the number of clicks on an ad by the number of impressions (the number of times the ad was shown). It tells you how often people are clicking on your ads. A high CTR indicates that your team is targeting qualified leads, while a low CTR could indicate that you are targeting the wrong people or that your ad is not appealing.

- **Cost-per-thousand impressions (CPM):** this is the cost of reaching 1,000 people with your advertisement. It is calculated by dividing the total cost of advertising by the number of impressions. This metric can help you determine how efficient your team is in targeting a large audience.

- **Conversion rate:** this metric tells you how many people who saw your ads actually clicked through to your website and became customers. It is calculated by dividing the number of customers acquired through an ad by the number of people who saw the ad. This metric can help you determine how effective your ad campaigns are at generating leads.

- **Bounce rate:** this metric measures how many people who clicked on your ad left your website without converting OR staying on your site to browse.

- **Digital ROAS:** your return on ad spend (ROAS) is your total revenue generated from your digital advertising campaigns divided by the amount you spent on those campaigns. This metric tells you how profitable your digital advertising campaigns are.

Digital advertising is easy to measure in the short term. Longer term, it is important to keep tracking the results of these ads. For instance, perhaps you generated a lot of leads from a campaign, but none of those leads converted. In this case, you will want to revisit your targeting criteria to make sure you are reaching the right people.

Paid search metrics

Measuring the performance of your paid search campaigns is essential in order to make sure you are getting the most out of your investment. Here are some key metrics to track:

- **Cost-per-click (CPC)**: this is the amount you pay each time someone clicks on one of your paid search ads. It is calculated by dividing the total cost of your advertising campaign by the number of clicks on your ads. This metric can help you determine how efficiently your team is spending your advertising budget.

- **Click-through rate (CTR)**: this metric tells you how often people are clicking on your ads. It is calculated by dividing the number of clicks on an ad by the number of impressions (the number of times the ad was shown). A high CTR indicates that your team is targeting qualified leads, while a low CTR could indicate that you are targeting the wrong people, using keywords that are too short-tail, too long-tail, or misaligned with search intents, or that your ad is not appealing.

- **Cost-per-acquisition (CPA)**: this is the amount you pay for each new customer you acquire as a result of your paid search campaigns. It is calculated by dividing the total cost of your advertising campaign by the number of new customers acquired as a result of your ads. This metric can help you determine whether your campaigns are profitable. CPA varies widely across industries. If you are an ice-cream shop bidding on "ice cream shop near me," your CPA may be under $5. A logistics company bidding on high-CPC B2B terms could see a CPA over $100 as reasonable. It is important to look at the average CPC for your keyword set to benchmark a realistic CPA.

- **Conversion rate**: this metric tells you how many people who saw your ads actually clicked through to your website and became customers. It is calculated by dividing the number of customers acquired through an ad by the number of people who saw the ad. This metric can help you determine how effective your ad campaigns are at generating leads.

- **Bounce rate**: this metric measures how many people who clicked on your ad left your website without converting OR staying on your site to browse. It is a red flag with PPC campaigns, since it means you are spending money on ads that no one is converting from. If you have a high CTR on an ad campaign but also high bounce rates, it is time to A/B or multivariate test those landing pages. You are getting clicks to your site, but what consumers see once they are there leaves them cold.

- **Cost-per-thousand impressions (CPM)**: this metric tells you how much you are paying for each 1,000 impressions of your ad. It is calculated by dividing the total cost of your advertising campaign by the number of impressions (the number of times your ad was shown). CPM is a useful metric to track if you are interested in increasing brand awareness rather than generating leads or sales.

- **Paid search ROAS:** your return on ad spend (ROAS) is your total revenue generated from your paid search campaigns divided by the amount you spent on those campaigns. This metric tells you how profitable your paid search campaigns are.

Measuring the performance of your paid search campaigns is essential in order to make sure you are getting the most out of your investment. Fortunately, PPC platforms still provide a strong range of metrics to do so. As automation and AI play a role in more and more PPC campaigns, platforms are shifting away from showing you as much data as before. However, the above metrics are still essential to understanding and optimizing your campaigns and continue to be available to marketers.

Organic search metrics

We dive deep into organic search on its own in Chapters 6 and 7 on content marketing. Here's let's take a look at a few of the additional metrics that track organic search health:

- **Search visibility:** this metric looks at how often your website appears as a result of certain search queries on which you should be appearing. These are searches using keywords that are relevant to the content on your page.
- **Domain authority:** this metric looks at the strength of your website's link profile, and a host of other ranking factors to determine how likely it is to rank overall in organic search.
- **Organic traffic:** this metric looks at the number of visitors coming to your website from unpaid search results.
- **Rankings:** this metric looks at how your website is performing for a set of target keywords, relative to your competition.
- **Rankings lost and gained:** this metric looks at how much movement your website has experienced in the search engine results pages (SERPs) for certain target keywords.
- **First-page results:** this data looks at the number of your keywords for which you are ranking in positions ranging from #11 to #1, generally the first page of the SERPS.

While you can track all of these metrics manually, there are a number of tools that make the process much easier, including Moz's Pro Tools, Ahrefs, and Semrush. All of these tools allow you to track your website's visibility using these metrics and more.

Social media metrics

Social media metrics can help prove the impact of social on your brand. Of all the channel metrics that you cannot afford to sleep on, social media reach and engagement are the ones that merit not only constant tracking, but continuous testing and experimentation. With routine platform algorithm updates a fact of life, it is crucial that you regularly measure how well your social media posts are getting to your audience. Here's how to do it.

REACH

This metric is calculated as the number of people who saw your post. It only tells you how many people saw your post. A high reach indicates that your team is targeting a large audience, while a low reach could indicate that you are targeting the wrong people or that your content is not appealing.

It is important to remember, though, that reach is determined by each social media platform's algorithms. These algorithms change periodically, without notice. Thus, your reach will vary regardless of your effectiveness at social media marketing. For instance, in its early days, Facebook's algorithm showed a business page's followers all of that page's posts. Today, research shows that the average brand's Facebook post is seen by less than 7 percent of their followers.

Algorithms also change the priority with which they show posts in different media. In 2022, for instance, Reels reach more users on Instagram than static posts. This means that you need to monitor reach regularly. When you see dips in reach, you need to test different approaches to see if your reach changes. For instance, when brands saw their reach drop for photos but grow for Reels, many brands kept testing Reels to confirm that the engagement was not a fluke, and then shifted their strategy to using Reels.

ENGAGEMENT RATE

This metric is calculated by dividing the number of engagements (likes, shares, comments) by the number of reach. It tells you how engaged people are with your posts. A high engagement rate indicates that your team is creating content that people are interested in, while a low engagement rate could indicate that you are targeting the wrong people or that your content is not appealing.

Engagement is a byproduct partially of reach—and we know that reach changes with each platform's algorithm adjustments. Thus, it is vital to track and experiment frequently to optimize your social media.

Let's see this in action: our bespoke notebook company, WriteWit, has a Facebook page with 10,000 followers. In a given week, they have 1,000 post reach and 100 engagements (likes, shares, comments).

Another notebook brand, CheapNotebooksNow, has a Facebook page with 1,000 followers. In a given week, they have 100 post reach and 10 engagements.

In this example, WriteWit's engagement rate is 10 percent (100 engagements/1,000 reach), while CheapNoteBooksNow's engagement rate is also 10 percent (10 engagements/100 reach).

WriteWit's social media strategy relies heavily on Facebook polls. While this works for a while, Facebook changes its algorithm to show image posts first. As a result, WriteWit's reach drops, along with engagements. With engagement now below 5 percent, they need to shift tactics.

CheapNoteBooksNow, on the other hand, continues to post the same types of posts (text only) and sees a marginal increase in engagement (2 percent).

While both brands are seeing low engagement, WriteWit acts quickly to test out new post types. They start doing Lives, which results in a jump to 20 percent engagement.

It is important also to remember that engagement is relative to your audience. What's considered high engagement for a brand with a small following might not be as impressive for a brand with a large following.

Thus, it is vital to track and experiment, benchmark, and test. This way you can ensure that your social media posts are engaging your target audience.

FOLLOWERS

Your number of followers is a vanity metric. It is important to track to see if your follower count is growing, but it doesn't tell you anything about how engaged those followers are.

This is why it is important to track engagement and reach. They give you a better indication of how well your content is resonating with your audience.

SENTIMENT

A high sentiment score means that most of your posts are getting positive responses, so you are doing something right. Sentiment is a great way to measure the overall tone of your social media content.

You may have noticed that leads, sales, and revenue are not included in this list of channel metrics. That's because they are not often the direct results of social media for many brands. However, social media can help you increase leads, sales, and revenue indirectly by building brand awareness. Like many other channels, it is important to see it for what it is, using metrics that track its true indicators of success, which are often more about getting the word out.

Influencer marketing

Influencers are critical to today's marketing landscape. They can help you reach new audiences and drive engagement.

Influencer marketing should be tracked like any other paid channel. While some brands treat it as a hybrid between paid and earned, it is wiser to treat influencers the way you do advertising channels. This is why it is important to track the following metrics when working with influencers:

1 **Reach/impressions**: this is a good metric to track to see how many people an influencer is reaching.

2 **Engagements**: this is a good metric to track to see how many people are engaging with an influencer's content.

3 **Sentiment**: this measures the sentiment of an influencer's content.

4 **Cost-per-engagement**: this measures how much you are spending to get an engagement with an influencer's content.

5 **Conversion rate**: this measures the percentage of people who take a desired action after being exposed to an influencer's content.

6 **ROI**: this measures the return on investment for working with an influencer.

When tracking any of these metrics, make sure to track them over time to see how they are changing. This will help you determine whether or not your efforts with influencers are paying off.

Video content metrics

Video marketing is core to your brand. You've been creating videos for a while, and you're starting to see some success. But how do you know if your video marketing is working?

View rate

This metric is calculated by dividing the number of people who watched your video by the number of people who saw it. It tells you how many people watched your video. A high view rate indicates that your team is creating content that people are interested in, while a low view rate could indicate that you're targeting the wrong people or that your video isn't appealing.

It is important to remember, though, that views are also determined by YouTube's algorithms. These algorithms also change periodically, without notice.

Average view duration

This metric is calculated by dividing the total watch time of your video by the number of views. It tells you how long people are watching your video on average.

Percentage of completed views

This metric is calculated by dividing the number of people who watched your video all the way through by the number of people who watched it. It tells you how many people watched your video all the way through.

A high average view duration and percentage of completed views indicate that your video maintains the audience's interest throughout the video. A low average view duration and completed views can mean that your video looks interesting at first, but viewers soon either get bored or find the information they want and move on.

Reach/impressions

This metric is calculated by dividing the number of people who saw your video by the number of impressions it received. It tells you how many people saw your video.

Engagements

This metric is calculated by dividing the number of engagements your video received by the number of impressions it received. It tells you how many people interacted with your video.

A high reach/impressions or engagement rate indicates that you are targeting the right people with your video, have used the right keywords as tags, and have a compelling description, title screen, and title. Low reach/ impressions or engagement could mean that you are targeting the wrong people, the wrong keywords, you haven't optimized your video for YouTube search, or that your video's title and title screen are not appealing.

Conversion rate

This metric is calculated by dividing the number of people who took a desired action after watching your video by the number of people who watched it. It tells you how many people took a desired action after watching your video.

Click through rate

This metric is calculated by dividing the number of people who clicked on a link in your video by the number of impressions it received. It tells you how many people clicked on a link in your video.

Email and text metrics

To determine whether your email program is performing effectively, look at the following big-picture metrics:

- **List growth:** is your list growing over time? By what percentage? List growth of 10 percent is considered healthy; anything above that is very strong. A list that is growing steadily is a healthy list.

- **What efforts are driving list growth**—in other words, where are our subscribers coming from? List signups at the point of sale in exchange for a discount are different from those that take place on the website in order to receive regular company updates. The former is a convenience signup, made in the moment. It may not indicate a future engaged subscriber. The latter, on the other hand, is much more indicative of a possible longer-term relationship.

- **Open-rate trends:** your list is growing, but are your open rates holding steady? If you are seeing list growth while maintaining or even increasing open rates, your new subscribers are an engaged, high-quality audience. On the other hand, if your open rates decline as your list grows, take a look at how you are acquiring these new subscribers. You may also want to re-examine your segmentation. Your previous emails may have worked well with your existing subscribers—your new readership may have different expectations.

- **Click-to-open-rate trends:** similarly to your open rates, your click to open rate (CTOR) is a long-term indicator of email program health. Are your CTORs holding steady or growing? If they are in decline, is it across your list or only with particular segments? What topics are still getting high numbers of clicks? Where are your messages struggling to generate interest? Be prepared to look critically at your email's content. In addition, even if you are happy with your current metrics, there is always room for improvement. If your CTOR is 8 percent right now, can you drive it to 15 percent? What offers or content are already attracting that volume of clicks and how can you replicate that more?

PR metrics

PR is, in short, earned media. It is the result of a good story, well told. And, like all effective marketing endeavors, it takes time and effort to cultivate relationships with the media. As a result, you can spend a lot on PR before it results in ROI. For most brands, direct ROI is not, therefore, their key metric. Earned media is about amplifying your brand's reach and reputation.

Imagine a bespoke notebook brand, WriteWit. If a journalist writes about the company and its unique notebooks, that would be earned media. If WriteWit ran a contest on the joys of handwriting and the winning essay was featured in a national newspaper, that would be earned media. If the company was mentioned on a popular business blog as a useful organizer, that would be earned media, too.

These mentions may lead to sales. But, even if they don't, the brand is reaching a new audience, gaining visibility, and building its reputation—all of which are essential to long-term success. Thus, measuring that success means looking at the exposure the brand gained.

Traditional measures of PR success include:

- **Quantity of media placements:** a high quantity of media placements is a good indication that your story is getting out there. This metric is seldom a focus of PR measurement today, but it is used at times and it is important to know that it is used in some organizations.

- **Brand impact:** a brand impact study measures how people feel about a company after reading or hearing about it in the media.

- **Share of voice:** this metric measures how much attention a brand gets compared to its competition. For example, let's say a company gets mentioned in 10 percent of all articles about a certain topic. That would give the company a share of voice of 10 percent in relation to its competitors.

- **Sentiment analysis:** this metric looks at whether people are talking about your brand in a positive or negative way. You can use software to automatically track this, or you can manually review.

- **Editorial quality of media placements:** not all media placements are created equal—you want to make sure that you are getting quality coverage as well. This metric looks at things like the reach of a placement, the tone of the article, and how prominently your brand is featured. This metric also looks at the reputation of the media. For instance, getting mentioned in the *New York Times* is more prestigious than a mention on a local news site.

There are also several digital-focused PR metrics that can be useful in measuring the success of your campaigns:

- **Web traffic:** this metric looks at how much web traffic is coming from your PR campaigns.

- **Social media shares:** this metric looks at how many times your content has been shared on social media.

- **Inbound links:** this metric looks at how many inbound links you are getting as a result of your PR campaigns.

- **Email subscribers:** this metric looks at how many people are signing up for your email list as a result of your PR campaigns. For instance, did visitors who clicked on a link in a media article sign up for your emails?

- **Domain authority:** this metric looks at how authoritative your website is in relation to others, especially in an SEO context. Sites with more inbound links tend to have higher domain authority.

- **Social media reach and engagement:** this metric looks at how many people post about your earned media reach, as well as how engaged they are.
- **Traffic to website or landing pages from PR efforts:** this data looks at how much traffic links within earned media drive.

Sales or leads generated from PR campaigns may be considerable, or they may not happen. The important thing when measuring PR success is to use a variety of metrics that will help you understand how well your campaigns are performing at generating buzz for your brand.

TV, radio, out-of-home

Marketing research is a traditional way in which brands measure the impact of marketing campaigns that cannot be directly measured. Surveys and other market research (MR) studies can indicate whether consumers who were exposed, or likely were exposed, to ads have an increased propensity to like or buy from the brand. This propensity is often measured through these metrics:

- **Brand lift:** a measure of how much a campaign has increased the awareness or positive sentiment of a brand. It is often measured through surveys in which respondents are asked if they have seen the ad, if they know more about the brand, and so on.
- **Purchase likelihood:** a measure of how likely it is that a person who has seen the ad will buy the product.
- **Attitudes:** advertisers often want to know if their ads are changing people's opinions about a product in a positive way. This can be measured through surveys that ask things like "would you consider buying this product?"
- **Recall:** a measure of how much people remember an ad after seeing it. It is also measured via surveys.
- **Lift:** a measure of how much a campaign has increased the sales of a brand. It involves subtracting the baseline (typical) sales expected at a given time from the amount of sales that occurred after the ad ran. For instance, let's say you run a gaming store. Your weekly sales are US $1 million. After running a TV ad, your sales are $1.5 million the next week.

That $500,000 is lift. Put another way, you achieved 50 percent lift—sales increased by 50 percent after the ad. Lift can also apply to awareness or positive sentiment of a brand. In such cases, it is often measured through surveys in which respondents are asked their opinions before and after the ad is run.

- **Brick-and-mortar traffic:** measuring whether there has been an increase in physical traffic to a store is another way to measure the impact of marketing campaigns. This metric can be difficult to track, as there are many factors that can contribute to changes in traffic (e.g. weather, seasonality, etc). Use benchmarks for normal traffic to measure your lift.

Many of the metrics used fall under branding metrics, looking at overall attitudes toward the brand before and after a campaign. Indeed, many of these measures, because they cannot be captured through digital channels, must rely on surveying people who have been exposed to various forms of marketing. For more on brand metrics, see Chapter 5 on metrics-driven brand strategy.

Digital metrics for lift created by TV, radio, and out-of-home

In addition to lift of purchase intent, brand attitudes, and other data that can be measured via surveys, effective TV, radio, and out-of-home ads should create lift in your digital metrics as well. They especially are drivers of:

- **Web traffic:** ads on TV, radio, and out-of-home can all direct web traffic to your website or specific landing pages.
- **Social media:** paid or organic social media amplification of your TV, radio, or out-of-home ads will result in increased engagement with those posts. In addition, you should see growth of followers and increased engagement with your brand as a whole.
- **Search:** if you are running TV, radio, or out-of-home ads that are also supported by search engine optimization (SEO), you will see an increase in organic traffic and impressions. Watch for growth of branded keyword searches, and in particular, look for branded searches for any products mentioned in an ad.
- **Email marketing:** TV, radio, and out-of-home ads can inspire people to sign up for your email list.

All of these digital channels are important to track in order to determine the full effect of a traditional media buy. When measuring the impact of your TV, radio, and out-of-home campaigns, be sure to use a variety of metrics that will help you understand how well they are performing. This will help you make better decisions about where to allocate your advertising budget in the future.

Television advertising metrics

Before we dive into TV advertising metrics, it is important to define what we mean by television. Today, the two main forms of TV technology are linear and over the top (OTT). You may also hear the term CTV (connected TVs). Linear TV is old-fashioned broadcast programming, whether it gets to your TV via an antenna or cable box. OTT is the universe of streaming services, such as Netflix, Disney+, and Hulu. CTVs are the smart TVs or standard TVs equipped with streaming devices such as a Fire TV stick.

Measuring linear TV has traditionally been more challenging than measuring digital advertising that has a more immediate connection to audience action, such as social media ads. Today, the TV ratings and analytics powerhouse Nielsen has developed a digital ad ratings product to provide a measure of how many people saw an ad and how often, but it is still in its early days. Other ways of measuring TV ad viewership have become easier with the advent of OTT. Platforms such as:

- **Gross rating points (GRPs):** this is a measure of the reach of an advertising campaign. It is calculated by multiplying the frequency of an ad by the percentage of the target audience that saw it. For example, if an ad is aired 10 times and 100 percent of the target audience sees it, the GRP would be 1,000.
- **Television viewer rating (TVR):** the metric that tells us the relative viewership of a show; this indicates how popular a show on which you advertise is.

But viewership is only a quarter of the story in TV metrics. The real metric is ROI, as with any other channel. Quantify lift in terms of ad spending: did your lift justify the amount you spent on the ad? Be careful to look for lift over a relatively long period. It is not enough to have a great week after running an ad—you need to look at cumulative lift. If the week after running an ad is not spectacular, but your sales double over the following quarter, you still have lift.

To track TV metrics, you also want to refer to the metrics for tracking TV, radio, and out-of-home noted above. Measuring brand lift, lift of purchase intent, and ad recall are all vital to understanding the impact of TV viewership.

Radio and podcast ad metrics

Radio and podcast advertising, like television, is seeing a resurgence with the advent of streaming services. The two main ways to measure the success of these ads are through reach and engagement:

- **Reach:** this is the number of people who hear your ad. It is calculated by multiplying the frequency of an ad by the percentage of the target audience who are listening to the radio or podcast at that time. For example, if an ad is aired 10 times and 100 percent of the target audience is listening, the reach would be 100 percent.

- **Engagement:** this is the percentage of people who hear your ad and react to it in some way. Engagement can be measured through actions such as clicking on a link, calling the number, or visiting a website. For example, if 100 people hear your ad and 10 of them visit your website, the engagement would be 10 percent.

Most radio and podcast spots have a dedicated URL to make it easier to track listener response. Let's say you're listening to a movie podcast; we'll say it's called *Popcorn Predictions*. WriteWit runs an ad with this podcast, read by the host. At the end, she may say: "To get 20 percent off your own WriteWit notebook, go to WriteWit.com/popcornpredictions. This URL is not WriteWit's main URL; its sole purpose is to track traffic that comes to the site in response to this ad. Most of the time, such dedicated URLs don't lead to a special landing page, even—instead, they simply redirect to the main site. Nonetheless, web analytics will track visits to the site that originate with this URL, even if it just redirects immediately to another page. This simple method is currently the most reliable way to measure the success of a radio or podcast ad campaign.

Print advertising metrics

Print advertising is seeing a resurgence, too, as brands shift more of their budget to offline channels. The two main ways to measure the success of these ads are through reach and engagement.

- **Reach:** this is the number of people who see your ad. It is often roughly estimated by the circulation of the print publication. For instance, if a magazine has 30,000 subscribers and an additional 10,000 non-duplicative news-stand purchases, its monthly circulation of 40,000 is your print ad's reach.

- **Engagement:** like radio and podcasts, print ads can contain a special URL to track responses, or a QR code. This can be used to measure how many people visit a website or take action after seeing the ad. For more on using dedicated URLs and QR codes, see the section below. Other direct tracking mechanisms are dedicated phone numbers or old-fashioned response coupons. The important thing is to make sure you are tracking response rates and not just reach.

Out-of-home metrics

This is a catch-all term for all the different ways people can see or interact with your advertising outside of traditional media. This could include signage, bus stops, and other out-of-home placements. The most important metric for out-of-home advertising is engagement, which is measured by the number of people who take some kind of action as a result of seeing the ad. This could be anything from visiting a website to making a purchase.

Geopath

As with TV and audio media, out-of-home (OOH) can be measured using dedicated URLs. It also can be tracked using techniques such as brand lift. One newly emerged way of measuring some OOH is Geopath. Geopath measures viewership, demographics, and reach of billboards and related media using a combination of roadway traffic analysis, household demographics in a region where an ad is located, and population movement metrics to estimate how often a billboard was seen and by whom. Created by a nonprofit, Geopath is becoming an industry-standard method of measurement technology.

Geopath draws on a range of metrics, including US Department of Transportation traffic metrics, mobile-phone location data, US Census demographic data, eye-tracking studies, and more. It is in continuous development, and you can learn more about it here: https://geopath.org.

QR codes, dedicated URLs, and measuring out-of-home marketing

QR codes are a quick and easy way to measure the success of OOH advertising. When someone scans the QR code, it takes them to a landing page where you can track their activity. Alternatively, brands can use dedicated URLs to track OOH responses.

QR code and dedicated URL metrics focus on understanding how OOH messages in which they are embedded drove results:

- **Traffic:** how many people scanned the code.
- **Landing-page engagement:** how long they stayed on the page.
- **Conversions:** what actions they took.
- **Repeat visits:** how many users returned to your site after originally finding you via the outdoor ad and scanning the code.

Once visitors scan your QR code and visit your website, they can naturally be tracked using all your conventional digital metrics. That can be incredibly useful in understanding the impact of your outdoor ads that bear QR codes. For instance, once consumers who see your outdoor ads and scan the codes come to your site, you can measure the usual web metrics with regards to them and see how consumers acquired via outdoor channels compare to those acquired on other channels. Metrics to compare include:

- **Length and depth of session:** do OOH consumers visit for shorter or longer visits than other site visitors?
- **In-market and affinity segments:** what psychographic segments does Google categorize them under?
- **Conversion rates:** does this audience convert more or less than, say, social media visitors?
- **Loyalty:** do customers who convert after out-of-door acquisition return at a higher rate than other channels?

OOH advertising is a great way to reach people who are not reached by traditional media. For example, customers who are too busy to spend much leisure time on the web or consumers you are not targeting online. Measuring the success of this type of advertising can be difficult, but with the right tools it is possible. By using QR codes and dedicated URLs, you can track the success of your out-of-door campaigns and see how well they are working.

Channel metrics for marketing program optimization

Now that we have a sense of the metrics we use to optimize different channels, let's look at how we might optimize a marketing program that uses multiple channels. In particular, we'll look at a scenario where a company has two goals: increase brand awareness and generate leads.

WriteWit want to expand their B2B sales. The company begins by looking at their customer data to determine which channels are most effective at reaching their target customers. They find that LinkedIn, Instagram, and out-of-home have netted B2B leads in the past. They then allocate more budget to those channels and run campaigns in them to increase brand awareness and generate leads.

After a few months, the company reviews their data to see how well their campaigns are performing. They find that their brand awareness is increasing, but their lead generation is not as high as they would like. However, out-of-home is delivering the most leads, as measured by QR code and CRM data. LinkedIn is a close second, generating 50 leads in the past quarter. They then adjust their strategy by allocating more budget to channels that are more effective at generating leads and reducing the budget for channels that are not as effective. This allows them to focus their efforts on those channels that are most effective and improve their overall results. By the end of the year, they have made US $3 million in B2B sales to offices.

This is just one example of how a company can use channel metrics to optimize their marketing programs. By understanding which channels are most effective at reaching their target customers and allocating budget accordingly, they can improve the performance of their marketing programs.

Channel metrics are an important part of any marketer's toolkit. By understanding which channels are most effective for your business and using that information to guide your marketing efforts, you can improve the results you see from your marketing programs.

Conclusion

Understanding the health of your channels and how they relate to your business is critical for any marketer. By using the appropriate metrics, you can determine which channels are most effective and allocate your budget accordingly. This will help you focus your efforts on those channels that are delivering the best results for your business.

In this chapter, we looked at the different types of channel metrics and how they can be used to optimize marketing programs. We saw that by understanding which channels are most effective for your business, you can focus your efforts on those channels and improve your results.

We looked at the importance of the PESO model to this type of measurement, and how it can be used to understand the different channels that are most effective for your business. We also looked at some of the ways you can track the success of your out-of-home campaigns. We also learned how to apply lift to a range of metrics correctly, and, in turn, to use it to measure various channels.

While ROI is the key metric, daily optimization requires that we look at other factors such as reach, engagement, and leads. By tracking which channels are most effective for reaching your target customers, you can focus your marketing efforts on those channels and improve your ROI.

05

Data-driven branding

Before we talk about data-driven branding, we first need to define branding. This is important because it is a marketing term that has a range of definitions. To management outside of marketing, branding is often about visuals only: logo design, the selection of specific colors that represent your brand, and fussing over your fonts. Brand design is, indeed, a key part of branding. A strong visual identity is key to helping consumers identify your organization. It can convey your organization's top values, such as being green and sustainable. It also helps present your brand image, whether you wish to appear trendy, or fun, or professional.

Branding has a more significant purpose, however, than simply making your organization look sleek and stylish. You can establish a strong brand through compelling logo design and color selection, but it is where all of these elements come together to communicate your organization's values and goals that makes branding important. This is why we're going to focus on the bigger picture of branding.

First, let's break down some of the main disciplines within branding:

- Brand design is the creative process behind how to visually communicate your brand. Your logo is the most critical element of your brand design, but it is not the only one. Other elements include typography, color palette, illustration style and tone, organization or product name, taglines or slogans—or any part of how you visually identify yourself as an organization.

- Brand identity is the end result of brand design. It is the collection of elements that creates an experience for your audience. Identity elements can include a logo, color palette, tone, and style—and even the personality you want to convey. The materials that communicate these parts of your identity are typically collected in a brand book, which is a tool for all of your designers to follow.

- Brand architecture is a framework you create to classify and organize all the components of your brand—identity elements, audience personas, messaging, tone of voice, and any other important elements. This framework comes in handy when you begin to communicate your brand identity across many mediums. You can reuse pieces or create new ones for each unique situation—but the experience will all feel cohesive because it is all part of the same system.

- Brand guidelines are directions that instruct members of your creative teams on how to apply the brand identity and architecture to specific materials, such as ads.

Those are the tactics of branding. The strategic side of branding, however, is also vital to measure. Your brand strategy is the process of how you will use your brand to achieve specific business goals. This could be improving customer retention, increasing website traffic, or growing sales—these are all examples of strategic objectives that branding might help you achieve if done well.

Utilizing both tactics and strategy for branding requires planning and research. You need an understanding of your brand's purpose, audience, and the larger business goals. You need a thorough understanding of your brand architecture and how all the elements fit together in a cohesive way that will help you achieve your strategic objectives.

Brand strategy consists of a range of sub-disciplines, such as brand associations. They are just as measurable as tactics. Indeed, unlike most other marketing disciplines, branding is a field where strategy often has more granular metrics than tactical work.

The strategic aspects of branding include a range of measurable activities that you want to track:

- Brand touchpoints are individual consumer experiences with a brand that help them form an opinion of that brand. These experiences can vary greatly between consumers, and often are only partially influenced by the visual brand.

- Brand awareness is a measure of the degree to which consumers are aware of a specific brand, and can be influenced by both visual and non-visual brand touchpoints. This includes both your company as a whole as well as all individual parts of your branding, such as: logo, slogan, color scheme, packaging design, etc.

- Brand associations are often intangible things that people think about when they think about a certain brand, such as "Coca Cola is refreshing," or "Adidas is #1." These are often subconscious on the part of consumers, dated, or based on a personal experience. For example, a person might think that Coca-Cola is the best soda because it was their favorite as a child. They may not even realize that this is the reason for their preference, but that doesn't make it any less strong an association. These layers of conscious, unconscious, and outdated associations make brand associations important to measure, since they can influence consumer behavior in ways brands can't anticipate by looking at their current brand positioning.

- Brand perception is a consumer's opinion of a brand, which is made up from their individual touchpoints with the brand.

- Brand equity is the brand value in a specific market. Brand equity can be positive or negative, and ultimately provides an economic base for the business that does not directly derive from its products or services.

- Brand recall refers to how easily consumers can connect with your company or product when speaking about it (without looking at any reference material to help them).

Metrics will help you measure both the creative and strategic impacts of your branding efforts. It will help you stay focused on your customers. You cannot have a good experience if you don't know what your customers want! "Mission statements" only scratch the surface when it comes to branding. They are a statement of your own values as an organization, but they are often less useful in figuring out who your customer really is. Metrics-driven branding is key to creating a brand that goes beyond your internal team's creative vision to what resonates emotionally with your consumers.

Part of the complexity of measuring branding is that all aspects of branding are complex. A logo, for example, is a visual representation of your brand identity—but not the only one. If you also use typography or color palettes consistently throughout your materials, these are other elements that comprise your identity. All together, they create an experience that engages and inspires your customer. But of all these creative elements, how do you use metrics to learn which aspects are creating the most emotional impact?

Goal-driven brand metrics

It is important to note that when you start out with your branding initiatives, the primary objective should be to grow awareness in your target market. Once you have a better understanding of your customers, you can begin building relationships with them.

You have to invest the money necessary to reach the people who will become loyal customers. One great way to do this is by investing in your brand's visual appearance, which includes everything from posters and business cards all the way up to your corporate website.

The most effective way to measure the impact of your branding is to monitor and analyze conversions (i.e. sales, requests for information, etc) as they relate to all aspects of your brand's image. To do this effectively, you should start collecting data before you begin any sort of rebranding.

Measuring brand equity

Brand equity is when an organization has created a significant competitive advantage in the minds of target customers that results in measurable financial outcomes either through charging higher prices or earning premium margins without costing more to produce. The value of this association is in the minds of consumers, and it can be measured using surveys.

Accurate metrics of brand equity include:

- Revenue-based metrics, such as increased revenue, increased operating income and increased net income.
- Recommendation metrics, such as Net Promoter Score.
- Comparative price data, indicating a premium price in comparison to competitors.

In order to track any of these accurately, you need a baseline. You will need to know what your company's current performance is in order to measure the impact of your rebranding efforts down the line. To do this, you can track overall revenue growth as well as brand awareness and equity measures over time.

Measuring price premium vs profit premium

Let's say you discover that you are comfortably charging a premium price for your product, thus indicating strong brand equity. The next question is whether you are charging an affective premium, or whether you are earning an innovation premium.

Affective premiums indicate a superior product or service experience while innovation premiums reveal a sustainable competitive advantage, which can be sustained even as a business scales. If your product speaks for itself so that consumers are convinced it is better than the competition, you have an affective premium. If you have a sustainable competitive advantage that allows you to charge more—innovation premium—then consumers may be paying more not on the basis of an overall perception of quality, but because of that specific competitive advantage.

To understand which premium is at work, you need to measure your brand perception and your brand associations. Those metrics will tell you whether your consumers associate words such as "luxury," or "value," or "innovative" with your brand. Think of Coca-Cola's brand equity (it has the highest level of familiarity, awareness, and share of preference) as an umbrella for all other premium categories. In most cases they are applying an affective premium across their product line—from flavored water to designer water. It's not that Coca-Cola beverages are especially innovative. Instead, their brand equity stems from emotional associations: the brand is an iconic part of Americana, it is associated with happy experiences in people's lives. Generic colas, on the other hand, are associated by US consumers with financial struggle—being unable to afford "name brand" beverages in tough economic times—or with niche beverages that are outside the mainstream and thus not iconic.

Apple, on the other hand, has brand equity that allows them to charge both an affective and an innovation premium. Their brand experience is top-notch, making their brand iconic. It is associated with technological sophistication, creativity, and elegance. At the same time, the products historically have been at the forefront of innovation, making consumers willing to pay a premium for features not available with competing products. As Apple's reputation for innovation has experienced erosion in the early 2020s, it will be interesting to see that erosion's effect on both types of premiums.

As for Samsung, they have been able to develop a decent brand experience in the smartphone space. It's associated with technological sophistication and high quality. However, it hasn't been able to command an affective premium due to its lack of creativity and elegance. That's why Apple continues to be successful even in markets where it charges much higher prices.

So, what can you do with metrics that indicate a strong affective bias to your brand equity? How do you act on that data? It means your consumers turn to you because your products make them feel something about themselves: wearing your clothing or drinking your beverages may make them feel glamorous, prosperous, or trendy. Your brand may give them feelings of nostalgia, stability, or health. The bottom line is that a brand with affective brand equity is selling a feeling.

It means your consumers feel they can trust you. And since it's a feeling, not a thought, your brand equity can best be reinforced through affective marketing. If consumers trust you, they believe in you. They need reminders of why they should continue to trust and believe in what you represent.

Brands with affective brand equity are well-served by marketing that includes:

- TV, print, and radio spots that focus on brand identity, associations, and perceptions—in other words, that sell the feeling. Affect can be triggered through more traditional media sources such as TV ads or through social media.

- Influencer collaborations that deepen consumers' connection with the brand.

- Content marketing that focuses on the consumer—their interests, likes and dislikes—rather than the product.

- Events that make consumers feel your brand is a good fit with their interests—activities and events they may participate in, be it a marathon or a popup store, a tech convention or a weekend retreat.

If you have affective brand equity, you share a deep connection with your consumers. Your key to success in the 2020s is to continue to nurture and build that connection through messages and experiences that trigger feelings associated with your brand, across all marketing channels.

With so much data out there about consumer behavior it would seem impossible not to know what pushes their buttons, but the reality is that tracking the details of affective brand equity usually requires old-fashioned tactics, such as surveys, focus groups, and individual interviews. It can also be measured using digital tools. Some of the best online data-gathering methods for understanding your consumers' emotions include social listening with sentiment analysis, keyword research, and text analytics. We will talk more about each of those methods later in the chapter.

Innovation brand equity, on the other hand, is often measured in terms of financial metrics that indicate a strong preference for a brand among consumers. Willingness to pay a premium price, the standard metric of brand equity, is the best measure of innovation equity. There are other metrics you can use to measure this equity, as well. These metrics include brand loyalty and the number of consumers willing to recommend the brand to others.

Innovation brand equity is about offering the customer something they feel enhances their life in some way or helps them achieve goals that no other product can. We can measure this aspect using purchase intent. It gives us insight into how likely consumers are to buy our product. We will learn about measuring purchase intent later in the chapter, in the section on survey tactics.

If you have innovation brand equity, your first step is to find ways to use your data to reinforce your best customers' perceptions about the value of purchasing from you. Look for patterns in customer behaviors and purchases. What do they spend money on? What web pages do they visit? How much time do they spend on those pages, and how often do they return? Let's look at an example: The Mercedes-Benz brand is one of the most iconic luxury car brands in the world. It has a rich history and a loyal following. In recent years, the company has leveraged data to better understand its customers and their needs. One of the things they learned is that many of their customers are interested in nature and outdoor activities. To appeal to this customer base, they created marketing campaigns with themes such as "Into the wild." TV ads, print ads, and social media content showed Mercedes-Benz cars being used in a variety of outdoor activities, from mountain climbing to kayaking.

The goal of the marketing content was to show customers that Mercedes-Benz understands their needs and interests. The ads were also designed to create a feeling of excitement and anticipation in viewers, showing them that owning a Mercedes-Benz is the ultimate luxury experience. The campaign was a success, with purchase intent for the brand increasing significantly.

Focus groups for brand metrics

Focus groups and one-on-one interviews can also help you understand what makes your customers tick. For instance, if you ask them to complete a sentence that begins with "I buy X brand because…" it might give you insight into their practical considerations in the purchase decision.

Brands with innovation brand equity are best served by marketing that includes:

- Inbound marketing driven by SEO, paid search, and event marketing channels that consumers turn to when they seek identified solutions to practical needs.
- Content marketing that focuses on product applications, research and development, and case studies.
- Information-based social media marketing channels such as LinkedIn, Reddit, and YouTube.
- Events that are more experiential and product-focused, including tradeshows, conferences, roadshows.

Innovation brand equity is the better type to have if you are a business to business (B2B) product, are in the high-tech sector, or produce high-ticket, necessary items such as appliances, cars, and so on. This is not to say that affective brand equity is not important—it can also be a key predictor of purchase intent and loyalty. However, the reality today is that we buy for both emotional and practical reasons (even if we don't always understand why we do what we do). Innovation brand equity is about products that are useful, new, and/or of high quality. It is the type of branding that your top customers seek.

Trust equity

There's a third type of brand equity: trust equity. This is when you inspire the trust of consumers, such that they are, again, willing to pay a premium for your service, recommend you to others, and/or show high loyalty. It is the brand equity that services require. We need to trust our accountant, our physical therapist, our mechanic. The increased fees, loyalty, or word-of-mouth propensity that a trustworthy service can command are its trust equity. Trust equity is also in play in B2B products, where the consumer is another business organization. For example, in IT consulting services, consultants are often required to build trust with your clients before they can be considered for purchase.

To measure trust equity, look at metrics that indicate how much people appreciate your brand. Here's a list of those metrics:

- Net Promoter Score (NPS)—the percentage of promoters and detractors who recommend you to other consumers. The difference between these two groups is called the Net Promoter Score. For reference, NPS for Amazon is 69. Learn more about NPS here: https://www.netpromoter.com.

- Favorability—a brand attribute metric, this is the percentage of consumers who like your brand and associate it with positive qualities.

- Purchase intent—the percentage of those who like your brand and agree that they might purchase from you.

- Customer satisfaction score (CSAT)—how satisfied are customers with the quality of your products and services? This is measured on a scale of 1–5. CSAT tells you how well you are currently doing in keeping customers happy. To learn more about CSAT, visit: http://www.zendesk.com/satisfaction.

- Word of mouth—the number of people who have talked about your brand in the last six months.

- Brand advocacy—how likely are customers to recommend you to others? This is measured on a scale of 1–10.

- Referenceable customers—how many customers would be willing to serve as a reference for you?

- Customer effort score—the amount of effort that customers need to engage in to resolve a service issue. This is measured on a scale of 1–10. The higher the effort they must make to resolve their problems with your brand, the lower their trust will become. By contrast, fast, easy resolutions of service issues grow trust.

- Customer loyalty—do consumers buy from you again after their first purchase? If so, how much time passes before they buy your product again?

Brands reliant on trust equity are best served by marketing efforts that include:

- Inbound marketing based on blogging, thought leadership pieces, videos, podcasts, and webinars.

- Channels that consumers turn to when they seek personalized recommendations for solutions to their problems or questions. Focus on customer-centric channels such as Twitter chats, livestreams, and social media groups.

- Relationship marketing when you host in-person events that are informal and allow consumers to interact with your brand one-on-one.

- Events where consumers get hands-on experience, such as trade shows and the like. This is because trust is built through experiences, not through brand messaging. When you actually show consumers how your product works, it increases the likelihood they will purchase from you in the future.

Marketing efforts that revolve around building relationships are effective for services that rely on trust equity. It is important to have a website and social media presence that is straightforward, free of heavy sales pitches, and more conservative in its visual branding. You want to push for a warm tone with consumers, not the stuffy image of an old-school brand. However, you want to avoid being too trendy, instead aiming to project stability, trust, and authenticity.

> Pro Tip: Even though trust equity is the final brand equity type we will cover, it is also the most challenging to build. It takes time for consumers to learn about your brand and come to appreciate its value proposition. That said, there are some practices you can use to help speed up this process of demonstrating why consumers should trust you. The above tactics, executed with transparency, will help showcase your integrity while building buzz.

Measuring brand perception vs brand awareness

Brand awareness is when a consumer recognizes the brand, while brand perception goes beyond that to involve other associations in the mind of the customer, such as positive feelings about their experiences with your product or service. While you can measure brand equity as a function of revenue, to measure brand awareness and perception you need to go outside your organization, straight to your consumers. Surveys are the traditional means of assessing these metrics.

A brand awareness survey needs to sample a wide cross-section of consumers. If you are a niche brand, the sample to whom you deploy the survey can be your target niche. For instance, if you are a baby-product company, your target audience is parents of infants and expectant parents. While knowing whether the general public is aware of your brand is nice, you need to know if the target market knows about you. Brand awareness surveys often select specific samples of respondents who meet the criteria of belonging to a particular demographic or to a psychographic segment. Ideally, you can separate out your existing consumers when deploying an awareness survey. You know they are aware of you! What you want to know is whether those in your ideal segment who have not yet become your customers know you exist.

A key question a brand awareness survey needs to answer is whether customers associate your brand with a specific value proposition, and one that is unique to it. Your uniqueness is what will make customers buy. Thus, questions in such a survey should include questions of what values consumers identify with a brand. After all, if you only ask consumers whether they have heard of you, you will be in for a surprise if you later learn that all they have heard is negative buzz. You can also identify whether consumers have a misperception about your brand that might prevent them from becoming customers. For instance, your organic baby line might be quite affordable. However, consumers may look at your logo, colors, fonts, and packaging, and misperceive your brand as high-priced.

In a consumer context, surveying anyone in your target segment should work. In a B2B environment, you might look at "influencers"—people in key positions who will decide which brands to buy and recommend to their colleagues. Identify these people and get them on your survey panel.

Measuring brand identity

What are you measuring when you measure brand identity? There are several key areas to measure:

- Cognitive: awareness, comprehension, and memory for the brand.
- Emotional: how the consumer feels when exposed to your brand.
- Behavioral: what actions consumers take when exposed to your brand (e.g. purchase intent, word of mouth, willingness to consider).

The biggest mistake brands make when measuring brand identity is that they mistake it for brand awareness, leading them to only survey for cognitive reactions—whether their brand is easy to remember. Again, while being known is the first step, you need to understand what you are known for. If your logo is memorable for its ugliness, that is not a win. You need to understand how your brand identity is received, both cognitively and affectively.

The first step should be to include a measurement that captures what consumers think of your brand. Begin with the construction of an ad awareness scale, asking consumers how familiar they are with various marketing communications. Include questions about other aspects of your brand identity as well. Then include an affect scale, where consumers rate their feelings about the brand. Try to get at both positive and negative aspects of affect.

The next step would be to identify key associations around your brand identity. What is it known for? What are its key features? Key benefits? How does it compare to other brands in the category? What are its most important emotional terms that consumers think of when prompted to think about your brand?

Search data

Branded searches are another way to understand your branding. Look at how many times your brand is being searched for, and also look at how that changes over time. Look at related searches to see what other terms are being associated with your brand. If you offer a product or service, look at the branded search for that product or service as well.

You can also use Google's Keyword Tool to help you understand how people are searching for your brand. This tool will show you how many people are searching for a particular term each month, along with other related terms.

You also want to look at what words and questions are being searched in conjunction with your brand. Tools such as SpyFu will provide a list of questions that are commonly searched that include or are related to a keyword. This can give you a good indication of how people view your brand and what they are looking for when they search for it.

Once you have a good understanding of how people are searching for your brand, you can start to develop content around those topics. You can also use that information to help target your advertising efforts. You can also use it to develop new products or services that are in line with what people are searching for.

Monitoring brand reputation with social listening

Social listening is vital to modern brand metrics. Try to search for both positive and negative mentions of your brand on social media. Try to include sentiment analysis—do posts have a strong positive or negative sentiment?

When doing social listening for branding, you want to capture what people are saying about your brand, not just what they are saying about your products. You also want to capture the context of the conversation. Is it a review? A complaint? A discussion with friends?

You can also use social listening to track consumer perceptions of competitor brands. This can help you understand how you stack up against the competition and what positioning you might need to adopt in order to be successful.

Brand tracking software

A brand tracking software tool can give you a holistic view of how a brand is performing over time. This will help you understand how different marketing channels are impacting your brand awareness and perception. It can also help you identify any negative trends before they become too big a problem.

There are many different types of brand tracking platforms. Some are specifically for measuring online branding, while others measure both online and offline branding. Some tools, such as Latana, use AI to monitor online conversations, while more traditional tools such as Semrush provide a suite of search and social trackers. Make sure to select a platform that fits your needs: if you are primarily interested in online branding, there is no need to select a tool that also tracks offline brand metrics, for instance.

Acting on brand awareness metrics

Once you have measured your brand awareness, it is important to take action on the results. If you find that your brand awareness is low, you might need to invest in a marketing campaign to increase visibility. If you find that your brand is doing well but you want to improve certain aspects of it, you can use the data from brand tracking software to decide which marketing channels are worth investing more in.

If you are noticing negative trends in how people perceive your brand, you need to take action to correct that. This might involve changes to your marketing strategy, product development, or customer service.

Brand awareness is an important metric for any business, but it is only one piece of the puzzle. To really understand how well your brand is doing, you also need to track brand consideration, purchase intent, and customer satisfaction.

Here are some ways to act on your awareness metrics:

- Lack of awareness: when consumers just don't know about your brand, it seems easy to remedy the situation—just advertise more, post more often to social media, and, in general, promote more actively. However, it is not quite that simple. Yes, low brand awareness does signal a need for greater promotion, but those promotions need to support brand perception and associations. In other words, you need to promote in a way that builds your brand's reputation. In the long run, you will need to spend less on promotion once you have cemented your brand's reputation. It is much more expensive to establish a brand than it is to keep it strong. Thus, you want every penny you invest in promotion at the brand awareness-building stage to pay back double in both letting consumers know you exist, and helping them understand why you exist. A strong brand is your best asset, so make sure all your promotions work to build it.

- High awareness: when consumers are already familiar with your brand, you can't just keep shouting at them. It's tempting to think that the solution is to shout even louder, but it is not. You have to find new ways to create fresh associations between your brand and useful information. At this stage, you are really defending your brand: against new upstarts ready to unseat you, against the inevitable negative reviews that all brands garner, and against consumer apathy. You need to keep one step ahead of these threats to your brand. Thus, when the metrics tell you that you have strong brand awareness, that is your signal not to rest on your success, but to shift gears to keeping your brand relevant.

Strategies with brand equity data

Brand equity metrics are highly actionable when you know how to use them. Acting on your brand equity metrics can be complex, as brand equity is a complex concept. Here are a few strategies you can use:

- Low brand equity: this usually means that you are not making the profits you should, because consumers are not willing to pay extra for your brand. You may be at risk of commodification, or you might already be there. When brand equity is low, you need to shift into high gear to fight commodification.

- High brand equity: this means that you are making the most profits per dollar spent on marketing. However, when brand equity is high, it could mean that your consumers think about your product too much—they love it so much that they might start getting tired of you. The history of business is filled with once-premium brands that lost their equity. Look at your brand equity alongside your pricing strategy. Are you discounting to drive more sales? Are you trying to break into new markets by offering lower-priced versions of your products? Those can all be good strategies, but be careful of wasting your brand equity. You might be commodifying the brand perception that people have of your product, which means that you are becoming more and more like commoditized brands. A good rule of thumb is to keep your brand equity at 25 percent of the price. That means that 25 percent of your price should be a premium on top of your basic profit margin. If you are selling a $100 product, you should have at least $25 of equity folded into that price point—in other words, you should be charging a 25 percent premium successfully.

Let's break that down to see how it works: say you're an accessible high-end clothing brand. You sell a premium pair of winter gloves for $100. Your cost to make them is $35, and you would be profitable if you sold the gloves at twice your cost, $70. Thus, you are charging $30 more than you need to charge to make a decent profit margin. That $30 represents the premium you can charge because of your brand equity. Since a healthy premium for brand equity would be 25 percent of the selling price, or $25 in this case, your brand equity is strong if you can charge even more than that on top of your profit margin. You are charging $30 on top of your profit margin, an indicator of quite healthy brand equity.

If you are not selling enough units at that 25 percent premium, your equity is already eroding. For premium brands, it is even more important to build on your equity rather than letting it erode. You can do that by:

- Making simple changes like updated brand colors or logo design. Remember, your brand identity contributes to your brand equity.

- Adjusting your promotional strategy to target luxury consumers. For instance, you can shift your ad spend from paid search to print ads in fashion publications. Simply advertising in higher-end channels is seldom enough on its own to build brand equity. However, it supports brand equity by changing brand perception.

- Upgrading your customer relationships. Often, what distinguishes a higher-end brand from a commodified one is superior customer service. Service is a key element of "quality"—especially for luxury brands. It is one thing to make a fine product, but if the service doesn't match up, it will seriously detract from the brand's image. Working with your operations, ask yourself how you can upgrade your customer service to the level of a luxury brand. Improving your retail experience, if you have brick-and-mortar stores, can also shift your customer relationships to those of a premium brand. Remember, customer relationships are about more than customer service. Think in terms of the big picture. What is the customer experience like? Is it largely self-serve, or do customers receive personalized service from live human agents? How do customers feel about doing business with your company?

- Enhancing your packaging. There are many elements that go into producing high-quality experiences for consumers, and sometimes the most overlooked element is product packaging. Your packaging can help you to convey a higher-quality image. Luxury brands spend heavily on their packaging because it is an integral part of their client experience. The easiest way to do that is to ensure that your packaging is considered in your brand architecture. If you ship products in plain cardboard boxes, create branded ones instead, so that the brand experience starts the instant your merchandise arrives on customers' doorsteps. Change from bags to boxes, or thin boxes to more solid ones. Make sure that all packaging is in your brand colors, and decorated with your logos. Extra points if you include language on packaging that reflects your brand values. If you're in an industry where physical appearance matters, integrating packaging in your brand architecture is definitely an option worth exploring.

- Upgrading your product quality. This is about more than using better materials or better engineering and workmanship. Quality is often a function of a product's innovativeness. The highest-end brands are known for their exceptional products. You may not be able to do the same immediately, but if you are working on improving your product quality, make sure customers know about it. Building customer panels, engaging with your customer community, and inviting customer feedback on your product, can all help you innovate and improve.

- Increasing customer lifetime value. High-end brands are also known for their superior customer loyalty and retention rates. If you have strong customer relationships that continue even after the initial purchase, you are well on your way to building brand equity. There are many ways to increase customer lifetime value, but some key strategies include creating a loyalty program, developing engaging content and marketing initiatives, and providing excellent customer service.

There are many things you can do to build brand equity for your company. Using metrics that pinpoint challenges you have with your brand equity can set you on the path to improvement. Whether it is improving customer relationships, enhancing your product quality, or increasing customer lifetime value, taking action to improve your brand equity will pay dividends in the long run.

Conclusion

There are many different ways to measure brand awareness and identity. Which ones you choose will depend on your brand and what you are trying to accomplish. But, by using a variety of methods, you can get a well-rounded view of how your brand is performing.

It is important to understand what you want to measure and then select the right tool to help you get that information. Measuring brand identity is an ongoing process, and, as your brand changes, so too should your methods for measuring it.

When it comes to data-driven branding, it is important to use as many data sources as possible in order to get the most accurate picture. This includes using customer data, social media data, market research data, and data from other sources. Once you have all this data, it is important to analyze it and look for patterns.

From there, you can start to develop hypotheses about how to improve your brand equity. Using this data-driven approach is the best way to ensure that your branding efforts are effective and that you are making the most of your resources.

06

Content marketing metrics frameworks

Content marketing is the glue that holds a savvy company's marketing together. What do you post to social media? Content. How are you building your SEO program? Content. What do you send in your email promotions? Hopefully, some good content.

There is no modern marketing without content, so we need to use the right metrics to optimize it for maximum results. The impact of well-optimized content can be felt well beyond a smart organization's blog. Content drives results across all inbound channels.

This chapter is not about just measuring whether content is interesting to your readers. We do learn about that, including engagement metrics, finding the right keywords, and virality metrics. However, content marketing is about more than giving people something fun to read. It's about that, but it is also about changing minds, winning consumers' hearts, and ultimately changing behavior.

As marketers, we want to be sure that the content we are creating is successfully addressing our business goals. Right now there are two ways you can measure these results: descriptive metrics and actionable metrics. In this chapter, we learn about a third type: strategy metrics. I will introduce you to two tools I've developed that can create a measurable framework for your content marketing from the start. This chapter introduces theme mapping and content value score, the two metrics tools that help create a total content program with provable ROI, all while taking less time to create content that sells.

A few basic content marketing concepts

Before we dig into measuring our content, let's talk about the key activities we will be measuring:

- **Content marketing**: this is any type of content you produce or repurpose with the specific intention of driving traffic back to your site. This can include blog posts, case studies, video, infographics, white papers, etc.

- **Inbound marketing**: this is a process that uses online content to attract and engage customers for the purpose of converting them into leads and customers. This includes social media posts, website optimization for better search rankings, email campaigns where you send information directly to potential or current customers, and so forth. Inbound marketing rests on a foundation of content marketing, but the two are not interchangeable. Content is just one part of an entire inbound strategy. In this chapter, we focus on content within an inbound context.

- **Outbound marketing**: sending information via email, social media, flyers, and other means to prospects or potential customers in the hope that they will click a link or buy something. This is also known as interruption marketing.

- **Pillar pages**: a main page on your website that focuses on one of your key content topics. It often contains high-level information about a topic, and is used to establish context for other pages on your site related to that topic. It's a great way to give visitors an overview of a topic important to your brand. Think of the "About Us" page on any website—it's usually a pillar page. A good content marketing program will have several pillar pages, one for each key topic. This makes it easier for search engines and social networks to index your site because they will be able to easily understand the content on your page. Pillar pages improve search rankings, make it easier to organize your content, and showcase your firm's expertise in a subject. Another word for a pillar page is *content hub*. Regardless of its name, it is a place for visitors to go when they want more detailed information about a particular topic. It's typically a deeper-linked page that includes in-depth articles and videos about that topic, but can also include data sheets, presentations, images, and documents.

- **Evergreen content**: this is content that is not tied to a specific season or event. Evergreen content can be consumed at any time and used as a reference tool long after it has been published. It is also content that can be leveraged as a resource for other marketing initiatives.

- **Hub-and-spoke content strategy**: a hub-and-spoke content strategy involves creating pillar pages on your website, and then using those pillars to feed evergreen blog posts. This is an effective way to generate both high-quality and evergreen content. Confused about the difference between pillar pages and hub-and-spoke content? Hub-and-spoke is the strategy; a pillar page is the functional structure that makes it easy to execute on the strategy.

- **Keyword targeting**: keywords are words or phrases that people might use when looking for information on your website. The goal of optimization is to ensure that your pages are relevant for the phrases you choose. You cannot rank for a keyword unless it is on your page. Keywords are valuable because they help people find information they need when searching online.

- **Landing pages**: this is where users are sent when they click on an ad or go directly to a specific URL. Sometimes these pages are called "landers." The goal of a landing page is to get visitors who click on your ad or link over to your website and then convert them into customers or some other type of lead before they go anywhere else.

Okay, now we have the terms defined it is time to dig in and start optimizing our content with metrics.

What happens if we don't optimize our content? We lose traffic and rankings, which means we also lose customers. One of the biggest challenges in measuring content is that it takes so many different forms across so many channels. To arrive at a comprehensive view of content, we need to start with a framework. Let's start by looking at why content marketing is different to many other traditional channels in how it is measured.

Traditional marketing vs content marketing

Content marketing is significantly different from more traditional forms of advertising-based digital marketing, including PPC, display advertising, and text marketing. It is also different from the channels it supports, such as social media, SEO, email, and retargeting.

Advertising can work in a silo by itself (though that is not ideal), but content marketing can be integrated into all of your channels to deliver a holistic strategy that is greater than the sum of its parts.

Advertising is focused on driving sales while content marketing is focused on establishing thought leadership and building brand awareness. While many other forms of digital marketing focus on branding and awareness, content marketing is all about getting your audience to take action (i.e. engage with you), such as visiting your website or social profile. Content marketing is what makes a marketing program stable, substantive, and sustainable.

Content marketing is based on a long-term commitment to producing high-quality content and distributing it through multiple channels over an extended period of time, while advertising only provides a temporary boost. Yet, many companies see their investment in content as an expense instead of an investment because they don't fully appreciate the value of content marketing and the cost of not having it.

Content provides value as an investment over time. It serves to increase brand awareness, drive website traffic, and boost conversions. It can generate leads that can be converted into sales, but it is more often a contributor to conversions. That can make it tough to measure using the methods that work with other activities. The good news is, though, that the same metrics and tools will give you insight into your content marketing. All that changes is the way you look at the data—and that different lens starts with a new tool: thematic mapping.

Thematic mapping

To get actionable data from your content marketing, you first need to connect your content efforts to your brand values, customer segments, and value propositions. After all, content, as we learned, is not a channel but the expression of what your company does. It's the steak, not the sizzle. It makes no noise on its own, even though it's the main dish. So, you need to translate all that great content you are creating into something that can be measured. Enter thematic mapping.

The foundation of measuring content is theme mapping. This type of map organizes every piece of your content into relevant categories tied to your organization's main marketing themes. That translates content into measurable form.

When you create that thematic map, you identify the different topics your content addresses and the themes your marketing strategy revolves around. This includes things like who your audience is, what industry you serve, how you solve problems for them, what competitors are in the space, what business goals are behind your marketing strategy, and any other important considerations that affect how consumers find value in your products and services.

Let's look at an example. With the proliferation of food delivery services, let's say you decide to launch something new: a service that delivers the bread and fillings to make perfect sandwiches for busy workers. You decide to call this service SandWish. Each week, subscribers get a package with several gourmet breads, already sliced, plus an assortment of sandwich-ready meats or vegetarian fillings, sauces, and sides. Your core value proposition is delicatessen sandwiches at a fraction of the cost. Your promotions center around the fact that your customers can eat healthy on the go, if they work on site, without running out to spend on expensive lunches at work. For those who work remotely, they get the taste of a delicatessen sandwich at home. Core values are health, environmental sustainability (your products are locally sourced and the packaging is eco-friendly), and better living.

These then become your themes. You can think of them as a map, as shown in Figure 6.1.

FIGURE 6.1   An initial content map should outline both your key topics and the relationships between them

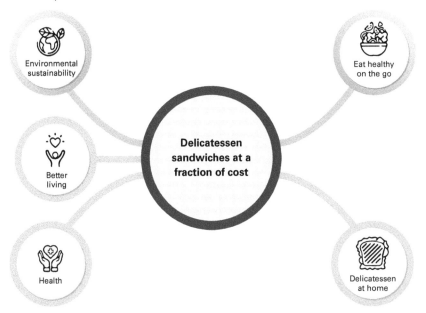

Once you have your basic themes outlined, you can conceptualize their priority and hierarchy. Those priorities and connections can be highlighted

by adding lines between related topics, making more important topics larger, color-coding, or all of the above.

In Figures 6.2 and 6.3 you can see that eco-friendly is one theme, because it's one of your core brand values. Taste is another, because what food company doesn't advertise their great flavors? Convenience is key, but it is smaller than savings, because often, making a sandwich in the morning is less convenient than buying one, but it is most often cheaper. You can see major themes are large sections, while less important ones are smaller.

When you map out your content, you can begin to see where similar topics appear. For example, if a lot of your content focuses on health and wellness, it is best to put those articles under one theme. But within that section, the types of articles should be further analyzed. Do they talk about eating healthy for moms? Busy office workers? Families? You may need to include specific target audiences as themes in your map, if they are a core focus in your content. Be willing to revise your initial map as you analyze what your content really talks about, as shown in Figure 6.4.

Stuck on how to define some themes? It is helpful to view your company as the audience would, looking at what you do from their point of view. This is not a simple map of what content you are creating, for whom. This ties that content to where it all fits into the bigger picture. It defines each piece of content by the brand values it embodies, the product message it carries, and the value proposition it reflects. Any core concept that you regularly try to communicate to your customers needs to be part of that theme map.

Thematic mapping is useful no matter what types of content you are creating. It can also help you measure all aspects of your marketing, though it is particularly helpful for demonstrating ROI.

Ranking themes for better measurement

Once you understand your content in terms of themes, give each theme a value. Assign it to one or more marketing goals that are important to the success of your company. This could be driving sales for a particular product or service, increasing brand awareness, or generating leads for a new product.

If your marketing goals are awareness, the themes with the highest value are those tied to your brand's core values. If your goals are leads, the themes related to customer needs will rank highest.

FIGURE 6.2   Start mapping additional connections between topics and scoring topics by importance

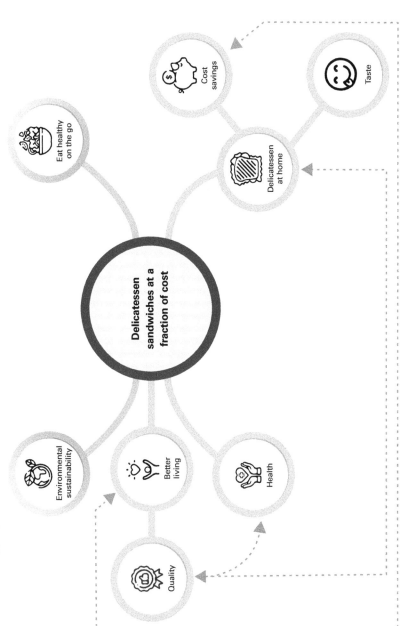

FIGURE 6.3 Add ratings to quantify the importance of different topics

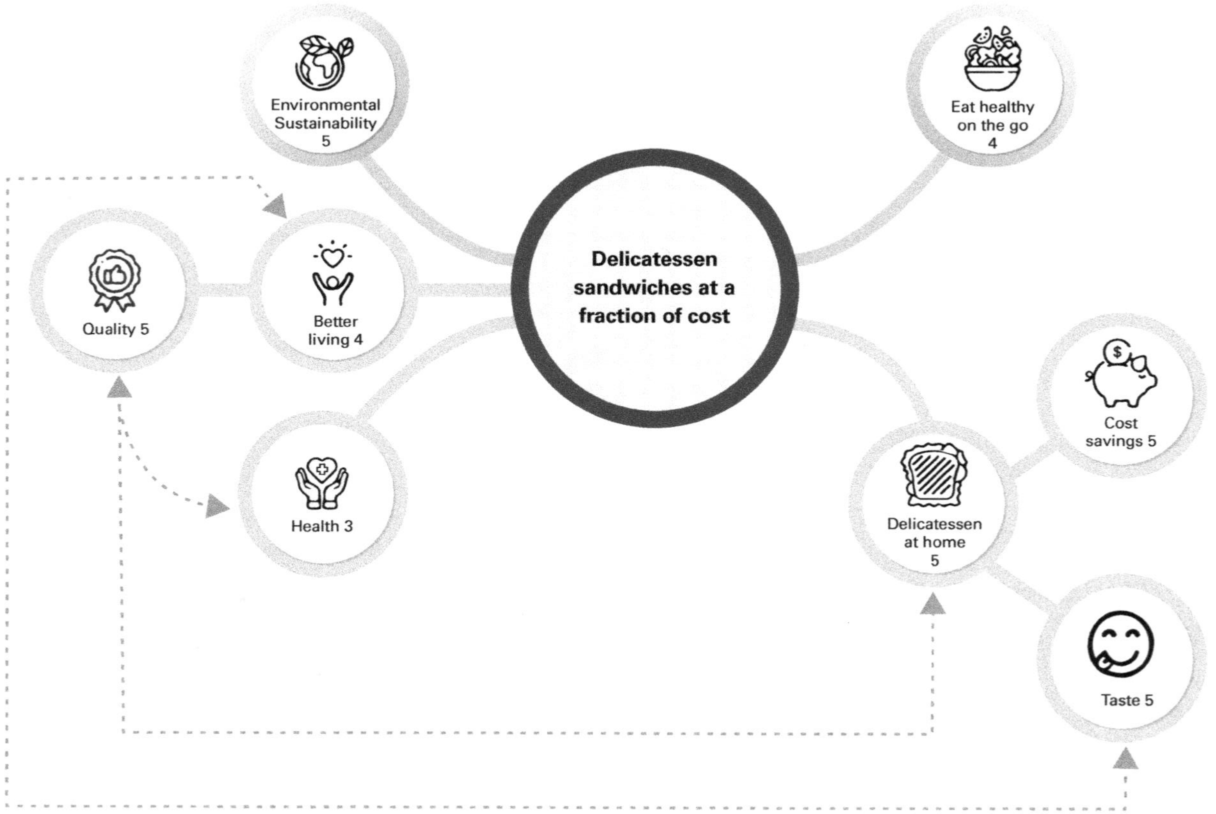

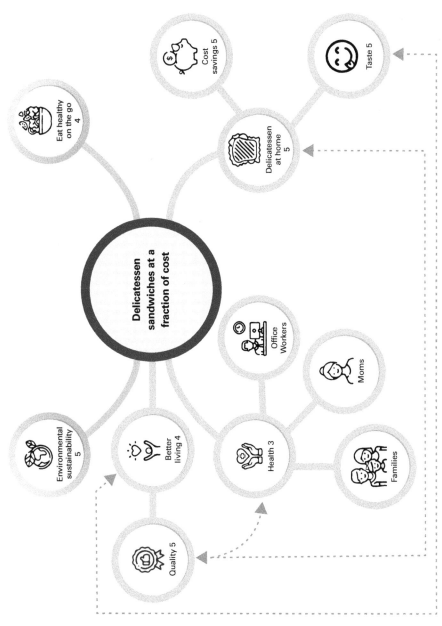

FIGURE 6.4   Revised map after further analysis

How does this work in practice? Let's look at an example from SandWish. You may already be aware that most food box subscriptions are focused on more elaborate meals. A chief obstacle in the market that SandWish needs to overcome is showing that their product brings consumers a complete experience that many consumers value. For many of us, a delicatessen sandwich is one of those meals we crave while staying healthy and going green. SandWish has a core value proposition: the deli comes to you, affordably. In this example, SandWish wants to achieve three marketing goals: increasing brand awareness, generating leads for a new product line, and overcoming consumer skepticism.

SandWish needs customers to know these messages so strongly that they will buy their product. They also need potential customers to feel that SandWish can solve a real problem for them. Finally, they need those who don't yet subscribe to feel that this is the right solution for their needs and values. So, they add themes of cost savings, quality, and taste. Those new sub-themes get assigned the highest values, as Figure 6.3 demonstrates.

Armed with this thematic map, the team is ready for the second step in content metrics: the content audit.

Audit your content by theme

Once you have a theme map, it is time to assign a theme to each piece of content you create. This helps you identify the topics of your measurable content, so that you can tie metrics to specific brand values, customer needs, and so on. Your audit should include all of your content, such as:

- blog posts
- social media posts
- videos
- email messaging
- white papers
- webinars
- newsletters
- new product announcements

As well as anything else you want to track toward your goals. When you look at your content, don't just look at blogs, social media posts, videos, and other "glamor" content. All of your basic content, such as e-commerce product descriptions, can also be mapped. You also must include content that talks specifically about your product, not just inbound, informational writing. If product features are a key part of your messaging, you need to include them in your theme map. If you are doing the more common messaging by benefits, those benefits belong in your map. If you are not tracking it, don't include it in the list. This takes time, but you want to do this for all of your content so you can better track performance across themes.

The content value score: measuring the value of content to your brand

The thematic mapping process will quickly give you a programmatic view of how your content is supporting your marketing goals. For example, let's say that being good value is key to SandWish's messaging. Yet, almost nothing on their blog talks about the financial benefits of packing your own lunch. Their social media posts don't call out the potential cost savings, their videos offer no content on saving on food. In other words, their current content is doing nothing to promote one of their core themes. In the daily process of cranking out content, the team had ignored part of the brand's core value proposition. Identifying this lapse allows them to rectify it. Thus, simply conducting an audit can be a powerful tool in content marketing optimization.

I call the results of this audit process the content value score. It helps you quickly score each piece of content for how well it helps drive your marketing message.

What is content value?

Content value (CV) is an advanced metric that takes theme mapping to a quantified level. It is a combination of:

1 Customer lifetime value (CLV).

2 Themes that most closely map to your overall goals and strategy (in other words, the message you want to communicate).

3 Relevance of content to high-value themes (more on that in a moment).

Let's break that down. To value a new piece of content, you need to tie it to revenue. The easiest way to do that is to identify the content themes of interest to your highest CLV segments. A new content piece does not have a track record, but you can predict its impact on ROI by identifying how well it attracts the customers who contribute most to your revenue. Thus, the first step in CV scoring is to assess all your content by its alignment with the needs of your customer segments. Themes that interest high-CLV segments should carry a higher rating than those that are less interesting to that valuable group.

Next, you already have your theme map. This tells you how well your content aligns with your company's goals. Ideally, themes core to your brand are also those most attractive to your best customers. However, in the real world, we know there are often gaps between what your brand has long been and the current needs of the market. A nimble organization closes this gap as quickly as it can, but let's face it, there's often a gap. Thus, you want to rank your core brand themes again, but this time include the factor of how important each theme is to your high-CLV customers.

You can calculate your CV score with a spreadsheet. First, rank all of your themes in order of importance to your brand, with 1 being "not that important" to 5 being "critically important." Then, you score each piece of content based on how well it performs for that theme on a scale of 1 to 5, with 1 being "doesn't address the theme" to 5 being "focused on the theme." For example, a blog post that briefly mentions working from home, but doesn't really focus on it as a core topic, might get a score of 2. Another post that offers tips for organizing your home office, "Create a productive home 'coffee shop'" might get a 5, since it is completely focused on the work-from-home theme.

Now that you have a score for how well each piece of content covers a theme, you can multiply that number by the importance of that theme. For instance, if "work from home" is critical to the brand, it's a 5 in importance. A blog post that focuses on that theme completely will rate a 5 for its theme coverage. This is a post that covers your most important theme really well. It's a 5 in its level of coverage of a theme that is also a 5 for importance. Then, you multiply the theme coverage score by the theme importance score. For this post, you have the highest rating: $5 \times 5 = 25$. This is a highly valuable piece of content.

The goal with CV score is to identify how much of your content is truly high-value. Once you have CV scores for each content item, you are ready for one more step: rate each theme for the percentage of your total content that falls into that category. You will want to see your most important themes getting the most coverage.

While CV score has proven to be really useful for us, it does allow for freedom of creative expression for your team. Provided you have a strong content marketing program, you can make room for up to 10 percent low-CV content, provided it is on-brand. For instance, if 10 percent of your content is "nice to have" and 90 percent is focused on value, then you're doing fine.

Why use CV score?

There are several reasons why the content value score is valuable. First, it allows you to see how much value your content is delivering, in aggregate. If you don't track this kind of information, you could be wasting resources on low-value content. Tracking CV gives you an automated way to make sure that doesn't happen. Second, by quickly identifying the high-value content, you can promote those pieces via email newsletters, on your blog or on social media. This increases their prominence throughout your marketing promotional mix. Third, whenever content is falling short on any theme, it provides an opportunity for fine-tuning that piece of content to increase its value. Promoting more highly valuable content through all available channels is an excellent way to increase the impact it has for your brand.

CV scoring can also increase the impact of high-cost, long-term marketing investments such as SEO. We often hear clients saying that their past organic search efforts have been disappointing. Though the site was well-optimized technically, the SEO efforts didn't yield ROI. Looking at the site, it is often easy to see why: a lot of the content is low-value. If you optimize low-value content, you are wasting your money.

Another benefit of CV scoring is setting lead generation targets. If a certain group of customers is the most likely to convert, then that is your target audience. They are going to be interested in high-value content because it speaks directly to their interests and problems. Ranking highly with this group will increase your conversion rates. Content marketers can use CV scoring as a way to better identify which specific themes they should focus on for different lead gen initiatives. For example, let's say you are an HR software company that has good—better—best offerings for small, mid-size, and enterprise customers. Through customer metrics, you understand the needs of each segment. You have mapped those needs to themes.

But because of resource and time constraints, you only have the resources to focus on two types of leads: mid-size and enterprise. You can look at your high-value themes for those segments and use the CV score as a way to target which themes you should optimize for each customer segment. That way, your content is provably tailored to your target segments' needs.

In addition, CV scoring can also help with overall content governance. It is a common problem that many marketers get wrapped up in the latest trends and forget about their overall strategy. For example, let's say your overall marketing strategy at SandWish is to create 10 articles on every new product release from your company. You see a spike in organic traffic for a new release of gourmet mustards, which you are selling in jars on their own without the rest of the sandwich ingredients. So, you schedule 10 articles on that release. When the traffic spikes again next month, you schedule another 10 articles. But at that point, your content is getting lopsided: too much of it is focused on the new product release. Each new piece of content starts cannibalizing the traffic from earlier pieces. In addition, your overall content map is now filled with this one theme. Ironically, while the new mustard product release was important, it's a product that is a departure from your core brand. The theme most closely tied to it scores 3 in importance, and now you have flooded your site related to it, driving down your overall CV scores.

You can use CV scoring to prevent this from happening by identifying topics that are already high value for customers. Focusing your resources on promoting those pieces, you can identify the right balance of branded content that stays aligned with your company message. That way, you will reach more customers with existing content while also maintaining a balanced content calendar that focuses on your core product lines and supports your brand.

Measuring content by theme performance

The real magic happens, though, when you start measuring the performance of each theme across your marketing channels. This is how content metrics become a data point for understanding your branding, market positioning, pricing strategy, segmentation, value proposition, and customer acquisition channels.

When you measure content by theme, you start to see where you are doing well, where you can improve, and what themes may need tweaking or eliminating entirely.

Tracking content metrics shouldn't stop at text metrics, however. If you want your metrics to be actionable, you need to look at how themes work on specific channels, and with other creative, such as visuals. You also need to pair theme data with campaign metrics if you want a full picture of what you should be doing strategically. For example, if every piece of content around lunchtime at home is performing really well for SandWish, they might look at how their PPC funnel is converting by time of day and consider running ads around lunchtime hours or adding a call-out to their ads that says "at home" or "take a break from the couch." Like all aspects of marketing metrics, CV scores are part of the picture, working best in context.

Moving forward: on-page content optimization

Once you have identified themes in your content, you can start optimizing around them. This lets you turn CV scores into strategy. Here are some quick optimization tips.

Let's say that among SandWish's target markets are working moms who are looking for quick on-the-go lunches. The brand might create a dedicated landing page for these users that features images of women in business attire carrying their lunches, with copy about how to save time and money.

In the end, SandWish gets more leads from their optimized page, which includes a strong call-to-action for subscribing to the blog. This delivers even more revenue, a larger customer base, and faster growth. From not knowing how to measure content, they now see content as a major driver of marketing ROI.

Using CV scores, you can identify content themes and optimize your content to meet customer expectations. A poorly converting page may, for instance, cover the right theme, but not comprehensively enough. Look at coverage scores, and work to rewrite content to increase those scores on landing pages.

Optimize your call to action (CTA) based on themes, too. Content marketers know that the CTA is their last chance to convince a visitor to opt-in, make a purchase, or do whatever it is you really want them to do. It should be no surprise, then, that a weak CTA is going to turn customers away. So, look at your theme data and make sure that the copy on your CTA matches what you have been talking about in your content. In this way, you keep customers from getting turned off by confusing CTAs that do not connect to their needs. CV scoring is an efficient way to measure the causes of low conversion rates or poor messaging, and a roadmap to fixing them.

Another example of how to use CV scores is in keyword optimization. Many brands struggle to identify the perfect keywords when faced with thousands of search terms. Optimizing first for CV can help you narrow the focus of your keywords, bypassing a lot of trial and error. It is one step closer to better organic search optimization. Let's see that in action.

Let's say that 5 percent of SandWish's customers are in Massachusetts, which isn't many. The marketing team wonders why the state has such low interest in their subscriptions when they have advertised heavily and food subscriptions overall perform well in the market. When they look at their keyword data, they notice that many Massachusetts visitors are also interested in low-carb living, which is a theme the brand was considering. SandWish should add "low-carb" to their list of keywords, and it might help them close the gap between share of voice with other states. It is easier to optimize for content themes than thousands of search terms, which makes it easier to test out copy and measure results across a smaller set of terms.

You can use CV scores and content optimization to make changes and measure improvements. They go hand-in-hand so perfectly that it is impossible to imagine one without the other. Content strategy, after all, is meant to make content more connected, valuable, and relevant to visitors. As you continue along your optimization journey, always track CV scores.

With a thematic mapping and content value scoring framework in place, you have the basis for better content that drives ROI while also being valuable to readers. It will give you a competitive advantage and it will give your content strategy accuracy and direction.

When you start thinking about content as the intersection of themes and channels, then it becomes a much more actionable, easy-to-digest data point. And that is exactly what content marketers need in order to bring their metrics up to par with industry standards. Thematic mapping and content value scoring take content strategy out of the hard-to-measure realm of creative, into a more structured, quantified framework closely connected with ROI. With this new perspective and the right tools, you can connect your content strategy to your conversion rate optimization (CRO) efforts.

And just like that, we're done! You now have enough information to move forward confidently with thematic mapping and content value scoring for your own brand. In Chapter 7 we learn about more tactical content metrics that will help optimize your content across specific channels.

HOW TO IMPLEMENT A CONTENT VALUE SCORE

There are three steps to getting started with implementing a content value score:

STEP ONE

Create a spreadsheet with four columns: Theme, Rating (1–5), Actual Coverage, and CV Score. Next to the "Theme" column, list out all of your site's themes and give each one a rating 1–5, according to how important they are for your content. It is best to use the following scale, with 1 being low value and 5 being high value:

5—highly valuable

4—valuable

3—nice to have, but not essential

2—low value

1—no value

STEP TWO

For each theme listed, make sure you enter the theme's actual coverage. For instance, if your goal is to increase sales for Google Ads consultants, make sure you record each piece of content that covers this topic (choose between 1 and 5). Then multiply the "Impact" ratings by the number of times it appears on site. So if you have five pieces of content covering this topic, multiply it by four. This step ensures you are tracking both the quantity and quality of high-value content. Finally, calculate your content value score by taking the numerical average between all of your themes.

STEP 3

Look for gaps in your content coverage. If you have a high number of low-value themes, this indicates that you need to create less content on those topics or rework existing content, so it becomes higher value.

Use this framework to audit your existing content. Make adjustments, then use the framework as a guide each time you update your content calendar. Remember to update the values of different themes as your marketing evolves. For instance, if your branding shifts to emphasize being a value brand, update the ratings of all content related to value, cost savings, and other related themes.

The content value score becomes second nature as you develop skills in scoring. Be sure you are confident in your ratings—that makes scoring content quick and the resulting metrics reliable. Fairly soon you will have higher content ROI, with much less effort. Happy content scoring!

07

Content marketing: the essential metrics

In Chapter 6 we discovered a framework for building content marketing on a solid foundation of ROI metrics. In this chapter, we dig into the tactics of measuring content that you can use, even if you haven't fully implemented the framework. We will learn the basic content metrics, what they mean, and how to use them to optimize our campaigns. We also explore advanced ways you can track content success, including things you should never do!

You have a map, now get on the path: taking action with content metrics

Now that we have the basics of content marketing metrics, it's time to dig a bit deeper into using metrics to optimize our content marketing. In this section, we're going to talk about some of the actionable content marketing metrics that can help you supercharge your content efforts across the board. These metrics help more sophisticated marketing operations truly get the maximum value out of their content marketing by honing in on the top influencers, identifying their top formats in greater detail, and highlighting particular sub-topics that are generating the highest ROI moment to moment.

A word about B2C vs B2B content

Content marketing takes very different forms in business to business (B2B) vs business to consumer (B2C) marketing. B2B marketers often develop technical, long-form content, such as white papers, webinars, ebooks, and industry studies. This content is meant to be substantive, educational, and highly credible. It is also a substantial investment; a single sponsored analyst report package can run to tens of thousands of dollars. Thus, each piece of content needs to carry significant weight. Its ROI is easier to prove, however, since it is often gated content—that is, leads must provide extensive contact information in order to access it. That makes it easier to track the leads that a content piece generates. After that, we can easily track lead conversions, revenue per lead, and such key metrics as CLV. In B2B content marketing, the stakes are higher, but the measurement is much simpler.

B2C content is different. It is designed not to be a major investment of time or money, or a deep dive into a particular topic. It has the potential to go viral, so there is less control over resulting leads and conversions. And since B2C content is more geared toward branding than it is toward sales, measuring its impact can be very complicated. In some cases, B2C brands might gate content, or conversions can be otherwise tied to a specific content item: a coupon code available only in an influencer's newsletter, for instance. However, most of the time, measuring the ROI of B2C content requires our cleverest multi-touch, multi-channel attribution skills.

We'll be taking a look at both sides of the equation. Whether you are measuring traffic generated by your successful blog posts (B2C) or measuring leads generated via email (B2B), you can successfully optimize any type of content with the right measurement strategy.

What follows are some of the more popular contemporary metrics for measuring content performance. Remember, these are just examples. The best content metric for your marketing strategy is different depending on what you sell and to whom, so choose what is relevant to your organization's goals.

The fundamental five content metrics that matter

Let's start with several of the most important metrics to consider when analyzing your content's performance. At the minimum, measure these metrics for your top themes, for each piece of content you create:

- page views
- time on page
- bounce rate
- percentage of new visits
- conversions

These metrics will give you a baseline measure of whether content is resonating at all with your audience. They will also help you determine which content items are performing poorly and could be removed from your site.

Beyond this, the next most important metrics to monitor involve leads, conversions, and engagement. We talk about those more specifically toward the end of the chapter.

Content metrics by content type

Blogs, video, webinars, ebooks—content comes in a range of types. Each type has unique metrics that tell us how well it is performing. If you are looking to build up your content marketing, consider each type of format and think about the unique metrics related to it. Some of these metrics apply to blogs only (for example, post frequency), while others are relevant across different types of formats (such as social shares). Here is what you need to measure for each popular content type in order to get the full picture of your content marketing performance.

Blogs

The most common type of content marketing is blogging. It's easy to set up and it has a low barrier to entry, but that doesn't mean it isn't effective.

There are so many different types of blog and so many ways you can measure them: new visitors vs returning visitors, page views vs session duration. What direction does each metric provide?

NEW VISITORS VS RETURNING VISITORS

This is one of the best ways to see if your blog is growing. If you are seeing more returning visitors than new ones, then that means people are not only finding it but they are sticking around and coming back. If you have your content organized by pillar pages, track the rate of returning visitors to content associated with specific pillars. That will give you thematic data.

PAGE VIEWS VS SESSION DURATION

Page views measure breadth (how many articles on your site did visitors read?), while session duration assesses depth (how long someone spends on your site). Both are vital to understanding how engaging, useful, or controversial people think your blog is.

TOP ORGANIC KEYWORDS

This metric works by measuring the search terms people are using to find you. Content marketing, in essence, is all about influencing those search results. If people are finding you via organic search results (vs paid ads), then you are successfully influencing buyers' decision-making process with your content. However, some keywords are more powerful attractors than others. By looking at your top organic keywords, you can see which content topics are the most popular and make brand decisions accordingly.

BLOG-ORIGINATED LEADS

Of course, you can track which blog posts actually generate leads. To do this, use a tool like HubSpot and tie the source of the lead back to the content they found on your blog. If a lead's landing page was a blog post, attributing that conversion in part to that post is a reasonable way to quantify leads generated from your blogging. Multi-touch attribution should also include blog posts as touchpoints, especially when they occur early or late in the funnel, when content can make the biggest difference in buying decisions.

These blog content metrics pave the way to better optimization. Once you know which posts are the most effective, use those as templates for future content. Rearrange, rewrite, and repurpose these top-performing blog posts to turn them into pillar pages that can then become the seed content of your entire content marketing campaign.

Web analytics-based content metrics

Web analytics data is key to measuring any content that lives on your website—that's evident. However, it is also key to measuring the impact of off-site content, such as social media posts, videos, and more. Using your analytics to measure these types of content can tell you what content out on the web is most effective at driving valuable traffic.

BRAND THEMES BY REFERRAL SOURCES

This is a cool metric, because it tells you the type of content that drives traffic to your content. If you are seeing referral sources, it means people are finding your site on their own (via a link on another website) and then deciding to visit more of your content. What makes this metric a sneaky but brilliant content datapoint: it can really tell you the content on other sites that is driving traffic to your content—the great materials on your own site that you want consumers to read. That gives you insight into themes that resonate with your audience, even when you are not the one writing the content. More importantly, it can bring to light effective new themes you haven't considered. Let's get back to SandWish. Your business is growing. To boost brand awareness, you launch a PR campaign that garners strong earned media. By the end of the first week, you have mentions in five blogs: one for busy working moms, two focused on vegetarian cooking, one for project managers, and one for young workers at the start of their careers. The vegetarian and working-mom blogs were expected. But you're intrigued by why a blog for project managers would want to feature you. So, you check out the post. It turns out that the blog's readers have been having a lively conversation about team morale in a remote environment, given that team lunches are a big part of many organizations' morale building. Your service was called out as one way to provide team lunches even when teams work from home. This gets you thinking: you have a potential B2B market segment that you could tap for more revenue. You decide to explore marketing your subscription lunch packages as a corporate perk, opening up a new revenue stream!

Knowing this information also helps marketers plan their off-site content strategy. You can use these referral sources for future influencer outreach efforts, or to repurpose top content into other channels such as video.

HOMEPAGE ENGAGEMENT

This is an underrated metric because many marketers don't think of their homepage as content. And they're right—on its own, it's not really a content channel. However, heatmapping can show you which themes, as reflected on your homepage, get the most engagement. For instance, let's say that SandWish has three calls to action below the hero banner on their homepage: Eat Healthy, Save Money, and Deli Sandwiches at Home. A heatmapping tool such as CrazyEgg can tell you which of these CTAs gets more mouse hovers, where users click, and where they stop scrolling. This can provide data on how engaging they find these themes.

TOP ORGANIC LANDING PAGES

While keyword data provides insight into what search terms bring consumers to your website, this data is notoriously hard to obtain completely. Gaps in organic keyword data can be patched somewhat by looking at your top organic landing pages. This metric tells you what pages on your website get the most organic search traffic. If you have all of your webpages mapped by theme, patterns can emerge.

BOUNCE RATE

Perhaps the simplest and most straightforward metric to understand, bounce rate represents how many people leave your site after viewing only one page. It is often seen as a "lazy" metric because it doesn't give marketers much insight into what might be wrong; but in reality, it is great for identifying branding and content issues. The reason is that a bounce is evidence that users are not finding a page relevant, and they are also not interested in the CTA you have placed on it. This can be an opportunity to A/B test your content or re-evaluate what you are communicating on the page.

Social media metrics

Content marketing and social media are inseparable to the point that, for many organizations, they are one and the same. As a result, it is crucial to monitor social media success metrics. Here are some of the most important:

ENGAGEMENT BY THEME

The number of comments, shares, and links a post gets can provide insight into how well it resonates with your audience.

Social traffic by theme: if a video or Instagram post is doing particularly well in driving web traffic—if it has a lot of views, clickthroughs to the product page, and web conversions—you can tie those to specific themes as well.

SOCIAL SHARING

Using a tool like BuzzStream, marketers can easily see who is sharing their content and how often. This creates two benefits: it provides insight into the types of people sharing your content, and it helps you build relationships with these influencers to encourage future shares.

Let's see how these metrics work. One of the top Instagram posts from SandWish shows that they excel at creating shareworthy content. The post was seen over 800 times and liked more than 300 times (and counting). It's clearly resonating with the audience. What's the theme for this post? A dog watching their human eat a sandwich while working from home (WFH). While nominally classed in the "lunch at home" theme, the post may just be successful because of the cute dog. It is important to look at the average performance of many posts before declaring a trend. Looking back on the past 90 days, you find that, indeed, cute dog or no, posts related to working from home are among your most engaging. Clearly, your social media audience relates to content focused on your brand's value proposition of bringing better lunches to the WFH experience. Knowing this helps you craft your content strategy in a way that is focused on consumers' interests. And what could be better than that?

Email content metrics

Email is a chief content delivery platform for brands. In B2B especially, it is critical for getting gated content in front of prospects, assessing interest in a brand, and landing sales. Measuring email success is similar to measuring blog metrics, with one major exception: email data is also a vital source of individual consumer data. That is, through the content they engage with in our email marketing, we can build up a profile of each member of our email lists. At this level, the data becomes consumer data, which we learned about in Chapter 2. However, looked at across different types of consumers, such as converters vs non-converters, it can also provide a profile of the kinds of content that move leads through the funnel. It can also tell us whether specific content types work well for different demographics of leads, such as those in different industries.

Below are some of the core email content metrics. Remember, like all other marketing data, these metrics should be considered in the context of your business goals.

OPEN RATE BY THEME

Email open rates by subject-line theme can tell you the content topics that grab your consumers' attention the most. The reason is that the inbox is one of the most crowded of forums for getting that commitment to engage with your message. If a topic is of interest enough to garner precious time in that forum, it's a hot topic.

CTOR BY THEME

Email clicks by link theme can tell you the content topics that get your customers to move from interest to engagement. Just because a customer opens a message doesn't mean they will click on it, let alone go deeper into links and calls-to-action within the email. You want all that movement toward conversion. Email click to open rate (CTOR) by subject line theme can also tell you if your audience is getting bored with the same old messaging. If a change in topic results in an increased open rate, that's great. That means there was pent-up interest in that content topic and they are just happy to see it again after all this time. If those opens don't turn into clicks, then your theme is engaging, but maybe the content is not delivering on the theme's promise. For instance, if you use "sports" as a topic theme in your subject line and your messaging is about a lackluster sale or upcoming event, the email may be getting opened but then not clicked on. That's because your content is not delivering what it promised in the subject line topic. Your audience was interested in sports, but instead got something they were interested in less. In this case, you want to think more about your content quality. Clearly, you have identified topics that your audience likes. Now, you need to write content that they like, too.

OPT-OUTS AND SPAM COMPLAINTS

The percentage of emails that get reported as SPAM is an indicator of how engaged members are with your email content. This metric will not help you optimize for lead generation, but it does provide insights into whether or not people like your content at all. That said, zero opt-outs or complaints are so rare as to be a red flag of a different kind. As email marketers, it is our job to get at least some positive engagement. If you don't have any complainers, congratulations. You might be getting zero opens and zero clicks, but that also means your list isn't engaged with your content. That makes it highly likely you are sending irrelevant messages. Look for low, but non-zero rates of people leaving your list.

SEO content data

If social media and content are inseparable, then SEO and content are a tag team. At its most basic, SEO is about getting content ranked for search terms that your audience types into search engines like Google and Bing. Successful SEO is about writing great content and making sure it contains the right topics and keywords to show up for those searches. If you are doing search marketing, you are likely gathering vital content data all the time.

Now, most content on your site can be thought of as SEO content, but here we are talking about those content types that are mostly created to improve search rankings: pillar pages, FAQ pages, pillar page-linked blog posts, articles, guides, and infographics. These are the content types that you optimized for search engines first, with other content goals, such as engagement, as secondary.

For this dataset, you want to first look at three metrics:

- How much of your topical keyword space does each article/page/blog post occupy? (See Google's Keyword Planner Tool)
- What are the keyword densities of your most important pages? (See Yoast or Semrush)
- What keywords are customers typing into search engines most often? (See Google's Keyword Tool)

Here are some of the top keyword metrics that can optimize your content. Growth of new keywords can measure how successful you are at increasing the volume of content you are getting ranked for. If your company is new, then this number will be high because all your keywords are fairly new. But if you have been publishing content for years and haven't had any growth in keyword rankings, it may mean that your content marketing is stagnant. This is more a program-wide metric. It's a danger signal that your content is not staying as fresh as it should. You are not exploring new topics, so you are not ranking on new keywords.

EXISTING KEYWORD GROWTH

Ranking by volume can help you narrow down your target keywords. Are you getting ranked for any popular terms at all? Great, that means your content is targeting the right things. But are you regularly ranking for popular search terms? If so, then congratulations are in order! Your content is hitting the sweet spot of being relevant to what people type into Google and Bing. But if your content isn't ranking at all, then you need to check how relevant it is to what people are searching for. Get some user feedback and revise your content before trying search marketing again.

TOP ORGANIC KEYWORDS

The top organic keyword metric is a great example of why "listening" is so important in the content marketing process. This tells you what the top keywords are that are getting consumers to click when they find content from you on that keyword in search results. Let's break it down. Imagine SandWish ranks #1 on Google for three keywords: "keto sandwich recipe," "sandwich delivery," and "affordable food subscription." These keywords are all ranking #1, but they vary in how much traffic they deliver. "Keto sandwich recipe" gets the most traffic and "affordable food subscription" generates the least. This tells you that your audience is interested in recipes for low-carb sandwiches, but not so much generic meal kits or food delivery.

What does this mean? This means you should do more work around keto sandwich recipes instead of creating content on other food-related topics. You could write a book or create a subscriber list around keto sandwich recipes and send those people to this information from non-SEO sources, like social media posts. This is an example of using SEO as a method for content marketing rather than vice versa.

TOP ORGANIC CONTENT

Closely tied to top organic keywords, top organic content tells you what content people are reading once they find it through organic search. It is another valuable metric because it tells you what people are interested in beyond just finding your product or service. This is the content they are reading on your site, that they find via search. If you have all of your webpages mapped by theme, patterns can emerge. If your content is relevant, then it probably means that you are doing content marketing right!

ORGANIC LENGTH OF SESSION

Return to the strategy stage and think about what you want to get out of your content. Because SEO is just the path to getting found with your relevant content, it's not the end goal. You don't build audiences by being highly visible in search alone; you get them by getting people engaged with your content. Now that you are measuring top organic content, also look at how long people spend reading that content to see if they are staying engaged with it. Organic length of session tells you how long people stay on your site once they find your content in search engines.

Web education metrics

Webinars, Zoom meetings, virtual events—whatever you call them, whether you were doing them for decades before Covid or went online only in 2020, the online educational broadcast is a time-proven lead-generation, engagement, and loyalty engine. It is also costly to produce educational programming. A single webinar can require 8–20 hours of scripting, slide design, and production time per hour broadcast. It also usually requires the time of your highest-profile executives or subject-matter experts, adding to the cost. So you want to get these metrics right.

As with anything, your web education metrics will tell you what is working and where you should try new things.

REGISTRANTS

This is obvious. Be certain that you have de-duplicated registrant lists before reporting, since people often forget they signed up for free events and register again. Registrants are also a bit of a vanity metric. Don't fret if attendance is modest if you are generating leads, since, as with all content, many who consume high-value content are not leads. Also, keep in mind that the attendance rate for free programming is 50 percent of the registration list.

LIVE AND RECORDING VIEWS

This tells you the number of people who watched your broadcast. You can get this data through your video platform. It becomes tricky when you upload recordings to multiple channels. You need to know how many individual views you get across all of the different channels where you have uploaded your recording.

LIVE VS RECORDED VIEWS

How many people watched your live broadcast vs how many watched it later? You might fall into the trap of thinking that 100 percent of people who watch your event must have done so live, but this would be wrong. Many register for your event for later watching, either because they are in a low-connectivity zone or because they want to replay something to get more out of it.

AUDIENCE ENGAGEMENT

Watch time is the simplest measurement here, but some platforms provide a more sophisticated metric, tracking how many viewers had your session active on their screens, rather than working on another web tab or application while playing your webcast without watching it. You should also look at how many people took follow-up actions after viewing your webcast, such as registering for another webcast or completing a survey about their experience.

MOST ENGAGED TIME

This metric tells you how much of your webcast was engaging enough to be watched. It is a measure of the quality and effectiveness of your program, rather than just pure exposure. Were people watching live? Did they watch all the way through to the end of the recording? What segments had the most engaged viewers, and when did people tune out?

OPENS OF FOLLOW-UP EMAILS

Though the medium here is email, it is a measure of your webinar effectiveness. How many opened the follow-up email from the event? How did people take the desired action? Did they do so within a few days of watching your webinar or later on? What actions did people take and how were those tracked to be attributed to your webcast?

Gated content metrics

Ebooks, research reports, and other content marketing that you share with prospects only if they provide their contact information is called gated content. It's a lead generation mechanism. And it is high on the list of lead generation tactics because gated content converts at 5–10 percent, sometimes higher, depending on the industry and whether you offer something truly valuable in return for contact information.

Creating and distributing gated content is more than just putting up a form. It is about creating an integrated lead generation system where all the pieces work together to make sure you are targeting the right people, collecting enough information about them, and giving them quality content that will turn them into customers.

Gated content metrics are focused on conversions from offers of free or premium content. These metrics can be:

CONVERSION RATE

The percentage of people downloading a gated piece of content after visiting the landing page is the content's conversion rate. Unbounce reports that the average conversion rate for landing pages is about 5 percent. To beat that, you need to offer something of incredible value. What makes content worth downloading?

NUMBER OF CONVERSIONS

This is the total number of downloads in a given time frame (month, quarter, year) or since the page was created.

GENUINE LEADS

If you have ever run a gated-content campaign, you know that fake names and contact information are common. This number is the total number of real contacts you are left with after removing all those noneofyourbusiness@ noneofyourbusiness.com email addresses.

QUALIFIED LEADS

If you are creating good content, then lots of people want it. Many of those folks are not your perfect prospects. They may be students, journalists, or just curious readers excited to read your quality ebook or report. This metric is the number of leads who are your prospects (that is, they meet your criteria for what you are selling).

When it comes to gated content, these metrics will tell you whether your investment in this most costly form was worthwhile. They will also tell you how to adjust your marketing strategy to increase conversions and gather better information for future campaigns.

Acting on the data

The results are in. You know what themes are getting the most clicks on your blog. You know the email subject lines that garner the highest open rates, and the brand themes they reflect. You are measuring social media engagement tied to your theme map, and your keyword research is ongoing. Get ready to roll up your sleeves, because now the real fun begins.

Think of this as your cookbook for optimizing your content program.

Bounce-rate issues

The bounce rate is one of the most intuitive content metrics. If it is high, analyze the pages where your customers are leaving and see what you can improve to make them stick around longer. The bounce rate reflects how well your content performs to achieve conversions (i.e. download an ebook), leads (get a quote), or sales (buy now!). If the bounce rate falls in the 25–50 percent range, then your content is likely meeting its business objective.

Click-through-rate issues

Remember, the click-through rate reflects how relevant your content is to what customers are looking for. Optimizing it should be goal #1 if you are seeing CTR issues. You can do this by ensuring your content is thematically correct (i.e. is the content on cat food always about cats?) and constantly testing new headlines to improve engagement.

Open-rate issues

A low open rate can reflect email-list issues, including poor targeting or lack of segmentation, so it is not always about content. However, if you are confident your lists are well targeted, then use this data to determine the strength of your content. First, determine whether some themes in a subject line lead to strong open rates. Are all your emails suffering from lackluster opens, or just those on a few themes? If it is all your emails, your entire email program is at fault, and content is likely only part of the issue.

If you have strong performance for some themes and not others, then you have a roadmap to strengthen email content. Test whether increased focus on the themes that drive opens improves open rates across the board. It may be that your audience only wants as much of your most popular themes as they are already getting. In that case, increasing the number of emails that focus on that theme will disengage them. For instance, if you see that buy one, get one (BOGO) coupons get high open rates, then decide to send out only BOGOs in your emails, you may find consumers are tired of them. However, if a theme is more substantive, you can expand on it with fresh angles.

It is likely also time to increase your range of themes. Go back to your thematic map. Look at your themes and see if any suggest a relevant and engaging message. If so, adapt accordingly and test some new variants to find key opportunities.

Email clicks and click to open rate by link theme challenges

This data can help you understand if your readers see your company the way you do. It can also measure whether their priorities align with yours. To determine this, go back to your thematic map. The absolute number of clicks on links by theme should mirror the relative importance of each theme. For instance, if "saving money" is SandWish's most important theme, then links on that theme should be getting the most clicks. If they are, that's good news. It means that you have correctly identified your consumers' needs. If they are not, then there is a gap between your priorities and theirs. They may not be seeing the value in the content you are creating.

Brand themes by referral source inconsistency

If search engines, social media referrals and direct traffic all show similar company themes, it's good news. It means that your brand is presenting consistently across the web. Paired with a low bounce rate, it means people like what they see about you online, and when they get to your site they stay for more. But if search engines show a different set of themes than social media, it means you might have a problem. Inconsistency in brand themes across different channels can be fine in moderation. Think of how Duolingo presents itself on radio, for instance, in contrast with the madcap whimsy of their TikTok presence. If it's moderate, deliberate, and strategic, presenting different facets of your brand is usually not harmful. However, a lot of inconsistency in how people see your brand on different channels can lower your brand awareness. Repetition is key to branding. So, if consumers see completely different facets of your brand on different channels, they may have trouble forming an accurate picture of who you are. Look at how great the difference is among the brand themes driving traffic to your site from different channels. For instance, if most of your Facebook traffic originates from posts saving money, while your Instagram traffic is related to healthy living themes, then there is a significant disconnect either in how you are presenting your brand on these different channels, or in how consumers on the different channels are perceiving you.

Remember to make allowances for the audience that you know you reach through each referral source. If most of your Pinterest traffic comes from posts related to healthy living, while most of your LinkedIn traffic is related to remote team-building, that's reasonable. It's just important to understand that your brand is presenting itself differently on each of these channels.

Underperforming organic keywords by theme

If the keyword theme terms that send traffic to your site are similar, or consistent with, your thematic map, you're golden. You understand your consumers, your content is aligned with consumer needs, and your SEO program is making you visible on the right keywords.

But if they are completely outside of what you would expect for your company brand, then there is cause for concern. For instance, if most of your top keywords on your thematic map are related to some aspect of saving money, yet the keywords driving traffic to your site are mostly about gluten-free bread, it means that you are not getting across in your content what your company is about. It could also mean that your choice of keywords is not aligned with what consumers want from your brand. If this happens, look at how you can change your keyword research to better match what consumers are looking for.

Low growth of new keywords

This means that your content program is getting stale. If this is the case, it's time to host some brainstorming sessions with your team. Map new content to your existing themes, but branch out to explore themes from new angles. Better still, use referral source metrics to identify new themes present on sites that are driving traffic to your site. Because those themes are already part of your customers' journeys, you know they resonate with your audience. You get the freshness of a new topic, while still having data to prove that the topic is of interest to your audience.

As you might expect, low growth of new keywords also reflects poorly on your key performance indicators (KPIs). It is difficult to grow traffic if people are not finding your content via search engines. It takes time to build organic rankings, so you need a multi-channel strategy to become more visible on your new themes faster. In the short term, focus on increasing the volume and effectiveness of your social outreach strategies to compensate for this drop in visibility. You can also supplement with paid search or other advertising.

Low growth in new keyword rankings can also be a sign that your customer journey is not as well-defined as it could be. If the reason you are struggling to rank for new keywords is that you already optimize for hundreds of keywords across all of your content marketing, your keyword strategy may be a hodgepodge, rather than a well-crafted one. If you are spread too thin on keywords, you may be creating a fragmented customer journey or brand experience. So, look at how consistent the content themes driving traffic to your site are with the customer journey. If you notice gaps, try to pin down a more cohesive brand experience through your content. What keywords really matter to consumers at different stages of the journey? What keywords convert or increase engagement? If you don't yet have keywords mapped to the stages of your customer journey, now is the time to start. Paired with your thematic mapping, it can help you build a purposeful content marketing program that moves customers through the funnel.

Too many new visitors vs returning visitors

If you struggle to retain visitors this can mean your content lacks value. As a result, it fails to create brand loyalty, which sends customers looking for alternatives. This means you are losing your most valuable visitors—those who should have returned to the site after their first visit—because they didn't find what they came for on their first try.

To keep visitors returning, you need your content to be hyper-relevant to their interests at every stage of the customer journey. If you don't, they will click away. The first place to look to diagnose site stickiness issues is your bounce rate. If it's high, then you are likely losing visitors immediately. That first read of your content just isn't compelling enough to keep them on the site, let alone lure them back.

Sometimes, though, those initial visits seem to indicate an engaged user. They read several blog posts, raising the hope that they will return for more later. Yet, they never do. That can be frustrating. If the content was engaging enough on the first visit, why isn't our site sticky? Use your referral sources and keyword rankings to identify what paths consumers are taking across all content themes to your site. Once they are on the site during that first visit, look for places where visitors start to drop off in the funnel, or whether they even travel down the funnel. Visitors who engage with your content, but don't take the next steps to convert, may just be there to read your content.

If a user engages with your content, starts down the funnel to conversion on the first visit, then leaves, never to return, you are actually in a good place. Try retargeting ads to see if all visitors need is a push to return to your site. Alone, retargeting is the lazy way to increase site stickiness. Other tactics boost your chances of success:

- Test different site layouts to determine whether funnel leakage is due to poor UX.

- Re-map your customer journey to see whether conversion paths are longer or otherwise different than the ones you build your site for.

- Look at your pages that contain content for the next stage of the funnel or higher, trying to understand why they are not converting.

- Look at whether bounce rates change based on where users land in the sales process, as reflected in the content theme.

If you find that it's not users who are not sticking around, but rather prospective customers who make it through your funnel but don't convert, then it is time to look at your product or service. Is what you're selling the right solution? Are you reaching out to enough relevant users? Do they understand that you can solve their problem and feel confident in making a purchase with you?

This cross-platform analysis impacts a range of marketing functions. It helps product marketers identify the needs and feelings consumers have about their products across different platforms so they can craft the brand experience accordingly. Brand themes by traffic source can also help you learn if perception of your brand needs to shift, or is already shifting on its own. Take, for example, Duolingo. Their brand perception has shifted from one that was relatively serious to that of a cutting-edge, irreverent brand, thanks to their cheeky TikTok postings. Audience research may help them identify that people across all platforms now find their voice in TikTok charming and irreverent. They could then incorporate more of this tone into advertising on other platforms in order to build the unique Duolingo brand.

Knowing the root causes of poor content marketing ROI can be challenging. Part of the reason is that content does not exist in a channel silo. The same content that you are posting to LinkedIn is living on your blog, while an expanded version is part of a webinar and a gated ebook. That's why you need to look at your content strategy as a whole, even as you address specific issues. The key is to keep optimizing all the time. Try different approaches from this cookbook and see what works best for your business

Putting it all together: creating a content calendar

Once we have all these content metrics, what do we do with them? First, build a content calendar. This is vital to reconnecting with lost customers and boosting site stickiness. The following are the steps to building your content calendar:

- Identify steps in the customer journey on your site where content should play a key role. For instance, do consumers want to see recipes at the awareness stage? Do they engage primarily through your newsletter once they are further down the funnel? Does social media convert them?

- Review your thematic maps to locate your key themes, and look at your audit to find gaps in theme coverage.

- Know your sales cycle and industry calendar. For instance, if you are an online retailer, you will want to space out your content for upcoming holidays.

- Identify the best times of the year and/or months for publishing your type of content.

- Think about how much time it will take to research and create a piece of complementary content for each stage in your funnel.

With this prolog, we now have a plan for how to map out our content for the next few months. Content calendars will grow and change as you learn more about your audience's needs and what they want from your site. A metrics-driven content calendar may look like this:

- Content tied to days when consumers are most and least active.

- Content tied to most responsive customer segments.

- Content segmented by conversion targets.

- Channels aligned with the content that performs the highest on them.

Other factors are also worth considering when content planning, such as how much time you have to produce the content and whether your organization is more comfortable creating vs curating. As you finalize your calendar, map out the process for how the content will get created or curated. Who is doing it? What types of tools do they need? And what types of research should they do?

Conclusion

Measuring the impact of content marketing is more than just a simple ROI calculation. Content marketing is an investment in customer acquisition and retention, whether your content is gated or available for free. The goal of content marketing efforts should align with the broader vision of your business.

Measuring this impact requires you to think more like a marketer than an accountant. It's not just about measuring revenue; it's about understanding how all your content contributes to your branding, awareness, and lead generation efforts.

ROI is just one metric of interest to marketers, but there are dozens more that will help them understand how content marketing fits into the overall growth strategy for their business. In conjunction with the framework, the basic content metrics are essential to a product content marketing plan.

FROM THE FIELD: MICHAEL DEANGELIS

Michael DeAngelis is Vice President of Integrated Communications and a registered dietitian for New England Dairy. This nonprofit industry association for dairy farmers in the US New England region works to educate consumers about dairy products, promote sustainable agriculture, and serve as the voice of the region's dairy farmers. We talked with him about the role metrics play in his communications strategy to reach consumers.

THINKING BACK TO THE TIMES WHERE YOU HAVE LOOKED AT MARKETING METRICS, WHAT DO YOU FIND IS THE MOST HELPFUL TO YOU? OR WHAT HAVE YOU USED THE MOST WHEN IT COMES TO MARKETING METRICS?

"Great question. For our organization, we have leaned very heavily into social and digital. For the work that we do, being a nonprofit, those tend to be the areas that are most cost effective for us. So, social media analytics have become critical for us. We have been looking more into SEO: our keywords, how they are resonating, how we're appearing in search, and what terms are appearing in search that we can then tailor our content and our marketing specifically. We learn a lot. We do look at our web analytics. Our website is also a key hub for us when we're doing our marketing. A lot of our campaigns drive folks to our site, where we're able to really get the deeper engagement with content that we're offering, whether through blogs, or video content.

"We also focus on our newsletter analytics. We've used those analytics to better target some of our newsletter content, and then actually increase our open rates and click-through rate by using more of a targeted strategy by looking at our analytics. Analytics helps us be more efficient with our time, or effective with our communication. Also, it has helped us steer what kind of content we need to create.

"On our website, for example, when we look at topics that are being searched very heavily, looking at the Google Analytics, we see 'lactose intolerance' really comes up very high in the search list. So we created a content center on our website focused on lactose intolerance, and then targeted our social media to drive folks who are interested in the topic to our content center. Those are examples of where we really have let the data drive where we need to lean into. Now, this has been effective for us in terms of getting more readership and engagement."

"Our digital marketing manager is looking at reports weekly to bi-weekly. Especially as we're launching specific campaigns, she'll focus heavily on them, review, and make recommendations. She'll identify: here's where we need to dial up or here's where we need to alter course. And she also oversees the digital influencers we're working with. In this capacity, she analyzes how content is performing generally in order to steer what is being generated by our paid partners. She also adjusts the content we are putting out more organically.

"We also look at which content channels are resonating the most. Since we don't sell a product, as a nonprofit, we really sell information. We really are about engaging people and understanding the value that dairy brings to people's everyday lives, as well as what dairy farmers are doing.

"We're providing information and experiences not only in a digital context, but through in-person events. For those events, we have more rudimentary means of tracking how people are engaging with us in person, in events, or whether it be farm tours or other programming. But we also look at digital analytics, both pre- and post-experience, to see the impact of in-person events on our messaging engagement. At events, we try to capture folks' digital information, whether that is email address, or other data, then connect with them to draw them in—because that's where they get the deeper opportunity to interact with us vs the in-person events. It's kind of like casting a net, and then we're able to really target better.

"We know what we can share with them, what they are interested in, through in-person event data. If we met them at a farmers' market, they may be interested in more sustainability content. So how do we then target our content accordingly? It's a funnel strategy in a sense, where we are trying to bring them in through the experience, but then kind of really engage them more on the digital side with content."

"I can share two examples. One is with our newsletter, which is our only direct-to-consumer interaction from a marketing standpoint. We have good open rates, generally speaking. But one of the things we realized was there was specific content that seemed to perform really well, amongst a particular subset of our readership. And this was something that our marketing manager noted, looking for opportunities indicated by this data. She identified 'recipe content' that had a particular spike with a certain subset of our readership.

"With that data, we produced a targeted strategy. We publish a quarterly recipe roundup newsletter. For this newsletter, engagement and now open rates are in the

40 percent rate and click rates are in the 30 percent range, both of which exceed by far industry standards. We try to do that kind of looking and slicing the analytics to see other subsets of content that perform better with subsets of our audience, then asking how we serve up content that will grow their engagement.

"And of course, all those newsletters drive to our website, for more recipes, or for the recipe videos, so that newsletter content just opens the door for us to bring them in more. This is an opportunity in our marketing, and let's use that similar model going forward for how we can better target content.

"On the flip side, something that didn't work as well was Instagram Live. We did trials with Instagram Live with our dietician talking about nutrition, or with a partner talking about lactose intolerance. While we didn't really get great viewership, we did end up getting more followers.

"So, it seems to drive more followers than drive the actual eyes on the video. We re-evaluated the goals of Instagram Live, from immediate viewership to follower growth. That left a big question mark on Instagram Live. Is it really something we should invest in, because it takes a lot of our time. Is that really something we should be doing? For us right now, it's kind of a question mark about whether we go forward with it or not. So, I think that's an example of where looking at the numbers helps us decide what is not the best way to go in the future."

YOU SAW THE METRICS, YOU TOOK ACTION ON THEM AND MADE STRATEGIC CHANGES. WOULD YOU SAY USING METRICS HELPED MAKE YOUR MARKETING MORE SUCCESSFUL?

"It worked well, for us. It served our purpose in terms of building trust in dairy by helping people understand areas consumers have questions about. Our move on the newsletter definitely helped us with kind of improving that area. We have also been able to make other optimizations: we tried to increase the frequency of our newsletter, and began to see the opposite effects. We saw people dropping off in terms of open rates and clickthroughs. So, it was a little oversaturated. It helped us address the rhythm of that newsletter. For us, it's such an important piece of us connecting with people on a regular basis, that it was really important for us to readjust the rhythm for the newsletter for optimal performance.

"We're trying to be more purposeful on evaluations. You get the metrics, and that's great. That's good data. But what's the evaluative value of it and what do you do with it? As an organization we're trying to be more disciplined; we have conversations about the data. We routinely look at the data on our newsletters or on our website performance, looking at those content centers, and whether they are performing. And if something is not performing, can we figure out why it's not performing?

"We just completed a customer journey mapping for our consumer audience. We are seeing that we have some bottlenecks in that journey. That is leading us to do more data collection around that journey: how can we make the experience with our media better? Are we losing opportunities to engage with consumers? And what adjustments can we make, whether it be content, or a website, destination? Metrics have really helped us make decisions about stopping something, adjusting something, or asking continuous questions."

08

Data-driven product strategy

One of the traditional "4Ps" of marketing, product strategy has evolved into one of the most data-driven disciplines in business. From qualitative to quantitative data, in this chapter we will learn how to build a product roadmap driven by timely data, understand the product lifecycle, and create value for consumers across buyer segments. We finish by analyzing different product strategies using data.

Products do not exist in a vacuum; they are part of a larger system that includes the company, its customers, and the competitive landscape. In order to create successful products, it is important to have a deep understanding of all these factors.

You can think of product strategy as the set of decisions that determines how a company will meet their customers' needs. It is also a plan to help them compete in the market. It includes everything from what products to create and how to make them stand out, to what features to prioritize and how to price them.

The product lifecycle

Products have a lifecycle, just like people do. There are a few different stages that a product goes through as it moves from idea to obsolescence:

1 **Introduction:** this is the beginning of a product's lifecycle. In this stage, the product is new and there is lots of excitement around it. The company is trying to generate awareness and interest in the product.

2 **Growth:** this is the stage where the product starts to take off. Sales are growing and the company is starting to make money from it.

3 **Maturity:** the product is now well established and sales are slowing down. The company needs to find new ways to create excitement about the product and keep customers interested.

4 **Decline:** the product is no longer popular and sales are dropping. The company needs to find a way to get rid of it or else the company will go bankrupt.

The product lifecycle is not a straight line; products can jump from one stage to another depending on what is happening in the market.

Metrics play a role throughout the lifecycle. At the introduction phase, companies need to measure awareness and interest. In the growth phase, they need to track sales and engagement. In the maturity phase, they need to focus on profitability and market share. In the decline phase, they need to watch out for signs that the product is no longer popular, seeking ways to revitalize sales through strategies such as finding new markets, rebranding, or updating features, just to name a few.

There are a variety of metrics that companies can use to track their product's performance. The most important ones vary depending on the stage of the product lifecycle:

1 **Introduction phase:** in this stage, companies need to measure awareness and interest. They can do this by tracking things like website visits, social media mentions, press coverage, and sales leads.

2 **Growth phase:** during this phase, companies should track engagement metrics such as active users, pageviews, downloads, and time on site. They should also track conversion rates and customer lifetime value (CLV).

3 **Maturity phase:** in the maturity phase, companies should focus on profitability and market share. They can track metrics such as revenue growth, churn rate (the rate at which the customer base turns over through both gaining new customers and losing some others), gross margin, and customer satisfaction.

4 **Decline phase:** as a product moves into the decline phase, companies need to watch for signs that it is no longer popular. Companies should keep an eye on indicators such as market saturation, declining sales, and shrinking profits. They can track metrics such as declines in sales, market share, and brand equity. They may also want to measure customer satisfaction and loyalty to see if there is any way to re-engage customers.

Understanding the metrics to use at different stages in the product lifecycle is important for companies. It helps them track their progress and make necessary changes to keep their product competitive. To keep a handle on these metrics, many product marketers use frameworks to map data to specific product management goals.

The classic product metrics frameworks

There are several frameworks that product teams use to understand their products and make decisions. Three popular ones that are especially relevant to today's marketers are AARRR, HEART, and the Kano model. Each framework allows marketers to sort their data according to the impact it has throughout the product marketing cycle. Let's look at them all.

AARRR

Also known as the "pirate" metrics, AARRR stands for Acquisition, Activation, Retention, Referral, and Revenue. Developed by Dave McClure, a noted venture capitalist, AARRR looks at:

- **Acquisition:** this metric simply looks at your customer acquisition channels. We have looked at measuring acquisition throughout this book. Check out the chapters on customer metrics for a full explanation of customer acquisition.

- **Activation:** in the AARRR metrics framework activation corresponds to engagement. It is when users explore a product's features, start using more features, log in more often, or otherwise show indicators of growing loyalty.

- **Retention:** this is the rate at which users stick with your product. For instance, you might track the percentage of users who return to your product after a certain time period has elapsed. Or, if you are an e-commerce site, you might track the percentage of first-time buyers who come back and make a second purchase.

- **Referral:** the number of active users who introduce new users to your product. Referred customers are ones who have been brought in by someone else. This could be through social media, word of mouth, or any other marketing channel. Referral is when current users talk up a product to their friends, family, and colleagues. Word-of-mouth metrics can measure referral, but many brands take measuring this a step further by incentivizing referrals, giving unique links to existing users. This can both increase referrals and make them more measurable, so they are worthwhile even if their use is limited, since the process can be automated on any web platform.

· **Revenue:** of course, this is the most important metric for any business! Revenue captures how successful a company is at monetizing its user base.

Using AARRR, companies can drill down into which channels are most effective for them and focus on improving those. AARRR is a framework for high-level metrics, the ones most likely tracked by the C suite. While it is a good way of categorizing the metrics you collect, it is more a classification system for detailed metrics than a set of specific measures.

If your role is to increase acquisition, improve retention, or drive referrals, you will of course need much more specific metrics, such as UX data, survey data, focus groups, and web analytics metrics. For now, look at AARRR as a way to see how these detailed metrics fit together to show you the total health of your product. It is a way of getting a broad understanding of your product's performance.

HEART

If you are not feeling piratical, perhaps you prefer a set of metrics that is a bit more affectionate. For you, there is HEART. Created at Google, HEART is:

Happiness: the percentage of users who are satisfied with your product. This could be measured through surveys or Net Promoter Score (NPS), customer satisfaction scores (CSAT), other survey instruments, focus groups, or reviews and ratings.

Engagement: the average length of time a user spends on your product each day (or week, month, etc), or the number of screens they view, features they use, or articles they read. Engagement measures user activity: the number of times users interact with your product, for example, the number of logins, pageviews, or emails sent.

Adoption: the percentage of new users who continue using your product after a certain period of time, or the number of new users who sign up for your product in a given time period.

Retention: the percentage of active users who stick with your product over a period of time. It could be measured by the percentage of returning users or the number of active users who have been with you for a certain length of time.

Task success: consumers turn to any technology to accomplish certain tasks. Task success looks at how many of these tasks users complete vs how many they abandon. It also looks at how long these tasks take vs the expected time they should take. The more users can complete their tasks quickly, the higher the task success.

Like AARRR, HEART is a framework for understanding how individual, actionable metrics fit into a larger strategic picture. It can also help you set measurement priorities. For instance, you might track Happiness to see how satisfied users are with your product, then use Engagement data to determine which features are most popular and which ones need more work. Or you could look at Retention rates to see if you're losing users in the first few days, weeks, or months after they sign up. Depending on your product challenges, you can invest more in the aspects of HEART that will give you answers.

The Kano model

The Kano model is another popular framework for understanding product metrics. It was developed by Noriaki Kano, a Japanese scholar and professor in the field of product management. The Kano model looks at how customers perceive features and what drives their satisfaction with a product.

In this model, we measure proposed product features by the type of customer satisfaction they will generate. There are three types of customer satisfaction: basic, performance, and excitement.

Basic satisfaction is when a customer is happy with a feature because it does what it is supposed to do. A classic example is unlimited music streaming services. Offering popular artists and genres is a basic feature; it's why consumers use your product. Performance satisfaction goes beyond that; it's when a feature improves the performance of a product such that the consumer gets more use out of the product the more the product has that feature. For our music streaming service, a performance feature may be customization. Excitement satisfaction is when a customer is delighted by a feature because it does something unexpected or innovative. These features are the hardest to develop with metrics alone, as consumers tend not to ask for innovative features that they have not imagined. Skillful interpretation of what consumers say they need leads to excitement features. For instance, the iPhone's touch screen was an excitement feature when it was first released: people had never seen anything like it before.

You can gather data on whether a feature is basic, performance, or excitement from the methods explored in this chapter. Customer surveys, UX metrics, e-commerce data, and the other metrics listed in this chapter are especially useful in identifying basic and performance needs. However, data on excitement features often comes from user interviews and focus groups—but also from the imaginative ways in which your team interprets what your customers say and translates this into creative features.

Once you have a good understanding of the Kano model, it is important to prioritize which features to develop first. In the Kano model, basic and performance features are essential, while excitement features are nice to have. Product managers can use this information to make tough choices about which features to invest in—and how to allocate their team's time and resources.

Kano looks at two deciding metrics: how much you must invest to build the feature vs how much customer satisfaction it will produce.

Basic features should always be developed before performance features, as they are necessary for satisfying the market. An interesting thing about basic features is that they have diminishing returns; there is a point at which investing in the basics will deliver less ROI than you invest, because you are working too hard on improving features that just need to be there. For a music streaming service, investing in ever more obscure music to add to your catalog may provide diminishing returns, as few customers need that extensive a music library. Performance features are those that don't have diminishing returns—the more you invest in them, the more your customers will be satisfied. Finally, excitement features are those that provide increasing returns, the more you invest in them. For our music streaming service, that may be developing a new way to interact with the music that provides more engagement for the user. Maybe adding virtual reality (VR) concerts, or tuning the music you hear to the weather in order to improve your mood would delight users more, the more effective the feature becomes.

The Kano model is an important tool for product managers in understanding how their customers perceive features. It helps prioritize which features to develop first and understand where to allocate resources. By understanding the three types of customer satisfaction, you can make better product decisions that will delight.

Product strategy knowledge gaps

When it comes to using metrics in product strategy, gaps come into play when different teams impact product performance: product management, UX, engineering/design, and marketing are not on the same page. This is why today's marketers need a completely interdisciplinary approach in order to bridge these gaps and use data effectively.

Think about the last time you sat down with analysts from different departments to compare metrics on your product. In a healthy organization, there should be a back-and-forth discussion about what the data means and how it can be applied to product strategy. However, this doesn't yet happen everywhere.

Even when teams are communicating effectively, they speak different metrics languages, which can get in the way of understanding the valuable data each team holds. For instance, product management may focus on number of active users, while UX teams look at engagement levels. Sales may be looking at feature questions from leads, while marketing is focused on the competitive landscape. One of the biggest impacts marketers can have in the product space is learning these different languages and translating them so that everyone is on the same page.

Sources of product metrics

Product managers have traditionally drawn on market research when making product decisions. Increasingly, UX data, digital marketing sources, and statistical analyses such as market-basket research have become part of the product marketing toolkit. Let's take a look at each one.

Market research

One chief source of product data is market research. This can include surveys of customers and prospects, focus groups, interviews with customers or experts, and data gathered from online sources such as social media.

Focus groups are used to get a sense of what people like and don't like about a product or service. They can also be used to generate ideas for new products or features. In focus groups, a small number of people are brought together to discuss a product, service, or issue. The group is usually moderated by a researcher who asks questions and takes notes.

Customer surveys are used to find out what customers want and need from a product or service. Survey questions can ask about general preferences, how likely customers are to recommend a product, what features they would like to see added, and how satisfied they are with current offerings.

Interviews with customers or experts are used to understand why customers like (or don't like) certain features and how they use a product. This type of research can help you determine which features are most important to customers and how best to design products and services.

Many brands turn to market research firms to gather direct feedback from their customers. When working with a market research firm, it is important to choose one that understands your industry and your target market. Beyond surveys, focus groups, and interviews, market research firms can also provide data from online sources such as social media.

While traditional market research is still important, we are going to focus on some of the other, digitally focused metrics sources that brands can use to gain a competitive edge. These sources go beyond conventional product data to include ongoing monitoring through a range of media not available to marketers of past generations. With today's shorter product lifecycles, and the need to constantly innovate and delight customers, it is more important than ever for businesses to have a robust data-collection plan that includes a variety of sources. Let's look at the sources available to us.

User experience research

User experience research can help identify unmet needs. This involves studying how users interact with your product or service, what they like and don't like, what frustrates them, and what delights them.

Marketing analytics

Data analysis can help you understand the business context for your product. This includes understanding customer demographics and trends, understanding market size and growth potential, analyzing key competitors, and assessing the financial performance of your product or service.

Customer service data

Customer service data can help you understand how customers are using your product and where they are having problems. This data can also help you identify features that are causing support issues and need to be redesigned or removed.

UX Research

One of the traditional sources of product metrics is user experience (UX) research. UX research is often so siloed that not only marketers, but also other parts of the product team, such as many in engineering, are not fully informed of what UX metrics are telling a company about their products' reception in the market. Yet, UX metrics are incredibly valuable across an organization. They can be vital to product positioning, audience segmentation, and promotional strategy. For example, at one client, a Fortune 500 company, internal adoption of the organization's training platform was low; when team members did use it, it was at the insistence of their managers. Using a range of UX techniques, from user interviews to card sorting, we looked at the time it took users to complete key tasks in the portal, the features users wanted, and issues that they felt that the current software had. We used that data to redesign and relaunch the tool, which resulted in a 60 percent increase in adoption.

When designing or redesigning a product, it is important to consider the user experience (UX). The goal of UX design is to make sure that users have a good experience. Since that is also a big goal of marketing, it makes sense that the metrics both teams collect should apply to each other's work. UX data is frontline data about your product that can make your products more competitive in the market.

Understanding which UX metrics for marketing to track is a challenge. Here are a few of the UX research techniques that user experience teams use of relevance to marketing. It is not an exhaustive guide to this research, but rather meant to help you understand the metrics that your colleagues in UX are collecting that have direct bearing on your job:

- Field research is a form of UX research in which teams go out and talk to people in their natural environment. The goal is to understand how people use a product in the real world, what problems they encounter, and what solutions they come up with on their own. Field research can provide more information on how people use a product than surveys or focus groups, and it can also help identify new opportunities for product development.

- Intercept interviews are a technique for conducting user research in which you intercept people who are already using your product. This type of research is especially useful for understanding how people use your product and what tasks they find difficult or frustrating.

- Card sorting involves organizing product features into groups based on similarities and differences. Card sorting helps to understand how people think about group-related items. For instance, a card sort might help you understand how people think about features of a social network, such as friends, messages, photos, and so on.

- User interviews are one of the most common types of user research. In user interviews, researchers talk to users about their experiences with a product or service. Interviews can help you understand how users interact with a product, what they like and don't like about it, and what problems they encounter.

- Diary studies ask customers to track their usage of a product along with their thoughts and feelings about a product over time. Diary studies can help you understand how users feel about a product over the long term and how they use it in their everyday lives.

- Eye tracking is a technique that uses special glasses or software to track where users are looking when they interact with a product. This information can help you understand what features and designs are catching people's attention and which ones they are ignoring.

- Heatmapping is a technology that uses color to indicate how much attention a particular area of a web-based application is getting. Heatmapping can help you understand which areas of your product are most important to users and where they are spending the most time. If you use heatmapping in marketing metrics, this technique will be familiar to you.

- Task analysis is a technique that helps you understand the steps users take to complete a task with a product. By understanding the steps users take, you can learn what features they consider essential, how well typical users understand your product, and how user-friendly it is in real life. To conduct a task analysis, researchers watch people use a product and take notes on their actions.

As more and more companies focus on user experience, it is important for all members of the company to have a basic understanding of how UX research can help inform product decisions.

Product positioning

UX data can be highly valuable in product positioning. Positioning is the process of determining how a product should be perceived in the market. It involves creating a unique selling proposition (USP) and differentiating the product from competing products. UX data can help you understand what features are important to users and how users perceive your product compared to others.

For example, let's say you manufacture a line of high-end luxury watches. Your USP might be that your watches are handmade in Switzerland and are of the highest quality. However, if you find through user research that users are interested in features such as water resistance or durability, you might want to consider adding those features to your watches to differentiate them from other luxury brands. You are in an even better position if your product is already waterproof, but you have not done much to promote that feature in your advertising, on your website, and in your social media. You can shift the USP that you focus on in your creative materials to emphasize the water resistance of your watches.

You can also leverage UX metrics to improve differentiation when your product is similar to a competitor's product. This is a common tactic in B2B messaging and some B2C products, such as health, tech, and durable goods. Use UX data to create a feature comparison chart that shows how your product is better than the competitor's product. This type of information can be used to help you position your product in the market against similar ones.

Another way brands can apply UX metrics to product positioning is by building your content around features as content themes. For example, let's look at a company that makes insulated beverage holders. They find through card sorting that keeping drinks cold is twice as important to consumers as keeping foods hot. A content theme that could be based on UX data is "cold drink recipes." This type of content can be used on the company website, in blog posts, and in social media. It can also be used as part of an advertising campaign. They can also create short videos that show how the product is being used in unique ways, such as keeping a drink cold while skiing or snowboarding. UX metrics should inform your promotions comprehensively, connecting all forms of communication, from social media to web copy, directly to the features and benefits consumers want. Done right, this deep connection reinforces your product's value consistently for higher sales.

Audience segmentation

Positioning also refers to the way a product is marketed. You might find that users are confused about the target market for your product. Through user research, you can clearly define your target market and create marketing materials that appeal to them.

Let's look at an example. A company that sells a line of health-food probiotic bars might conduct a series of focus groups and a diary study to understand how their customers integrate their snack bars into their daily food consumption. They find that their users are mostly women over the age of 45, who take the bars with them while commuting, watching their children's sporting events, and other daily activities. However, their website and social media accounts are full of images of younger people engaged in competitive sports. This could alienate their target market and discourage them from buying the product. In this case, the company would need to re-evaluate their USP, focusing on family health, convenience, and value, rather than performance enhancement, as the reasons their product is superior.

User feedback can also help you understand which audience segments to focus on based on their level of usage. If you find that a certain segment is more engaged with your product, you can create marketing materials and product features that appeal to them specifically. Unlike CLV calculations, which depend on prior revenue data, UX research can identify high-value customer segments for new products, or those that are being targeted to completely new segments on whom there is little other data.

Segmentation metrics can best be identified through field research, focus groups, diary studies, and user interviews. These techniques allow users to provide more open-ended feedback that can upend a team's preconceived notions of who uses their product and how.

UX research in promotional strategy

When you sit down with customers, whether it's a card-sorting session, a field study, or an in-depth interview, you learn more than just the nuts and bolts of their product usage. You hear the language they use to describe your product, understand the way in which the product fits into their day, and see the problems they are trying to solve. You also get a view of how they feel about your product and where it fits into their lives. This information is gold when it comes to creating promotional materials.

When you know the words your customers use to describe your product, you can use them in your ad campaigns, on your website, and throughout your marketing. You can also create taglines that capture the essence of what your product does for customers. For example, for our health-bar company, they find in diary studies that users are writing "feeling great," "taking care of my health," and other positives about the personal health benefits they experience. The brand can develop a slogan such as "We make it easy for you to be your best self" to speak to the health benefits of using the product. The goal is to create a connection between the customer's problem and your solution that resonates in all aspects of your marketing. UX studies reveal consumer language naturally, so look to it for guidance on your promotional strategy.

Audience segmentation metrics naturally influence promotional strategy. In the prior section, we considered a company that changed its branding upon learning that mothers over 45, not young athletes, were their top customers. In addition to shifting their USP to focus on family nutrition at a great price, they will shift their visual branding, the overall design of their creative, and the language on their site. Their diary study found that mothers keep their probiotic bars in their bags, snacking on them while they go about their lives. Knowing this usage, the brand might change their tagline. From "Power to go faster, further, every day" they might shift to the more relevant "Good for you snacks everywhere, every day." The targeting of their digital ads will shift to women aged 45–55 with children at home, impacting their geotargeting as well with a new emphasis on suburban zip codes.

Another company might find that their target market is young men, and focus all of their efforts on marketing to that demographic. However, if they do user research and find that the product is being used by women as well, they could create specific content and images for their social media accounts that would better resonate with that audience.

So, what does this mean for your business? By understanding how users interact with your product and the language they use to describe it, you can develop a promotional strategy that resonates with them. UX research provides valuable insights into how customers see your product and how they want it to fit into their lives. Use this information to create campaigns that make an emotional connection with your customers and speak to their needs.

You may be asking, "why should we rely on our UX teams to gather data on consumer perceptions? Marketing can conduct surveys, focus groups, and interviews. We also have social media metrics, sentiment analysis, CRM data, and so on. Isn't this redundant?" That's partially the reason to use UX data. Rather than conducting extensive and expensive market research, you may find the data you need for positioning and segmentation has already been collected.

That's not the only reason to use UX metrics for marketing. UX research provides insights that go beyond what survey data can tell you. Surveys are great for understanding broad attitudes and behaviors, but they don't give you the level of detail you need to create targeted marketing materials. For example, if you want to know whether people feel positively or negatively about a certain product feature, a survey won't give you that information in as naturalistic a way as a field study will.

UX metrics in B2B marketing: the case of the "hidden" customers

UX metrics become especially important in B2B product positioning, since brands often lack access to the actual users of their products. Let's look at an example.

Suppose you are a B2B company that makes a CRM software. You have an impressive list of features, but don't know which ones matter the most to your end users. That's because your sales team mainly works with marketing managers, who are the ones making the purchasing decisions for software in their departments. End users, however, are more likely to be frontline marketing staff, or even workers outside marketing, such as sales staff, customer support reps, and logistics teams.

In this case, you would need to use UX metrics such as task analysis and user interviews to understand how your software is being used in the real world. You might find that frontline marketing staff only use a fraction of the features in your CRM, because their roles are different from those of marketing managers. This information can help you focus on the features that are most important to your end users, and de-emphasize those that are less relevant.

It is also important to consider how hidden customers can influence a product's positioning. Hidden customers are people who use or could potentially use a product, but are not the intended target market. For example, someone who uses an e-commerce site to buy products for their business, even though they are not the site's target market.

Hidden customers can be a valuable source of information for B2B companies. They can tell you about how the product is being used in the wild, and give you insights into how it might be used in the future. It is one more piece of data you should be tracking as part of AARRR, as it represents a key metric for retention.

Web analytics

Web analytics data is a rich source of product positioning, feature, and segmentation data. From what features consumers search for vs what products they buy, to their sentiment, demographics, and psychographics, your site analytics provide a detailed view of your customers. Let's take a look at how you can use web analytics to understand your customer's needs and wants.

E-commerce metrics

E-commerce metrics are an obvious place to look for product insights. To be sure that you are getting the most out of this data, break it down into at least the following:

PRODUCT TRENDS

You are probably already looking at what products are selling by season, and how demand is shifting over months and years. To get the most from this data, start breaking it down by categories that are readily available in your analytics.

What products are site visitors looking at vs which are they buying? This can give you valuable insight, especially when combined with other metrics. For instance, imagine you have an e-commerce site selling outdoor gear. You find that female consumers over 25 tend to view your snow boots but purchase your waterproof hiking boots about 10 percent of the time. This may indicate that they are looking for winter gear, but that the initial winter footwear they identify on your site doesn't meet their needs, but the hiking boots do. What is it about the second item that it's a more attractive product? Keyword data reveals that many of your hiking boot customers arrive at your site from a PPC campaign promoting "cold-weather boots." This means that they are not specifically looking for winter gear for a sport, but for winter weather. They clearly are not finding what they need when they see the snow boot promoted in your ads. What do they do once they are on your site to find the hiking boots instead? You look at site search data, and find that visitors in the female over-25 demographic who visit the snow boots product page search for "boots with traction" on your site. That brings them to the hiking boots, which provide superior traction to the snow boots. This may mean that you would be selling more of the snow boots if they had good traction, like the hiking boots. By combining page visit, keyword, demographic, and site search data with purchase metrics, you are starting to learn about the product features that different customer segments want. If you had just looked at product sales alone, you would have only known that hiking boots are selling better than snow boots. By taking a deeper dive into cross-sectional data, you are pinpointing the product features leading to this preference, thus identifying a segment's preferred features.

In the above example, we looked at purchase data with the following filters:

- **Views vs purchases:** examine what products consumers view vs similar ones they ultimately purchase in order to understand the features they value.

- **Shopping behavior:** compare product purchase data to shopping behavior data (e.g. acquisition channel, shopping cart adds, shopping cart abandonment) to understand more about how product touchpoints affect overall propensity to buy.

- **Site search:** use site search data to see what visitors are searching for on your website in order to better understand their interests and needs.

- **Keywords vs purchases:** identify the product features and product types that bring customers to your site. How do these align with purchase behavior? For instance, if a consumer comes to your site via a keyword search for a specific feature, such as "waterproof," or "comfortable," what products do they ultimately decide have those features?

- **Demographics and psychographics:** what consumer segments buyers belong to.

AFFINITY, IN-MARKET, AND DEMOGRAPHIC METRICS FOR PRODUCT SEGMENTATION

Google Analytics provides rich data on our users. It profiles their age, location, gender, shopping behavior, and general interests. When paired with your e-commerce metrics, this information becomes a way to understand product preferences, feature needs, and USP across segments.

You can also look at product engagement data by segment to understand how well your products are resonating with each segment. Remember to use keyword data, both acquisition and site search, to identify feature needs vs products purchased, as in the example. This data can help you determine product areas that need improvement to attract segments. Extrapolating from that feature data can get you closer to identifying the USP for each product for each demographic.

As a refresher, here are the three main types of data that Google Analytics provides on site visitors, including e-commerce purchasers:

- **Demographics:** age, gender, location.
- **In-market segments:** what consumers have been shopping for recently, for instance, in the last 30 days.
- **Affinity segments:** what topics people are interested in on the web.

You can use this data to gather fairly sophisticated metrics on how segments perceive your product—without having to conduct an expensive segmentation study. For instance, let's go back to our outdoor gear vendor. They look at their affinity segments for those women over 25 who have been buying the waterproof hiking boots. Surprisingly, they find that only 20 percent are in the sports affinity segment. Twice as many, 40 percent, are interested in fashion. This means that, while hikers are certainly buying the hiking boots, perhaps even more consumers are buying the boots for fashion and because they withstand wet weather. You already know that features such as waterproofing and traction are the top needs of consumers. Now, you also know that fashion features, such as being available in on-trend colors, also matter to your consumers.

Content marketing metrics

When looking at content marketing metrics, it is important to understand what needs matter most to your consumers. The content they consume on your site is a vital clue.

You can then look at the types of content being consumed in order to determine what needs are bringing consumers to your site. Do they want tips on how to stay safe while outdoors? Ways to make their favorite hobby more eco-friendly? Product reviews for the latest gear? This data can help you understand the product types and features that matter most to your consumers.

For instance, let's say your outdoor gear blog has posts on keeping warm during winter sports, staying safe while camping, and the best eco-friendly gear for a summer hike. If consumers are interacting the most with content related to staying warm, then that is an indication that this need is top-of-mind for them. You can note this as a further indication of "warmth" as a key product feature that attracts consumers to your brand. While you might not change the manufacture of your product based on data from blog readership, it presents more evidence of what your consumers need.

ACQUISITION CHANNEL DATA

Your acquisition channels can sometimes tell you a lot about the context in which consumers perceive your products. For instance, let's say that acquisition channel data reveals that the traffic coming to our site for those snow boots is from fashion blogs. This can tell you that:

- The target audience for your snow boots is interested in fashion.
- You may want to produce more fashion-forward designs.
- You should consider positioning your snow boots as a fashion boot, rather than as purely functional.
- The competition for your snow boot in the mind of consumers includes fashion brands, rather than sports brands only.

You can use this type of data to infer things about how different channels are driving traffic to your site and product pages. This data can help you learn more about how your products might be perceived by consumers. While you don't want to jump to conclusions based only on acquisition data, it is a vital piece of the puzzle when it comes to understanding the landscape in which your products compete.

SITE SEARCH DATA

We have talked a bit about site search data; here's why it's such a key source of product information. Site search data can also be helpful in understanding how different types of visitors are using your site. For example, if many people are searching for "red snow boots," that might tell you that there is a demand for red snow boots that you are not currently meeting. It could also suggest that you feature red boots more prominently on your site.

Similarly, if many people are searching for "men's hiking boots," this might suggest that you need to produce more men's hiking boots. It could also suggest that you market your hiking boots to men more aggressively.

Using the data that Google Analytics provides on site visitors, you can segment site search data by demographics, in-market and affinity segments, acquisition channel, and other data points. This can tell you a lot about how different types of visitors are using your site and which products they are interested in. Consumers engage in site search when they really want to find what they are looking for, so this data is a great indicator of consumer demand, especially unmet demand on which you can capitalize in your new product development.

Social listening

If you are not using social listening for your product strategy, you will love the data available from social. It can help you determine which platforms are driving product discovery and purchase, as well as what content is resonating (and not resonating) with your audience.

You can also use social listening to identify top-of-the-funnel keywords that people are using to describe your products. You might not be targeting these keywords yet, but they could give you ideas for future product development efforts. For instance, the outdoor gear company could see that a lot of people are using the hashtag "#adventure" to talk about hiking and camping products. They might develop a product line specifically for those who love adventure.

Acting on digital marketing data

When you have all of this data in front of you, it is important to remember that correlation does not equal causation. Just because a segment is interested in fashion doesn't mean they won't buy a hiking boot from you. However, understanding the correlations between different types of data will help you create hypotheses about how to improve product engagement and sales.

Once you have hypotheses, it's time to start testing them! While digital marketing data should not be used alone to develop a product strategy, it can help you get the most out of resource-intensive methods such as focus groups, surveys, and field studies. Digital metrics help you narrow down the questions to ask, giving you potential features to test, new products to evaluate for development, and customer segments to try. For example, if site search data tells you that there is demand for a specific product, you can commission a survey to determine how likely people are to buy it. Those digital metrics will help you find initial directions, rather than relying on instinct alone.

Digital marketing data is an essential piece of the puzzle when it comes to understanding your products and the market in which they compete. By using data from site search, social media, and other sources, you can identify correlations between different types of data and develop hypotheses about how to improve product engagement and sales, hypotheses that can then be tested directly with some data already behind them.

Competitor analysis

No discussion of product metrics would be complete without competitor analysis. Product metrics are an important part of competitor analysis. When you are looking at your competitors, you want to understand their strengths and weaknesses, as well as the features and benefits of their products.

You can use a variety of sources to gather this data, including:

- **Reviews:** what features are called out as strengths of your competitors' products? What features generate the most complaints? For instance, if your competition's reviews cite eco-friendly materials as a positive, while complaints center on the range of sizes, you know that eco-friendliness is a key differentiator for them.

- **Social media:** what are people saying about your competitors' products on social media? Are they loved or hated? If they are loved, what are the main reasons people love them? For instance, maybe your competition's products are high quality but inexpensive.

- **Bloggers and influencers:** what are bloggers and other influencers saying about your competitors' products? What do they like (or not like) about them?

- **Paid search data:** what feature-centric keywords are they bidding on? Do they invests thousands every month into "eco-friendly footwear"? Do they bid on terms centering on a specific set of features, such as waterproofing?

- **Organic search data:** do they rank organically on keywords related to features, positioning, or USP?

- **Product pages on their website:** what features are revealed by a text analysis of their product pages? Try running their product descriptions through a simple word cloud application such as Mentimeter to learn which words they use most to describe their products.

- **Backlink analysis:** what websites are linking to your competitor's product pages? This can give you some great ideas for content marketing or link-building campaigns.

Once you have all of this data, you can start to formulate hypotheses about how to improve your product. Maybe you realize that people love your competitor's eco-friendly materials, but they are not as interested in your more expensive products. You could develop a new line of eco-friendly products that are still high quality, but more affordable. You should also keep in mind that you don't have to compete on every metric. Maybe your competitor has a great social media presence, but they are not as strong when it comes to SEO. You could focus on SEO and let them dominate social media. Competitive analysis is less about taking on a competitor head to head; it's more about finding ways to position yourself in a market in ways that they are not.

When gathering competitive product data, remember to ask yourself the following questions:

- What are our competitors' strengths?
- What are their weaknesses?
- What features do people love (or hate) about their products?
- What keywords are they targeting in paid search?
- What keywords do they rank for organically?
- Which websites are linking to their product pages?
- What words do they use to describe their products?
- What's the positioning of their products?
- What USP do they advertise?

The answers to these questions can help you understand your competition and develop a strategy to improve your product engagement.

Once you have all of this data, it is important to create a new product-positioning statement. This statement will help you succinctly articulate the key strengths of your products in relation to your competitors. It will summarize the competing product data in a way that connects it back to how you position and sell your product.

It is also important to create buyer personas for your competitors' products. This will help you understand who their ideal customer is and how to reach them. This is a step few brands take, yet it can create the perspective you need to fully understand your competing products in context. This can, in turn, tell you who your true competitors are for your ideal customers, and who is just making products in the same space, but for different customers.

Competitive product analysis is an essential part of any successful marketing strategy. By understanding your competition, you can find ways to differentiate your products and reach new customers.

Market basket analysis

Ever wonder how e-commerce sites know what you want to buy before you even have an idea? What about the number of times you have gone into a mass-market retailer for one thing, only to leave with a bag of items you had to have? The secret is often in market basket analysis. This form of product metrics identifies the products most commonly purchased together, using sophisticated statistical analysis. It can then use these results to help suggest other products that would be of interest to the consumer, given the patterns it has detected.

Market basket analysis can tell a retailer, given a specific item, what other items should be listed as strong suggestions for buyers. For example, say most grocery shoppers tend to buy flour and eggs together. Market basket analysis would identify this pattern, and recommend selling both flour and eggs together as a packaged deal. It can also be used to discover which items are not commonly purchased together—giving the retailer insight into product combinations to avoid.

Market basket analysis is at work any time you buy an item online that has suggestions for related products beside it. It is part of the science behind store layouts, which pair displays for products often bought together, as a way of encouraging you to add that one more item to your cart. Think about those endcap displays of similar foods that you often see in the grocery store—those are usually the result of market basket analysis. Retailers use it as a form of product metrics to figure out what would be most valuable for their business and consumers, and then they test those ideas through merchandising efforts. It is also at work when you check out of a brick-and-mortar retailer and receive an ad insert with your receipt, full of coupons for items you did not intend to buy.

Market basket analysis is very useful for e-commerce sites, but can be used on physical retailers as well. When market basket analysis is used in retail settings, it is known as store auditing. It can also be used to find what is missing from store shelves, giving the retailer insight into product combinations that are being undersold, or products that consumers typically need to go with items the store already stocks. Picture a grocery store that stocks bread but not butter, for instance—consumers would find that grocery quite inconvenient. Thus, far from being just another excuse to upsell, this metric increases consumer convenience, in addition to growing your market share.

Market basket analysis is one of the most common types of product metrics you will encounter, because it is so versatile and practical for businesses—both e-commerce and brick-and-mortar stores.

Market basket analysis is different from most other product metrics in that it is performed at the retail level, rather than within the product management function. It is also different from behavioral targeting, which focuses on the consumer side of the shopping cart equation. Where behavioral targeting looks at your buying behavior, with your unique set of preferences, market basket analysis looks at what products are leaving store shelves together.

So how do you do a market basket analysis? First off, you need a really large dataset of transactions; tens of thousands are needed. Millions of transactions are even better.

Market basket analysis is built around three statistical concepts:

- **Support:** the frequency that an item combination is purchased as a proportion of all purchases. For instance, let's say you run a bookstore. You have noticed that people who buy romance novels often buy tote bags too. Every day, your store makes 100 sales. Of those 100 sales, 40 include romance novels and tote bags, bought together. Support for the romance novel and tote bag combination is thus 0.4 (40/100).

- **Confidence:** the strength of the relationship between two items. Confidence measures the proportion of times the presence of one item is accompanied by the second one, as compared to all transactions that include just one item. Let's say that, in addition to the 40 transactions in which both tote bags and romance novels occurred, another 10 transactions included romance novels only, and 5 were for tote bags only. That means a total of 55 transactions included at least one of the items (40 + 10 + 5). However, 40 out of 55 included both items. We calculate both numbers as a percentage of all transactions: 0.4/0.55 = 0.72. This means that 72 percent of all romance novel transactions included a tote bag. That's a compelling argument for the association of one product with another.

- **Lift:** the probability that both items will be bought together. To get at this probability, we have to do a bit of fancy math. We multiply the percentage of transactions containing only one of Item A by the percentage of transactions containing only Item B. For our romance novels and tote bags, we know that 10 percent of transactions have romance novels only, while 5 percent have tote bags only: $0.1 \times 0.05 = 0.005$. We then divide that by our original support number, in this case, 0.4, to get $0.4/0.005 = 80$. This means it is extremely likely that the next customer who walks in the door for *The Devious Duke's Downfall* will also buy that tote with a reading cat on it. You can also see products impact each other negatively. This means that, if a consumer purchases Item A, they are much less likely to purchase Item B. If lift is lower than 1, it means that buying one item implies that a customer won't buy the second one. Let's say tote bags have lift of less than 1 when paired with other tote bags. This means that a customer who buys one tote is extremely unlikely to buy another one on that same shopping trip.

You can use market basket analysis to find not just complementary items that can often be sold together but also substitute items. For instance, let's say you find that business books are second to romances in lift when associated with totebags. If you run out of novels about devious dukes, but you know that totebag buyers are almost as happy to buy *Leadership for Ethical Managers*, you can put business books next to your totebags to keep sales brisk while you await the next shipment of books featuring sexy Vikings.

As you have guessed, market basket analysis can also indicate how popular an item might become if it were placed near another, increasing its visibility.

Let's take a closer look at how to use market basket analysis in your business, and why it can be such an important part of your product metrics. Data sources typically used for market basket analysis include transactional data, point-of-sale data, loyalty card data and e-commerce metrics. The resulting market basket can provide retailers with valuable insight into product combinations frequently purchased together in order to help identify opportunities for upselling and cross-selling products.

For example, let's go to our outdoor gear company. Say the company has data that shows tents and sleeping bags are frequently purchased together. The market basket analysis might reveal that, when people buy a tent, they are also more likely to buy a sleeping bag. But when they purchase a sleeping bag, they are less likely to buy wool clothing. Armed with this knowledge, the company might decide to place tents closer to sleeping bags and winter clothing further from the camping gear. This strategic placement could lead to an increase in sales of both products.

Market basket analysis requires a fair amount of data in order to do it right, but it leads to insights you cannot get anywhere else.

Conclusion

When it comes to product strategy, data is key. By understanding how your customers interact with your products, you can make informed decisions about what features to focus on and how to market them most effectively. Make sure you're tracking the right metrics and using the right tools to get the insights you need!

UX metrics are important to track because they provide a snapshot of how people are using a product. They can help you understand whether people are encountering any problems with the product and what features users like and don't like. UX metrics can also help you understand how well your product is performing compared to your competitors.

Digital marketing metrics such as web analytics, social media, and search data can help you identify the most interesting product-marketing concepts to test. These sources can help you identify unexpected real-world needs, shed new light on how your products are perceived in the market, and refine your segmentation.

Market basket analysis is a great way to understand what products are being purchased together. This information can help you develop new product lines and better understand your customers' needs.

No matter what data you are looking at, always be sure to ask yourself why. Why do people like this feature? Why do they hate that one? What can you learn from your competitors to improve your own product? And most importantly, what does this data tell us about ensuring customer delight?

Building a great product strategy takes time. In this chapter, we learned about the different types of data you can use to inform your product decisions. We looked at how to track user engagement, digital marketing metrics, and market basket analysis. Finally, we discussed how to understand your competition using data. As you continue to gather data and analyze it, you will start to see trends and patterns that will help you improve your products and achieve greater success.

FROM THE FIELD: SIDE BY SIDE PET—WINNING CUSTOMERS WITH CRM

Side By Side Pet is one of the fastest-growing holistic pet food companies in the United States. Their brand caters to pet owners who are seeking healthier alternatives to conventional pet foods. Using CRM the right way, they were able to leverage data better for customer-centric marketing.

The company's marketing automation program had grown organically. Campaigns were initiated for customer onboarding, seasonal promotions, user experience, and customer service. While each campaign was aligned with customer needs, the automation program as a whole lacked a defining structure that would make it scalable as Side By Side grows. Thus, "we weren't really getting the maximum value from our investment in our technology," noted CEO Carol Bramson. "We needed to create a platform that would help us reach our customers through marketing automation in ways that were sustainable, simplified, and organized for the long haul."

The organization faced another challenge: data about marketing per-formance was housed across multiple platforms, creating silos that made it difficult to see the big picture of marketing ROI. Indeed, thanks to the different ways in which each platform reported on data, "it was a constant game of comparing apples to oranges, without any clear directional data, let alone those critical insights you need to drive successful digital marketing campaigns, product strategy, and customer experience excellence." Breaking down these silos was another step in being able to grow through smart marketing investments.

Side By Side Pet reached out to Thoughtlight to help them get a handle on their digital marketing infrastructure, with an emphasis on building a robust marketing automation implementation as well as mining their marketing data while providing strategic data insights.

GETTING STARTED: THE TECH STACK AUDIT

The first step was a tech stack audit. This is when the Thoughtlight team looks at every digital marketing technology that an organization uses, to understand where they are right now. "You need to know where you are with technology, so that you can map out the path to getting where you want to be," says Thoughtlight CEO Christina J Inge. "We sat down with the team to know each technology they owned: why they had it, what they wanted to accomplish with it, what was working well with it, and where they felt they needed help." With this information, Thoughtlight was able to provide Side By Side with an assessment of their technology needs that "cuts out the waste, the stress, the hassle to give them just the technology they need, without having to learn a ton of platforms or juggle too many vendors," notes Christina.

MARKETING AUTOMATION: BUILDING FOR PERSONALIZATION AT SCALE

Next up was a complete overhaul of the HubSpot marketing automation system. The Thoughtlight team first looked at the workflows, which are sequences of marketing automation actions, such as sending emails to customers or targeting website visitors with relevant ad messages. They found a 40 percent redundancy in automations, which is fairly typical for a firm of this size. This was leading to significant inefficiencies. Team members had to search for relevant workflows among dozens of different ones. The risk was present that, as the system grew more complex, customers would receive too many marketing messages. Sending the wrong ones was also a possibility. Organizing the automations such that they were easy to navigate and focused on customer needs was primary. The team was able to reduce the automations by 70 percent, taking the workflows from a complex, headache-inducing system that required hours to navigate to one that could be deployed with a few mouse clicks. "Cleaning up the workflows makes it easy now to give customers the right personalized messages, keep them engaged, and drive traffic to the site, without having to spend all day on it," says Allen Gonzalez, who heads up Side By Side Pet customer service operations. "It means that we can focus on keeping our customers happy, not wrangling the technology."

The Thoughtlight team also brought focus to customer onboarding, creating a smoother workflow for internal teams to know where customers are in their journeys, while providing customers with a more focused experience. They also created new workflows to target customers with special promotions, retargeting ads, and relevant content.

MARKETING ANALYTICS: MOVING FROM RAW DATA TO ACTIONABLE INSIGHTS

Breaking down data silos was the biggest challenge of the engagement. Data from the company's WooCommerce e-commerce store, Google Analytics, HubSpot, social media channels, advertising initiatives, Amazon store, and their custom Pet Health Assessment application were all living in different applications, with no central venue to see what products were selling, how customers were being acquired, what marketing channels were delivering the highest ROI, and how programs were performing. Thoughtlight's data specialist Jacqueline DiStefano set to work pulling data from these disparate data sources into a single dashboard, built using Google Data Studio. The dashboard provided Carol and her team with a comprehensive view of product performance, campaign results, and channel ROI. "Bringing all of Side By Side's data into a single dashboard gave us insights we just couldn't easily get any other way," recalls Carol.

"Simply presenting raw data, though, isn't what adds value," says Christina. "We are all about turning data into business insights. Our goal turns raw data into real insights that the Side By Side team can use to understand their opportunities in the market."

To that end, Jacqueline and Christina focused on Thoughtlight's Three Pillars of Marketing Analytics:

- Visualizations need to be intuitive, so you can understand the data at a glance, any time.
- Data needs to be curated, so that you're seeing the data that matters most.
- Analysis needs to be part of all projects, so it's connected back to business goals.

Jacqueline connected the siloed data sources to the dashboard, bringing them into a single portal, breaking down those historical silos. Then, she created intuitive visualizations within the Data Studio dashboard to make it easy for the executive team to see business trends, from product demand to revenue growth. Visualizations presented clear, directional data on:

- e-commerce statistics, including product sales, top product categories, and seasonal product demand
- social media performance, including reach, engagement, and post performance
- SEO impact, including content performance and ROI from organic search programs
- customer demographics, including sales by customer segments
- web analytics, including site visits and top pages

Thoughtlight also worked to ensure data quality, cleaning data outputs to the highest standards. The dashboard presented a comprehensive view into all of Side By Side's marketing. Users could quickly move through screens' detailed big-picture data, dig deeper into the specific performance of different channels, content, ads, posts, and products. Much of the data was real-time, allowing an immediate snapshot of what was happening in the moment. The dashboard also allowed users a full lookback at historical data for trendlining.

With data silos broken down, a comprehensive dashboard delivering real-time information, and historical data at users' fingertips, it was time to make that data go to work. Christina leveraged the data to present strategic recommendations to the team on marketing campaigns, branding, and customer growth. The result was a complete transformation of Side By Side's analytics from raw data to company-wide strategic insights. The new insights empowered the team to make informed decisions about ad spending, product assortment, target demographics, and marketing campaign planning.

"It was so frustrating in the beginning to have a variety of sources of data with no integration and limited ability to build connections for decision-making purposes. The efforts to link the information was challenging and we're still learning, but we know we're on the right track," says Carol. "Once full integration is complete, we are confident that we'll be better able to scale our marketing efforts, knowing that the data is there to measure the impact. Thoughtlight really helped us visualize where we could go with this dashboard and the ability to get to the next level with our marketing technology."

09

Price and place metrics

We learned in college that marketing consists of the 4Ps: Price, Place, Product, and Promotion. Yet, when we go into the world as marketers, often our only role is Promotion. We don't often see those other three Ps after our last essay is submitted as undergraduates.

Why is it that Price and Place are so often forgotten? It could be because they are more difficult to control. You can't just change a price or move a product to a new shelf without changing other factors in the business. They are often the responsibility, as well, of other departments within our organizations.

But, as marketers, we can't forget about them. They are essential to creating a successful marketing mix. Price is how we make money and set our prices for the products we sell. Place is how our products are displayed and made available to our customers. And, finally, Product is what we sell and how our customers perceive it. All three of these Ps need to be considered when making marketing decisions.

In this chapter, we address pricing models, pricing metrics, and some data about measuring place as part of the marketing mix. It's not designed to be a crash-course in economics. It's going to give you, however, a better understanding of how to think about pricing and place when making marketing decisions.

Pricing analytics is often not thought of as a marketing function. Yet, the classical "4Ps" of marketing include both price and "place," or distribution channels. Metrics play a strong role in both pricing models and distribution strategies, so we need to understand the metrics relevant to both these aspects of marketing, even if they are not part of our core job functions. Knowing how to measure the components of profitability with different pricing models is an important skill set.

One notable difference between "price" and "place" within the marketing 4Ps, is that most marketers have a fairly good idea about the connection between price points and sales, but often little control over a product's pricing. Thus, understanding pricing metrics is only part of the battle in using metrics to improve marketing performance in this case. On the other hand, we often do have a lot of say over many aspects of distribution. However, retail metrics, a form of place metrics, are within many marketers' areas of responsibility. They can tell us how well our products are being placed and what levers we can pull to improve retail sales. We will look at retail metrics in more detail.

Data for pricing strategy

Pricing analytics relies on data to estimate demand, set or adjust prices, understand margins, and other important metrics. To create your own pricing strategy, you need to analyze your market's unique parameters. To do this it helps to investigate trends in price (in actual dollars), price sensitivity among the different customer segments for your products, costs of goods sold, including marketing costs, and other factors.

To get started, let's take a look at some of the basic metrics we will be talking about.

When it comes to pricing, there are a few key metrics that can help us understand how well our pricing strategy is working. The first is gross margin percentage (GM percent). GM percent tells us what percentage of each sale goes towards covering the costs of goods sold (COGS) and leaves profit. A higher GM percent is better, as it means that we're making more money on each sale.

Another important metric is average selling price (ASP). ASP tells us how much we are making on each product sold. A higher ASP generally indicates a more premium product or one in high demand. It is important to note that, while ASP is a valuable metric, it can be influenced by a number of factors, such as discounts and sales.

Finally, we have unit economics, which looks at the costs and benefits of producing and selling each product unit. By understanding our unit economics, we can determine whether or not a product is profitable at different price points.

Factors influencing price

When it comes to setting prices, there are a number of factors we need to take into account. COGS includes the cost of materials, labor, and manufacturing overhead. It is important to keep our COGS as low as possible, as this will help us maintain a high GM percent.

Another thing to consider is customer demand. If we set our prices too high, customers may go elsewhere. We need to find the right balance between price and demand, so that we can maximize our profits.

In addition, we need to be aware of our competitors' prices. If they are lower than ours, we may need to adjust our prices in order to stay competitive.

Finally, we need to take into account our own costs, such as marketing and administrative costs. We need to make sure that we are covering our costs and generating a profit.

Price strategies

There are a number of different price strategies we can use to achieve our goals. We can set prices high in order to maximize profits, or low in order to increase demand. We can also use discounts and sales to move more product.

It is important to tailor our price strategy to our unique market situation. For example, if we're selling a premium product, we may want to set our prices high and not offer any discounts. If, however, we're selling a product that is not in high demand, we may need to set our prices low and offer frequent discounts.

By understanding our market's unique parameters and using the right pricing metrics, we can create a pricing strategy that meets our goals and maximizes our profits.

Measuring price elasticity of demand

What if you raised your prices? Would your profits go up? Or, would customers be so annoyed by the higher price, or unable to afford your goods, they would go elsewhere? Measuring the impact of pricing on demand for your product is key to profitability. If you can charge more for your products, yet consumers will remain eager to buy them, your profitability will rise. If you raise your prices and customers go away, there go your profits, too.

So, we need to know how much price affects consumers' interest in our wares. We do so by using price elasticity of demand.

Price elasticity of demand is a measure for the sensitivity of demand to changes in price. For example, if certain products or services are "price elastic," lowering prices may drive up demand, and vice versa (i.e. not as many people will buy if you raise the price). Price elasticity changes over time too. As a product gains competitors, it can become commoditized, that is, it can turn into a commodity—a product that consumers buy based on price alone. Examples of commodities include coffee, soap, and gasoline. "Wait a minute," you say, "I don't just buy coffee based on price!" That's right. Some brands have achieved sufficient brand equity that they have escaped the trap of commodification. They used the strategies in the chapter on branding to build a better brand, increasing demand for their product even with a higher price than their competitors. They also keenly understand price elasticity of demand.

The price elasticity of demand is calculated by dividing the percentage change in quantity demanded by the percentage change in price. For instance, if you increase your price by 10 percent, and your demand decreases by 30 percent, then your price elasticity of demand is 30/10 = 3 percent. This means that interest in your product is rather price sensitive. Interest in your product will decline predictably with price increases, and you should be careful about how you time and communicate those increases.

Products can also be "price inelastic," which means that demand is not all that affected by price. For example, if you are in the business of selling high-end spa treatments or specialized medical equipment, consumers will probably pay more because these products are in demand. This does not mean that higher prices will always result in greater revenue though—it means that when people want something, they are willing to take whatever steps are required to get it. Luxury goods are often price-inelastic.

If a product is price-inelastic, it doesn't mean that you won't lose some customers if your price increases past a reasonable point. It just means that you are not going to lose as many as you would if you were selling a price-elastic product.

How do you use the price elasticity of demand to grow profitability? Well, that comes down to what you want your business to do. If you are looking for greater market share, then lowering prices is the way to go. However, if you are trying to increase revenue and profits, raising prices may be a better strategy—as long as demand remains relatively inelastic.

Pricing models

Before we go too much further into pricing metrics, let's first understand pricing models. This will help illuminate how to measure pricing strategy in the first place. Here are a few pricing strategies that brands use.

Penetration pricing

One strategy is to charge a low price initially, then increase it over time. This strategy is called penetration pricing, also sometimes known as skimming. Penetration pricing can be risky because you risk undermining the strength of your brand if consumers feel that they are being "taken" by high prices on an established product. Nonetheless, there are times when penetration pricing works, particularly if you are introducing a new product in an already competitive industry.

Mobile phones are both price elastic and price inelastic. The more expensive handsets are relatively price inelastic—people want them so badly they will pay whatever the manufacturer asks. However, prices of US $100–200 for lower-end phones are price elastic—people will shop around among models at that lower end of the market.

You don't have to price something very low to use penetration pricing. Apple's wise use of penetration pricing has helped to build tremendous brand equity in its smartphone business. iPhone prices have slowly increased over time, yet the products remain very popular.

Good—better—best pricing

Another strategy based off consumer psychology is to offer a high-end product at a premium price, but also offer an "economy" version of the very same product. The theory behind this approach is that people feel better about buying something expensive if they think it's worth it—and, if not, having the economy option makes them feel as if they got a great deal.

Economy cars are fairly price elastic—people who can afford it will usually prefer to buy the more expensive model, but if the economy car is good enough, those who normally could not afford a car at all might now be able to. Luxury cars tend to be relatively less price elastic because there simply is a greater desire for them.

In the airline industry, business-class seats are often "sold" as being three or four times more expensive than coach, but in reality they are not that much more expensive at all. Business-class tickets might be 10–15 percent higher than coach prices, which is far less than people perceive them to be. What metrics will tell you if good—better—best will work for your product? If you have moderate price elasticity of demand, this can be a good strategy. When a competitive analysis reveals that most of your competition is at either the low or high end of the market, good—better—best can help you capture market share at both ends, while also engaging hesitant consumers in the middle, who were reluctant to try cheaper brands due to quality concerns and cannot afford the luxury products.

Freemium pricing

Simply put, freemium is a pricing method that tries to give away your product for free in order to create an initial userbase or brand awareness, then charge for premium features later. It has worked well for Canva, Zoom, and Slack, all software platforms that launched apps with many features free. The key here is that you must be very clear about what features are free and which ones are paid—if you are not, you risk the trust and loyalty of your free users.

What metrics would tell you that freemium may work for your product? Freemium pricing is most effective when there are a great deal of usage differences between free and paid features (more than 100x), when the market size is large (at least tens of millions), when the average revenue per user is high (more than US \$100/year) and when there is a low-friction payment process.

Premium pricing

Premium pricing is simply what it sounds like—selling your product at a premium price. Many people assume that if they charge more for their products, they will automatically sell fewer units and make less money. But this is not always true; some people (like the Tesla Model 3 buyers) will pay more for a product they really want or like. Premium pricing can work both ways—if you have something truly unique, you might be able to get away with charging significantly more than your competition. Luxury sports cars follow this strategy—people are happy to pay extra for features they know they cannot get in cheaper cars.

What metrics would tell you that premium pricing may work for your product? If you want to try premium pricing, it is usually best when there is either a certain level of novelty (i.e. the company is not well known or the market is new, such as with electric cars); demand is not price elastic, clearly, for at least the high end of the market; and if you can prove that your company is in fact offering something unique.

Loss leader pricing

A loss leader is when a retailer sells a product at cost or even below in order to attract customers and hopefully turn them into repeat buyers. This strategy has been working well for beauty retailers like Sephora, who offer prestige brands at low prices to catch your attention, then get you to purchase their own brands in addition to impulse buys. Another example is when airlines sell tickets at rock-bottom prices but make it back up in extra fees.

What metrics would tell you that loss leader pricing may work for your product? Companies should use this strategy when the price elasticity of demand is high, people don't have a strong preference for your product or brand, and when the company has room to discount prices. It is a common pricing strategy with commodities, too.

Discount pricing

Discount pricing is also exactly as it sounds—offering products at a discounted price from regular retail price. This strategy works well for retailers who need to sell off excess stock after a holiday, product discontinuation, or store remodel. It is also an effective way to get rid of slow-moving inventory—if you can't sell them normally, discount them! Discounts are often used when there is a strong seasonal element in the product (such as holiday-themed gifts) and sometimes for limited time deals (Black Friday).

What metrics would tell you that discounting would work for your brand? The most successful discounts are when discounting is infrequent; demand for this type of product exists all year long yet there is a well-defined seasonality in the market (e.g. back-to-school or holiday); and price elasticity of demand is high.

Questions to ask when looking at sales data after you do a discount promotion include:

- Did a discount attract a new segment? A discount that brings you new business can be successful as long as it is not cannibalizing your existing sales.

- Was the discount deeper than you had planned? If discounts are becoming too commonplace, it devalues your brand and erodes profits in the long run.
- Did you see an increase in repeat purchases? A discount that encourages customers to buy more of your product can be successful.
- Were sales increased at a time when they typically slow down?
- Did the volume of discounted sales compensate for the lower profit per unit?

Discounts cannot be applied just to drive some sales without a long-term strategy. Look at these metrics as a way to plan how discounts work in the context of your long-term acquisition, segmentation, branding, and growth strategies. They are not just a way to get some fast revenue. You need to be purposeful and deliberate.

Cost-plus pricing

In cost-plus pricing, the company adds a fixed percentage (or markup) to the cost of goods to arrive at the selling price. This pricing strategy is often used by companies that make or sell unique products, because it is difficult to compare costs and prices between different companies.

What metrics would tell you that cost-plus pricing may work for your product? Retailers and manufacturers may use this strategy if they have high fixed costs, such as for production or research and development. Additionally, if the company has a low margin on the product, it may need to use a cost-plus pricing strategy to make a profit.

Questions to ask when looking at sales data after you institute a cost-plus pricing strategy include:

- Are there any competitors that are using a different pricing strategy?
- Do you have a low margin on the product?
- Do you have high fixed costs, such as for production or research and development?
- Do you think the customer perceives the product as having a high value?
- What are some other pricing strategies that may work better for your product?

If you answered "yes" to any of these questions, cost-plus pricing may be a good strategy for your product. However, if there are other pricing strategies that could work better, it is important to test them and see which one performs the best.

Market-based pricing

In market-based pricing, the company sets its prices based on what the market will bear. This strategy is often used in oligopolistic and monopolistic markets where there is little price competition. (A monopolistic market is one that has only one significant vendor; an oligopolistic market is one that has a few significant vendors.)

What metrics would tell you that market-based pricing may work for your product? If a company is using market-based pricing, it is likely because it sells a unique product that customers are not able to find anywhere else.

Additionally, a company may use this strategy if it has a low margin on the product. In this case, the company sets a price that is higher than its costs in order to make a profit.

Questions to ask when looking at sales data after you institute a market-based pricing strategy include:

- Do you have a unique product that customers cannot find anywhere else?
- Do you have a low margin on the product?
- Does the company have a monopoly or oligopoly in the market?

If you answered "yes" to any of these questions, market-based pricing may be a good strategy for your product. However, it is important to test different prices to see what the market will bear.

Competition-based pricing

In competition-based pricing, the company sets its prices based on how it compares to the competition. This strategy is often used in markets with many competitors.

What metrics would tell you that competition-based pricing may work for your product? This strategy is often used when the company has a high margin on the product. In this case, the company sets a price that is lower than its competition in order to gain market share.

Questions to ask when looking at sales data before you institute a competition-based pricing strategy include:

- Do you have many competitors in the market?

- Do you have a high margin on the product?
- Is the company selling a commodity product?

If you answered "yes" to any of these questions, competition-based pricing may be a good strategy for your product. However, it is important to test different prices to see how they compare to the competition.

Value-based pricing

In value-based pricing, the company sets its prices based on how much the customer values the product. This strategy is often used in markets where the product is not a commodity.

What metrics would tell you that value-based pricing may work for your product? This strategy is often used when the company has a high fixed cost, such as for production or research and development.

Questions to ask when looking at sales data before you institute a value-based pricing strategy include:

- Does the product have unique features that customers value?
- Is the company selling a product with high fixed costs?
- Does the company have a monopoly or oligopoly in the market?

If you answered "yes" to any of these questions, value-based pricing may be a good strategy for your product. However, it is important to test different prices to see how much customers value the product.

There are a few key things to consider when deciding whether or not to use premium pricing, loss leader pricing, or discount pricing. Each of these strategies can be successful, but it is important to understand what the metrics are that would tell you they would work for your product.

Dynamic pricing

Dynamic pricing is interesting, because it is a purely data-driven pricing model. In dynamic pricing, the price of a product changes depending on the current market conditions.

What metrics would tell you that dynamic pricing may work for your product? A company using dynamic pricing is constantly adjusting its prices based on data from the market. This strategy is often used in markets with a lot of volatility, such as the stock market or commodities market.

As you can see, a range of pricing models are available to you. It is important to select the pricing model that is best suited to your product and your market. By understanding the different pricing models, you can make sure you are selecting the right one for your business.

Digital marketing metrics

Now that you know some pricing strategies, it's time to think about the digital metrics that will help you gather data on what strategies work best for customer acquisition and customer retention. You're going to need A/B testing strategy, a CRM, and a tag manager.

Testing pricing models for acquisition

A/B testing is a great way to figure out the most effective channel for acquiring customers, we know. You can also use it to test the most effective pricing for acquiring new buyers. Run an A/B or multivariate test with different pricing clearly presented in the ads. For instance, if you are running social media ads for a new line of yoga pants, make sure that your "Buy One, Get One Free" message is prominent in both the text and graphics, then test a non-discounted, high price just as prominently featured in the control ad. This way, you can see what price point works best for acquiring new customers. Alternately, if your business model is lead-generation based, run an A/B test with different pricing options presented in the landing page—and see which one generates more conversions.

Test all the different pricing strategies you're considering on all the different channels you use. Ensure that the same creative is used, except for the price messaging, which should be placed in the exact same way across all creative of the same type. Prices should be in the same font, with the same graphics, in the same location, with the same colors, in all visuals. They should be mentioned at the same time, in the same tone, in all radio/podcast and TV spots. It is important to test pricing across your full promotional mix, isolating price alone as the only thing different about each message.

As with any marketing, you may find that particular combinations of channel and pricing model may yield different results. For instance, your Instagram organic traffic may be inclined to view you as a luxury brand, while your podcast audience wants discounts. Avoid the temptation to craft too complex a pricing and channel strategy. It can dilute your brand. Pushback may ensue, as well.

Which metric is most important for measuring the success of your pricing strategy? Click-through rate (CTR) is the most important early metric that will measure the success of your pricing, channel, and creative strategy. It is best measured by A/B testing price messaging on different channels. Conversions and sales will follow. But if you need early data, CTR is the best way to see whether your audience has reacted positively or not.

Retention metrics for pricing strategies

One way to get quite complex metrics on the price vs product features is conjoint analysis. In a conjoint analysis, consumers rate the relative value of different product features when considered in the context of all the other features the product has, as well as its price. For instance, if you are considering adding a folding screen to your phone, you would ask people to choose between different phones that vary in price but also by varying features. Perhaps a folding screen has little value on its own, but becomes valuable when paired with a lighter weight. Conjoint analysis pinpoints the mix of features consumers see as related to each other. It also identifies the feature combinations that represent a value, mid-range, or luxury product in consumers' minds.

You can then see whether the addition of one feature is enough to make people happy with their purchase or not, based on how much they are willing to pay for it. Conjoint analysis is most useful when you have a dataset of many different products or services with both price and product features. Pick your top segments, along with the desired product feature sets, and send out a survey to make sure you get the price sensitivity metrics you need.

Price sensitivity metrics

Other metrics that take into account price sensitivity include discounts and promotions data—how much revenue is lost from discounts and promotions? This helps marketers understand the impact of discounting on customer acquisition costs.

Testing price with advertising: multivariate testing with price in the mix

Testing marketing creative with price as a variable also helps brands identify their most profitable customer segments. A higher price point in an ad converts better, overall or with some targeted segments. This can tell you that specific ad creative appeals to customers who are more price-sensitive, less price-sensitive, view the brand as good value, or view the brand as a luxury brand. This can help you eliminate creative that appeals to customers who are not likely to pay your target price. For instance, if you find that specific graphics or text appeal to the price-sensitive, you might want to steer clear of using those elements in your ads if you don't want to attract bargain hunters.

If you have ever worked in a retail store, you know that some customers only come to you when you're running a huge sale. Some loyal customers, on the other hand, probably take advantage of any discount or coupon you offer them, but keep coming back even when there is not a sale. In an ideal world, your pricing strategy would be able to distinguish between these two groups. This is where segmentation comes into play.

The price sensitivity of each customer segment is important to take into consideration when developing a pricing strategy. For example, different groups may have very different ideas about what product or service qualities are very valuable, and those differences can influence how much they are willing to spend.

Segmenting customers by price sensitivity

Once you understand how price sensitivity varies among your customer segments, you can tailor your pricing strategy to match. For example, you might choose to offer discounts and promotions to attract new customers, while charging more for products and services with premium features that are more important to your most price-sensitive segments.

Or you could segment your customers by how much they are willing to pay and then offer different versions of your product at different prices. This is known as price discrimination, and it is a common way to increase profits.

Price sensitivity is a metric that can tell you more than just what price customers are willing to pay. It can also indicate how much consumers value your products or services. We learned this the hard way at Thoughtlight, as do many agencies. We found that the most price-sensitive clients are often the toughest to work with. They often were underresourced to the point that they could not fund advertising programs, or continuously asked for free work. Ask any retailer about customers who demand top service at low prices. Such highly price-sensitive consumers often have negative CLV.

Overhead costs remain fixed, while the contribution margin (price minus variable costs) declines as discounts are offered to these customers.

High-tech products may not find consumers profitable who require extensive customer support, as the cost of providing such support would exceed the revenue generated from these customers. Value-seeking customers can be so unprofitable that it's not worth pursuing them.

However, by understanding price sensitivity, we are able to better target our most profitable customer segments and adjust our prices accordingly. Look at price sensitivity as more than a metric in its own right: it is also an indicator of the types of customer segments you should focus on.

For example, a company that sells laptops might find that its most price-sensitive customers are those who are not interested in premium features, such as a faster processor or more storage space. In this case, the company could offer a lower-priced version of its product that excludes these features. However, if the buyers of this low-cost laptop require just as many support hours as those who get the pricey laptop, the company will actually lose money on these customers.

There are many different ways to measure and act on price sensitivity. By understanding how this metric varies among your customers, you can develop a pricing strategy that maximizes profits while satisfying the needs of your most price-sensitive segments. So what are you waiting for? Start collecting data and start increasing profits!

Additional price sensitivity metrics

Other metrics that take into account price sensitivity include:

- **Discounts and promotions data:** how much revenue is generated from discounts and promotions? How much do customers value your products or services when they are discounted?

- **Customer lifetime value (CLV):** what is the lifetime value of a customer who is highly price-sensitive? What is the lifetime value of a customer who is not price-sensitive?

- **Revenue per user (RPU):** how much revenue is generated per user? How does this vary with a user's price-sensitivity?

- **Variable costs:** what percentage of your variable costs is associated with customers who are highly price-sensitive?

- **Fixed costs:** what percentage of your fixed costs is associated with customers who are highly price-sensitive?

- **Discount duration:** how long do discounts typically last? Do they have a greater or lesser impact on customers who are more price-sensitive?
- **Customer segmentation:** what customer segments are most and least price-sensitive? How do you tailor your prices to appeal to each group?

There's no one-size-fits-all answer to pricing. By taking into account a variety of metrics, including price sensitivity, you can create a pricing strategy that is tailored to your unique business and customer base.

DECIDING ON GOOD—BETTER—BEST PRICING: METRICS THAT MATTER

A popular way to segment a market by price is good—better—best. As you may recall, this strategy is used in auto insurance, software, fashion, beauty, and many other industries.

In this strategy, your best customers are willing to pay the most, and as a result contribute the majority of profits.

The first step in setting up a good—better—best pricing structure is to identify which customers will be willing to pay more for additional features or benefits. These customers will often have a high CLV, but they will be less numerous.

This presents a problem for many organizations. While they want to provide the best possible experience and products to their best customers, they also need to offer a product that is affordable and accessible to a larger number of people.

One way to solve this problem is to offer different high-quality versions of your product at different price points. It's good—better—best for a reason, rather than bad—good—best. Even the basic version of your product needs to be something that customers would be happy with.

Another option is to focus on increasing the average revenue per user (ARPU) rather than the number of customers. This can be done by increasing the price for products and services with premium features that are more important to your most price-insensitive segments.

You can also increase profits by increasing the number of products or services you offer at each price point. This will allow you to attract a larger number of customers without sacrificing profits.

However, there is no easy answer when it comes to pricing. You need to consider your costs, the features you are offering, the competition, and a variety of other factors.

Using data analysis to set prices

Earlier in this chapter we talked about conjoint analysis. We learned that a way to determine which features are valuable is to survey your customers and ask them what attributes are most important. This method looks at the combinations of features that are related to one another in the mind of the customer.

Conjoint analysis can help you determine how much value customers place on different features and whether the addition of one feature is enough to make people happy or not with their purchase, based on how much they are willing to pay for it. For example, a customer might be willing to pay more for faster shipping but not for a longer return policy. However, if faster shipping and longer return windows are offered together, they both become more attractive.

Conjoint analysis is most useful when you have a dataset of many different products or services with both price and product features. Pick your top segments, along with the desired product feature sets, and send out a survey to make sure you get accurate results.

Once you know what features are important to your customers, you can start to think about how to price your product. You should also think about what features could be bundled together at a reduced price or at a premium one.

There are many different ways to set prices, and the best way to find the right one for your company is to experiment. One thing to keep in mind is that you should always be measuring the results of your changes so that you can continue to improve your pricing strategy.

One way to set prices is by starting with your high-end price and working your way down. This ensures that you are making a profit on all of your products and services.

You will also want to make sure that you are pricing your products at a fair value. This means that you need to make sure that the cost of your product is less than the benefit to the customer. Ideally, you want to find a price point where you are making a profit and the customer is happy with the purchase.

Loss leader metrics

Typically, for a loss leader to be profitable, it needs to lead to increased sales of other products. That is the purpose of a loss leader; indeed, it is its definition! To know whether a loss leader has driven higher, profitable sales, look at these metrics:

- Cross-selling: the percentage of customers who buy more than one product.
- Upselling: the percentage of customers who buy a more expensive product.
- Average sale price: the average sale price of products sold to customers who were attracted by the loss leader.
- Margin: the percentage of gross profit on the sale of products to customers who were attracted by the loss leader.
- Volume: the number of units sold as a result of using a loss leader.

In measuring the effectiveness of using a loss leader pricing model, look at metrics like cross-selling and upselling rates, as well as average shopping cart value. If you can find a profitable balance between attracting new customers with discounts and selling more expensive products to your existing customer base, you will be in good shape!

Exploring price elasticity of demand

Price elasticity of demand is an important metric for businesses to understand, as it shows how likely customers are to change their spending habits in response to price changes. By measuring price elasticity, businesses can identify which prices are most likely to result in a change in demand (either an increase or a decrease) and adapt their pricing strategy accordingly.

For example, a company in a market with a low price elasticity of demand might be able to raise prices without fear of losing customers, while a company with a high price elasticity of demand would need to be more careful in making changes.

There are three main types of price elasticity:

- **Price elasticity of supply:** measures how much the quantity supplied changes in response to a change in price.
- **Price elasticity of demand:** measures how much the quantity demanded changes in response to a change in price.
- **Cross-elasticity of demand:** measures how much the quantity demanded for one product changes when the price for another product changes.

It is important for businesses to understand all three types of price elasticity, as they will each have a different impact on how a business prices its products.

For example, understanding our cross-elasticity of demand can tell us how much we can raise the prices of our one of our products without negatively impacting sales of another. Let's take the example of WriteWit, a bespoke notebook company. They make elegant notebooks from sustainable materials. Originally a B2C brand, they are now expanding into being a B2B vendor. They are also expanding their product lines to become a full-scale office paper vendor.

In their early days, they found that they were able to price their notebooks at US $10 and people would buy them. However, as they started to become a B2B vendor, they found that their customers were more price-sensitive. Added to this price sensitivity is cross-elasticity of demand. To test the waters, they raised the price of their notebooks to $12. They found that there was a very small decrease in sales (3 percent) of the notebooks. However, sales of related products bought with the notebooks, such as their bamboo pens, plummeted by 20 percent with the price increase on the notebooks. This means that WriteWit not only has to account for price elasticity of demand in their product pricing, they also have to take into account the cross-elasticity of demand for their products.

MEASURING POTENTIAL UPSIDE FROM PRICE INCREASES

A common mistake in pricing strategy is to focus exclusively on the potential downside from price increases. However, if you have a good understanding of your price elasticity of demand, you can also measure the potential upside.

For example, if you know that a 10 percent price increase will lead to a 20 percent decrease in sales, you can be confident that increasing prices by more than 10 percent will lead to a net loss in revenue. However, if you know that a 10 percent price increase will only lead to a 2 percent decrease in sales, you can safely increase prices by more than 10 percent.

While it is important to take potential losses into account when making pricing decisions, it is also helpful to understand the potential for increased revenue. By understanding your price elasticity of demand, you can make more informed decisions about your pricing strategy. Price increases can also be part of a decision to attract a different market.

When it comes to setting prices, it is important to find the right balance that will maximize revenue without alienating customers. The right data can help you be proactive rather than reactive in your pricing, resulting in a pricing strategy that integrates with your other 4Ps.

Price sensitivity in B2B marketing: how price sensitivity impacts decision making

Understanding price sensitivity is critical for making informed pricing decisions in B2B markets. Let's take an example. Our notebook company, WriteWit, has expanded into an office supply company, supplying companies with a range of paper goods. One customer, Company A, is a supplier of industrial machinery, and Company B is a supplier of office furniture.

Company B's purchasing decisions are largely driven by price, while Company A is more concerned with the quality of the products. In this case, WriteWit can charge a higher price to Company A without losing any sales, while they may have to offer ever-deeper discounts to Company B to keep their business. Remember that price elasticity of demand is a big-picture metric, but price sensitivity can vary greatly by customer.

In B2C marketing, it may not make sense to measure the price sensitivity of each and every customer. It may be enough to assess price sensitivity of different segments. Paired with overall calculations of price elasticity of demand across your market, that measurement can be enough to help you make informed decisions about pricing.

However, in B2B marketing, it is important to understand the price sensitivities of each and every customer. Decision makers in B2B markets are often more involved in the purchasing process, and they may be more likely to switch suppliers if the price is too high or too low.

It is also important to remember that, in some cases, the price of a product is not the only factor that affects a purchase decision. In the example above, Company B may be willing to pay a higher price for a product if it means they can meet their sustainability goals or if it comes from a reputable supplier. It's important to consider all factors when it comes to price sensitivity in order to make the most informed decisions possible. Like all metrics, it doesn't exist in a vacuum.

Pricing conclusion

When it comes to setting prices, it is important to find the right balance that will maximize revenue. A range of pricing models are appropriate for any given brand; metrics will tell you which pricing model is more effective at attracting customers while growing revenue.

Price elasticity of demand is an important metric for businesses to understand, as it shows how likely customers are to change their spending habits in response to price changes. By measuring price elasticity, businesses can identify which prices are most likely to result in increased revenue, and which can reduce demand and drive down revenue. Pricing models are essential parts of a brand's marketing strategy, and are important for marketers to understand.

Place metrics

Understanding the distribution strategies that work best for attracting and retaining customers can be challenging. A range of features, prices, and places (geography) need to be considered. The following metrics will help you understand how well your distribution strategies are working compared to each other.

- **Customer acquisition cost (CAC):** the cost of acquiring a new customer on each channel. For instance, to attract customers to your e-commerce store, you may rely on affordable social media ads, while growing brick-and-mortar traffic may require more expensive marketing efforts, such as billboards or sponsorships.

- **Customer churn rate:** the percentage of customers who discontinue doing business with you in a given time period. Does one channel have higher churn than another?

- **Customer lifetime value (CLV):** the total revenue a customer is predicted to generate over the course of their relationship with your company. Measure the CLV of different channels and customer segments to see which ones are most profitable.

- **Cross-selling:** are you more effectively cross-selling and upselling in person or online?

- **Customer satisfaction:** how satisfied are your customers in-store vs online?

By understanding these metrics, you can begin to make more informed decisions about where to allocate your marketing resources for the greatest impact.

Point-of-sale data

No discussion of retail metrics would be effective without a breakdown of point-of-sale (POS) data. This is data that is captured at the moment of purchase and can include items purchased, prices paid, customer demographics, and more.

Using this data, you can answer important questions around the effectiveness of your promotions, the impact of price changes, and customer behavior. With POS data, you can begin to make more informed decisions about your product mix, pricing, and marketing efforts.

POS data can help you answer a range of marketing questions:

- Campaign effectiveness:
  o Which campaigns are driving the most sales?
  o What are the average purchase values for customers who were exposed to a particular campaign?
  o How many new customers did each campaign bring in?
  o What percentage of customers return after being exposed to a campaign?
- Pricing strategies:
  o Are customers more likely to buy a product when it is on sale?
  o What is the impact of discounts on overall sales?
  o Do customers prefer to buy products in bulk?
  o What is the optimal price point for each product?
- Product mix:
  o Which products are selling the best?
  o What are the bestselling combinations of products?
  o Are there any products that are not selling?
  o Should we discontinue any products?

- Location strategies:
  - Which locations are selling the most products?
  - What is the average purchase value at each location?
  - Are there any locations that are underperforming?
  - Should we open more stores in certain areas?
- Marketing strategies:
  - What is the average order value for customers who purchase products through our website?
  - What is the most popular product on our product mix?
  - What are the demographics of our store customers?

This data is vital in understanding the overall performance of your marketing programs if you have a brick-and-mortar presence.

It is also important to compare POS data to e-commerce metrics, to understand the differences in merchandising, customer behavior, price sensitivity, popular times of day for shopping, product mix, and impact of marketing campaigns between the brick-and-mortar and e-commerce channels.

When it comes to understanding retail metrics it is important to look at data from a variety of sources. By compiling data from different channels—such as e-commerce, POS, and customer surveys—you can paint a more accurate picture of your business performance. With this data in hand, you can make more informed decisions about where to allocate your marketing resources for the greatest impact.

Loyalty card data

Loyalty card data is another important source of information for understanding customer behavior. This data can include purchase history, frequency of visits, and other engagement metrics.

Loyalty card data can help you answer questions like:

- How often do customers visit our store?
- What are the most popular items among our customers?
- Who are our most loyal customers?

- What products are popular with different customer segments?
- What are the most and least visited times of the week?

Loyalty card data can also help you track your customers' purchase journey from start to finish. This information can be used to improve your marketing efforts by understanding where customers are dropping off in the buying process.

Let's say you're an e-commerce brand of shaving products, recently expanded into brick-and-mortar stores. You want to understand how your e-commerce business is doing in relation to your physical stores. You can use POS data to measure the impact of your marketing campaigns on in-store sales, and compare that to e-commerce sales. For example, you may find that online ads are driving more traffic to your website, but in-store sales are higher for customers who were exposed to print ads. This information can help you make more informed decisions about where to allocate your marketing resources.

You can also use loyalty card data to understand customer behavior. For example, if you notice that customers are purchasing more expensive razor handles at your store, you can look at their purchase history to see what other items they have bought. Perhaps they buy the most expensive handles, but buy your least expensive shaving cream, and never buy aftershave. By contrast, e-commerce buyers are mostly acquired via a social media ad that uses your least expensive handle at an even steeper than usual discount, as a loss leader. However, they often buy your organic, high-end shaving cream. They also not only buy your exclusive aftershaves, but also purchase subscriptions for your creams and aftershaves, making these a recurring source of revenue. Your online customers become your highest CLV customers, even though their initial purchases have a lower value than your brick-and-mortar shoppers.

This information can help you understand what products are most popular among your customers who shop different channels, and adjust your product mix accordingly. You can also look at purchase data to see what price points are most popular in brick-and-mortar vs e-commerce. With the CLV and shopping cart data above, you decide to try to entice brick-and-mortar shoppers into subscriptions, to no avail. Then, you adapt your promotional pricing, offering regular Buy One, Get One Free (BOGO) promotions in-store, along with a new loyalty card to access these offers. CLV grows 30 percent for your store in the following year due to this change. Using the loyalty card data, you then see that brick-and-mortar shoppers are more likely than online shoppers to purchase certain scents, such as sandalwood or cucumber, so you increase your stock of those items. You also use market basket analysis to see that customers who purchase your midrange razors tend to buy organic shaving cream as well, so you put those in the same aisle.

Price and place are two important factors that influence customer behavior. By compiling data from different channels—such as e-commerce, POS, and customer surveys—you can paint a more accurate picture of your business performance. With this data in hand, you can paint a more accurate picture of what pricing strategies work for your brand, as well as what distribution channels. You can make informed decisions about how to price your products, how to get them into customers' hands, and who your ideal customers are based on your pricing and distribution models.

Compiling data from different sources can be a daunting task, but it is essential for understanding the overall performance. This is where dashboarding becomes essential. By creating a dashboard with all of your data sources, you can easily compare and analyze the information to see what insights it reveals. Having all of this data in one place makes it easier to identify trends and make decisions about where to focus your marketing efforts.

Comparing POS and e-commerce data can help you make informed decisions about where to allocate your marketing resources—for example, if a particular product is selling better online than in-store, you might decide to focus more of your marketing efforts on that product. Conversely, if a product is selling better in-store than online, you might invest more resources in getting that product in front of potential customers online.

Using metrics to assess place options

We've looked at POS data as a way to understand overall retail metrics for existing locations. What about using metrics to help decide where to place a new retail establishment?

Let's consider the example of a grocery store. One way to use metrics is to measure population density—that is, the number of people living within a certain distance of the store. This can be done using tools like the US Census, in the United States. With this data, you can see not only how many people live near each store, but also what their spending power is. US Census data tracks median household income by area, for instance, so you can get an idea of how much money people in the area have to spend on groceries. You can use this data with your internal data to make predictions of where a store will be successful.

Another metric that can be used is average household size. This tells you how many people are likely to be shopping in a store at any given time. If you have two stores that are equal in terms of income and population density, but the average household size is different, the store with the larger average household size will have more customers at any given time.

You can use a range of internal data to determine whether a physical location makes sense:

- **CRM metrics:** do your customers have significant presence in some ZIP codes? Do they spend more or less in certain regions?
- **Competitive intelligence:** what are your competitors doing in terms of brick-and-mortar locations? How does this impact your ability to reach new customers or sell complementary products?
- **Google Ads data:** are there geographies where you are bidding on keywords but not receiving many clicks (indicating that there is not a lot of demand there)? Conversely, are there areas where you are not bidding aggressively but receive a high number of clicks (indicating that there is significant potential for revenue growth)?
- **Consumer surveys:** ask customers where they would like to see your business expand. This will give you a sense of the regions and neighborhoods where demand is highest.
- **Web analytics geolocation data:** do your site visitors concentrate in specific areas? This can indicate demand for a physical store in those areas.
- **Behavioral data:** understanding customer behavior can help you identify patterns that indicate when people are more or less likely to buy your product. This can help you determine possible location options. For instance, if your shoppers buy early in the morning, then placing a store on a busy commuting route may make sense. Just remember that online and offline behavior may not correlate. Before making any decisions, be sure to analyze your data!

Comparing locations

With a physical presence, it is also important to compare the metrics of different locations. This can tell you which stores are doing well and which ones need improvement. Let's look at an example for our shaving supplies company. They have three locations:

- Location A, in a suburban shopping center: higher customer acquisition costs (CAC) with expensive search and social ads, but a high lifetime value.

- Location B, near a busy urban train station: lower customer acquisition costs due to foot traffic, but a lower lifetime value.

- Location C, in a small city's downtown district: comparable customer acquisition costs and lifetime values to Location A.

By comparing these locations, they see that Location A is more profitable than Location B over the past two years. High CAC is offset by high customer loyalty, resulting in higher CLV. While Location C is new, it looks promising, with similar metrics to Location A.

This analysis can help the company make better decisions about where to expand next. Perhaps they will focus on suburban locations, as they have seen that these generate more revenue than city locations. Alternatively, they may choose to open a new store in a location similar to Location C, as that appears to be equally successful.

Understanding retail metrics is rarely so simple. But armed with the right data, you can make sound business decisions that will help your bricks-and-mortar store thrive.

Common metrics for retail include:

- **Sales per square foot:** a measure of how much revenue a store generates per square foot of retail space.

- **Average transaction value (ATV):** the average amount of money spent on a purchase in a given time period. ATV is a measure of a store's overall profitability.

- **Average customer visit duration:** a measure of how long customers spend in a store on average. This metric can help you understand whether customers are browsing or buying, and can help you optimize floor layout and product placement.

- **Percent of sales from returning customers:** the percentage of total sales that come from returning customers.

- **Customer conversion rate:** the percentage of customers who make a purchase when they visit the store.

- **Inventory turnover:** the number of times a store sells its entire inventory in a given time period. For instance, if a store has an inventory turnover of 10 per year, that means it sells all of its inventory 10 times over in a year.

- **Return on investment (ROI):** the amount of profit generated by a store relative to the amount of money invested in it.

- **Net profit margin:** the percentage of revenue a store earns after accounting for all expenses.

- **Gross margin return on investment (GMROI):** a metric that measures the profitability of a store's inventory. It is typically measured by taking your sales revenue, deducting your cost of goods sold (COGS), and dividing that by your average inventory cost. I swear it's easy. GMROI measures the ROI of your investment in your inventory, after accounting for associated costs. In other words, it measures how profitable the inventory you carry is. Let's take an example, as GMROI is important and simple:

  o You have a store that has revenue of US $100,000 with a CoGS of $20,000. Your average inventory cost, that is, the average amount you have invested in inventory, is $90,000. Your GMROI would be ($100,000 – $20,000) / $90,000 = 0.89. This means that for every dollar you spend on inventory, you earn 89 cents in revenue. You are losing money at this location.

When choosing a physical location or comparing retail stores, it is important to look at more than just sales numbers. You also need to consider things like customer acquisition costs, lifetime customer value, and competitor activity. By using CRM, competitive intelligence, Google Ads, and other metrics in addition to point-of-sale (POS) data, you can paint a more accurate picture of how well a store is performing. With this data in hand, you can make more informed decisions about where to open new locations—or whether to shutter underperforming stores.

When expanding your business, it is important to consider all the factors involved in making a good decision. By analyzing customer data, you can optimize place decisions with comparable accuracy to the rest of the 4Ps.

Conclusion

There are many different ways to set prices, and the best way to find the right one for your company is to experiment. One thing to keep in mind is that you should always be measuring the results of your changes so that you can continue to improve your pricing strategy.

Pricing models range from cost-plus to value-based, and each has its own benefits and drawbacks. Whichever model you choose, make sure that you are able to accurately track the results so that you can optimize your prices over time.

Price elasticity of demand is an important metric for businesses to understand, as it shows how likely customers are to change their spending habits in response to price changes. By measuring price elasticity, businesses can identify which prices result in increased revenue and which prices lead to a net loss in revenue.

While it is important to take potential losses into account when making pricing decisions, it is also helpful to have a long-term outlook and to focus on the overall profitability of your business. In order to do this, it is important to measure things like return on investment and net profit margin.

When selecting a brick-and-mortar location, it is critical to consider more than simply sales figures. You should also consider factors like how much it costs to attract new consumers, the value of each client over their lifetime, and how competition is.

It is vital to consider all of the elements you will need in order to make an informed decision: CRM, competitive intelligence, Google Ads, and other data need to be used in conjunction with POS data.

10

Marketing performance metrics

In previous chapters, we looked at various channel metrics. We learned about different ways to test and measure the performance of these channels. In this chapter, we focus on how to use these metrics to plan and optimize your campaigns for better performance.

Testing is an important part of any marketing campaign. You need to test different elements of your campaign such as the offer, the target audience, the ad copy, etc.

We can use metrics to continuously improve a campaign's reach, ROI, conversions, and other critical aspects of its performance. We use campaign metrics to continuously improve our performance within a specific channel. Of course, we also use additional metrics to improve larger overarching aspects of our marketing such as our branding, our product offering, and our target audiences. However, when it comes to optimizing campaign performance within an agile environment, marketers look to their testing in order to perfect their campaigns, driving more conversions, more ROI, and ultimately more sales.

Critical to optimization is testing. In testing, we experiment with different aspects of a marketing campaign within a specific channel in order to determine what approaches deliver the highest ROI. For instance, let's picture the optimization team at StyleTech, a sustainable brand that creates more ethical trendy fashions.

StyleTech's optimization team is constantly testing different methods for acquiring new customers. Recently, they have found that a new Facebook video campaign is driving a higher ROI than other channels such as Google Ads. However, the team is not sure that this win is indicative that video ads are going to be ongoing drivers of sales. Past videos have not been as successful. Might this recent success be the result of the content of these videos? They need to pinpoint the right kinds of videos that drive sales as compared with those that don't. How can they understand what videos will drive results?

An email marketer on the team might test different subject lines, different images inside an email, or different colors of buttons for the call to action to determine which one causes more conversions. Their goal is to test out different creative, measuring the results by which option gets consumers to click, visit the website, and ultimately make a purchase. In social media, the team might test different times of day for posting, different audience targeting, or different visuals. In testing, our aim is to experiment with multiple different approaches to identify the best offers, creative, logistics, and audiences, or other factors in driving conversions.

There are two main types of testing that we're going to explore in this section:

A/B testing happens when you test a single aspect of your marketing and compare two different options for that aspect. For example, an A/B test might test two different ads on social media. One offers a discount and the other offers free shipping. They measure which one delivers the most sales. The team tests one variable, in this case, the offer type.

There is also multivariate testing. In multivariate testing, you test combinations of variations in order to find the perfect combination of factors. For instance, let's say you start to wonder, after that initial A/B test of different offers, whether you could get even more conversions if you also timed the offer promotions right. Perhaps even a combination of the time of day when people see the discount, as well as the images in the post promoting the discount itself, can be more powerful. You feel these combinations of different factors—the discount, the time of day, and the imagery—interact in complex ways to produce a click through.

Let's see that in action. At StyleTech, a 50 percent-off discount with a very trendy item might actually backfire. Because consumers perceive the item as something new, they will question its value if it is heavily discounted. However, a more classic item promoted with a 50 percent-off discount would be welcomed by consumers as something realistic and attractive.

An A/B test wouldn't help to determine the factors that combine to get clicks. Instead, the team needs to resort to multivariate testing. This more sophisticated form of testing allows them to look at the way different factors interact to produce results, while identifying what those specific factors might be.

WHEN TO USE A/B TESTING

A/B testing works best when you are often fairly confident that you know what factors inspire results. For instance, you may have strong evidence already that it is the image or the product alone that increases clicks for StyleTech's social media ads. Thus, it makes sense to test which specific image—for instance, a trendy or a classic sweater—gets the most clicks in an ad. When you know exactly what to test, an A/B test can get you answers very quickly.

WHEN TO USE MULTIVARIATE TESTING

With A/B testing, you usually need to have a strong theory that you are going to test. With multivariate testing you may have only a vague sense of what factors are particularly influential on your consumers.

A/B testing

A/B testing rules

A/B testing must focus on only two variants. They are a focused type of test. Typically, these variants are different only in one element, such as the headline, images, or call to action (CTA). A/B testing allows you to determine which of these elements is most effective in driving your desired outcome, whether that is clicks, conversions, or some other metric.

To run an A/B test, you need to be able to randomly split your audience into two groups. One group will see the original campaign, while the second group will see the variant. You can then measure the difference in outcomes between the two groups to determine which element had the greatest impact.

There are a few key points to keep in mind when running an A/B test:

- It is important to have a clear goal for your test. What are you trying to learn?
- The test should be statistically significant. This means that the difference between the groups should not be due to chance alone.
- There should be a large enough sample size in each group.
- The test should be run for a reasonable amount of time.
- The test should be controlled for other factors that could impact the results.

STATISTICAL SIGNIFICANCE

In order to determine whether a difference between two groups is due to chance alone, you need to calculate the p-value. This is a measure of how likely it is that the difference could have occurred by chance; p-value is calculated by taking the probability of the observed difference occurring, given that there is no difference between the groups, and dividing it by the probability of the observed difference occurring, given that there is a difference between the groups. Don't worry—most testing platforms will do this for you.

A p-value of less than 0.05 indicates that the difference is statistically significant, meaning that it is very unlikely that it was due to chance. When calculating the p-value, you need to be sure to control for other factors that could impact the results. This includes things like time of day, day of the week, and weather conditions.

Designing an A/B test

When designing an A/B test, the critical first step is truly identifying a single variable to test. Too many tests actually should be multivariate tests or a series of A/B tests. When designing an A/B test, you want to make sure that the change you are making is small so that it is easier to isolate the impact of that one change on results.

To run an A/B test, you randomly split your audience into two groups. One group will see the original campaign, while the second group will see the variant. You can then measure the difference in outcomes between the two groups to determine which element had the greatest impact.

When testing two versions of a campaign, always make sure that the only difference between the two is the element you are testing. For example, if you are testing two different headlines, make sure that the only difference between the two headlines is the text. Do not change anything else, such as the font, color, or size.

When testing different elements, it is important to make sure that each version is displayed at an equal rate. For example, if you are testing two different images, make sure that each image is displayed at the same rate.

Running an A/B test: once you have determined what you want to test, the next step is to randomly split your audience into two groups. One group will see the original campaign, while the second group will see the variant.

It is important to make sure that both groups are as similar as possible. This means that they should be from the same target audience, have the same demographics, and be from the same location.

Evaluating A/B test results

Once you have collected enough data, you can use it to determine which element had the greatest impact.

You now have data on the difference in outcomes between the two testing groups. This includes metrics such as clicks, conversions, and engagement. These datapoints can tell you:

- Which variant performed better.
- The impact of the change on results, both in terms of the effect and the size of the effect. For instance, did the variant result in a 10 percent increase in clicks or a 50 percent increase in conversions?
- How long it took for the variant to start producing.
- Whether the change was statistically significant.

You can also use qualitative data to help you determine which element had the greatest impact. This includes things such as customer feedback and surveys.

Once you have these results, you can use them to make more informed decisions about your campaigns. For example, if you find that a particular variant performs better, you will naturally use it in future campaigns. Let's go back to StyleTech. They decide to test two different subject lines for their next campaign:

Version A: "The best T-shirts you will ever wear"
Version B: "New and improved—negative-carbon-footprint Tees!"

The results of the A/B test show that Version B had a statistically significant impact on click-through rate. This means that the change was not due to chance, and that it is very likely that the change had an impact on results. Version B was also the clear winner in terms of conversions. This means that it resulted in more people clicking through to the landing page and completing a purchase. They conclude that more specific subject lines, with a clear connection to their sustainability mission, result in better performance.

This is a reasonable conclusion, but there are other explanations for the lift. Maybe the change in wording created a more positive feeling about the brand, which then led to more people clicking through and purchasing. However, it may be the different spelling of the word T-shirt, the length of the headline, or the punctuation that was used. StyleTech cannot know for sure without further experimentation. It is important to note that an A/B test is not definitive. It can help you make a decision, but it should not be the only data point that you consider. You should always use your own judgment when making decisions about your campaigns.

They then test two different subject lines:

Version A: "Great Casual Fashion—T-shirts made with love"
Version B: "T-shirts that help the environment"

The results of the A/B test show that Version A had a statistically significant impact on click-through rate. This means that the change was not due to chance, and that it is very likely that the change had an impact on results. This winning headline is longer, just like Version B in the first test. And it doesn't mention sustainability. Perhaps it is longer subject lines that consumers prefer! Repeated testing will help the organization see if this is in fact the case.

StyleTech now knows that using specific, longer subject lines works. With more testing, they may also confirm that those lines with a clear connection to their sustainability mission result in even greater clickthroughs. Even as they continue testing, they use this information to focus their creative efforts on the types of headlines that are most likely to be clicked. This will help them improve their click-through rates and, as a result, their bottom line.

It is important to remember that campaign performance metrics should not be used in a vacuum. They should be used in conjunction with other datapoints, such as customer feedback and surveys, to help you make informed decisions about your campaigns.

Multivariate testing

What is multivariate testing (MVT)? It is when you have more than two variables in a test.

Say you want to know if using one of two videos or two images on your landing page will increase conversion rates. You would create four variants of your landing page, with each combination of video vs image. That would be a 2×2 matrix, and would be considered a simple multivariate test.

If you want to test even more variables, you could create an 8×8 matrix, with 64 different variants. This would be a more complex multivariate test.

With multivariate testing, you can test more than just images and videos. You could test the wording of your headlines, the colors of your buttons, or the placement of your CTA. You can also test different combinations of these variables.

In the example above, you might want to test whether a video headline results in higher conversion rates than an image headline. Or, you might want to test whether a green button converts better than a red button.

Multivariate testing allows you to test all of these different combinations, and find the best combination of variables to increase your conversion rate.

Interpreting multivariate test results

Once you find the combination of factors that result in the highest conversion rate, you can then focus your efforts on further testing that particular combination. Look at how the different elements interacted with each other, and try to find any patterns. For example, if using a video headline resulted in a higher conversion rate, did the video itself play a role in that increase?

Look at the goals for your test. Were you trying to increase conversions, shopping cart size, or something else? Try to determine which of the variable combinations had the biggest impact on your goal.

Let's see an example. You are a nonprofit whose goal is to increase the number of people who sign up for your mailing list. In a multivariate test, you test four different variants of your sign-up form, with each variant containing a different combination of input fields.

1 Variant 1 has a name and email field, and a video headline.

2 Variant 2 has a name, email, and postal code field, and a video headline.

3 Variant 3 has a name and email field, and an image headline.

4 Variant 4 has a name, email, and postal code field, and an image headline.

Variant 1 had the highest conversion rate, at 42 percent. Variant 3 had the lowest conversions, at only 27 percent.

From this data, you might decide to focus your efforts on Variant 1, as it had the highest conversion rate. You could then further test different video headline message themes to see if you could increase the conversion rate even more.

When interpreting multivariate test results, it is important to keep in mind the type of test that you're running. In the example above, we were testing the impact of different combinations of input fields on the conversion rate. But, you could also run a multivariate test on different types of headlines. So, you might test a video headline, an image headline, and a text headline to see which one results in the highest conversion rate.

You can also use your results to create a hypothesis for future tests. For example, if you found that a video headline resulted in higher conversion rates than an image headline, you might want to test whether adding a video thumbnail increases conversion rates even further.

It is important to remember that not every combination will be successful. In fact, most combinations will likely not be successful. This is why it is important to always have a control group in place. This way, you can determine which variables did have a significant impact on your KPIs.

Now that you understand what testing is, let's take a look at how you can actually conduct a test.

How to run your tests for best results

THE CAMPAIGN TESTING CHECKLIST

There are a few things you need to consider before you start a test, whether it's an A/B or a multivariate test:

1 Have a clear goal for your test: what are you trying to achieve? What is the outcome you're looking for? Is it higher conversions, higher CLV, higher shopping cart values? Identify the goals for your test.

2 Choose the right variables to test: not all variables are created equal. You need to choose the variables that will have the biggest impact on your goal.

3 Have a hypothesis: what do you think will happen in your test?

4 Know your audience: who are you targeting with your test? What is their demographic? What are their psychographics?

5 Make sure you have enough traffic to conduct the test: multivariate tests work best when you have a large sample size. You need to have enough traffic to get statistically significant results. That is usually 5,000 visitors per variable. So, if you have three variables, you will need to get 15,000+ site visits before you can trust your MVT results.

6 Choose an appropriate testing tool.

7 Design your test.

After reading this, you should have a good understanding of why relying solely on metrics can be dangerous for your campaigns. Use data to plan and guide your campaigns, but be sure to use your intuition and testing as well!

Finding the right testing tools

Today's marketers have a range of tools available to allow them to run tests. Among the most popular are:

- **Google Optimize:** a free tool from Google, it has a learning curve but an unbeatable price. Popular and well-integrated with Google Analytics, it's a good starter tool that can also grow with your testing practice.
- **Unbounce:** this landing-page testing tool is more complex to use than other tools on the design side, but makes it very easy to read the data itself. Its strength is partly its rich library of prebuilt landing-page templates. If you have a landing-page-driven business, it's a time-saver.
- **Optimizely:** if you need a content management system for your website as well as a testing tool, Optimizely is an excellent choice. Because it is a CMS, too, there is no need to fuss with integrating your testing with your CMS—it is already done.
- **Adobe Target:** part of the Adobe suite of marketing products, Target offers enterprise-level tools for highly sophisticated tests. It can test advertising, web pages, and mobile apps. It claims that its network ensures that tested content is delivered quickly, preventing one of the drawbacks of testing web and app content: slower page-load times.

Conducting effective tests is much more about your strategy than your tools. We recommend that you keep things simple and start with A/B testing.

You don't need to use all of the tools on this list—just pick one or two that seem most appropriate for your business, experiment with them for a couple of months, and then decide whether to expand beyond what they offer. You may find that some tools are more intuitive, while others provide greater accuracy.

When tests don't offer clear results

Our clothing company has a theory that classic clothing lines get fewer clicks than trendy ones when shown in ads. So, they run an A/B test. They create one set of Instagram ads with their trendiest clothing modeled by the most popular influencers. At the same time, they run an equal number of ads completely identical for the offer, time of day, budget spent, and even the models—all other factors. The second set of ads differs only from the first set in the types of clothing featured. This second set of ads has much less trendy clothing. These clothes are classic, simple. The question is: all other things being equal, which ads will get the most clicks?

In this A/B test, the company has isolated a single factor: clothing type. They also have a specific question that the test should answer: whether trendy clothing gets more clicks than classic clothing. For a true A/B test all the other factors must absolutely be kept equal. You cannot spend more budget on one set of ads or the other. You cannot run one set of ads longer than the other. You cannot run them at a different time of day. You must isolate the one factor that is different and test only that. Only then can you be sure that this was the one variable that influenced the results and not something else.

In the case of our clothing company, the results are inconclusive. There was only a 2 percent difference between the number of clicks the classic clothing ads received vs the ones with trendier clothing. The slight edge for trendier clothing was not statistically significant. The ads all told only got 220 clicks, so a slight difference might be accidental. The marketing team continued to run tests pitting classic clothing against trendy clothing. Over time, they began to collect more data and the results became conclusive. Despite their gut instinct that trendy clothing is more popular, the opposite proved to be true. Over repeated tests, classic clothing inspired 10 percent more clicks than trendy clothing. The theory was proven incorrect. That's not bad news. Now the organization knows to focus on classic clothing equally or more than on trendy clothing in their Instagram advertising. The lesson here is threefold:

- You need sufficient traffic for a test to be valid.
- Any test results are "good" news if they provide actionable metrics.
- It's normal to need to run multiple tests.

That last point bears repeating. One of the things about A/B testing that is important to remember is that you need to repeat it often. Marketing trends change and this year's results may mean nothing in 12 months' time. You want to be continuously testing: at least once a month in order to stay on top of trends. Keep your data current and be informed about what your consumers need the most. This is the way to make testing into a vital planning tool, rather than just an assessment tool.

Our clothing company goes back to A/B testing next month. They know that clothing trends change so quickly. In fact, they never stop testing. This means that they anticipate when trendy clothing is starting to go out of style well in advance of their competitors because they see how consumers' tastes change in their A/B tests. Months before their competitors catch on to the changing trend and shift their marketing strategy, this company is already promoting the winning variables, and thus the biggest trends. This gives them an edge that increases their sales by 16 percent over the next quarter. By continuously A/B testing the organization is constantly staying on top of trends and, more importantly, they are continuously optimizing their marketing operations.

Channel metrics in agile marketing

Channel metrics are vital to effective agile marketing practices. In agile, we work in sprints—fixed periods of time in which we try to accomplish the most we can without cutting quality or creating problems for the future through cutting the wrong corners. In an agile process, teams:

- Plan a sprint based on the work to be done in the next two weeks to 30 days—a sprint must be no longer than one month. It is important to prioritize.

- Do the work they planned. Typically, the team needs to maintain focus for those two weeks on the work they initially planned. While responding to emergencies and new opportunities, such as a media mention or PR crisis, is critical, the team should also avoid rushing from one imagined emergency to another. They must also avoid "shiny object syndrome," or the tendency to jump on every new exciting trend before completing needed work that is already under way. Focus is key.

- Assess the work that was achieved. At the end of a sprint, the team gathers for a retrospective, where they showcase the highlights of what they achieved, assess how the work was done, identify means of improvement, and measure their results.

As you can see, metrics are important to this process. Agile started out as a software development methodology. Software developers using an agile methodology typically build a feature of the software in a sprint, then test the feature in real-world conditions. Feedback from users then influences the new features that are built or improvements on current features. Marketers do something similar, except that the "product features" are marketing campaigns and the feedback is marketing metrics. Now, a lot of marketing metrics go into an agile process. First among them, of course, are sales—after all, if you are not growing your revenue, then all the clicks in the world don't make any difference.

So why should we bother with channel metrics if we're doing agile marketing? You're right that sales are the number one metric that many marketers are measured against. However, for many companies, revenue is a long way off. Remember, a sprint is a short, finite amount of time: it's a maximum of 30 days. In most organizations, it's half that—two weeks. If you're in B2B marketing, your sales cycle is measured in months, not weeks. So, how can you gather data for the vital feedback aspect of the agile marketing cycle? The answer is your channel metrics. Knowing your channel metrics gives you instant feedback on what's working in your marketing programs. It allows you to assess what worked at the end of each sprint, and plan for the next one, empowered with real data.

The agile marketing cycle: plan, measure, optimize, predict, and assess

The framework for marketing we use at Thoughtlight is a cycle: plan, measure, optimize, predict, assess:

- **Plan:** in the plan phase, we come up with hypotheses about what we think will work and what might not—we then use data to validate (or invalidate) our hypotheses.
- **Measure:** we then measure the early results of our campaigns to see what worked and what didn't.
- **Optimize:** based on what we learned in the early measure phase, we then optimize our campaigns to try and improve results.
- **Predict:** in the predict phase, we estimate how a change in one part of the campaign (e.g. increasing the budget by 25 percent) might impact other aspects of the campaign (e.g. impressions, clicks, conversion rate).
- **Assess:** finally, in the assess phase we look at the overall results of the campaign and determine whether it was successful or not.

Using this cycle we are constantly trying to improve our campaigns using data-driven decision making. Let's break it down:

PLAN

The first reason many brands want to start using metrics for marketing is to plan better campaigns. "If only we had the data on what works, we'd be better able to launch high-ROI campaigns in the future." There are a couple of problems with that outlook, though. For one thing, last year's, or even last quarter's, data will not necessarily tell you what will work now. Your customers may have moved on to new needs, your competitors have been catching up with you, and the world is rapidly changing. For another, growth comes through experimentation. Even if the world is the same as it was when you launched your last campaign (ha!), your customers' needs have not evolved, and your competition is letting grass grow under their feet—the best that repeating your successes will do is keep you in the same place, for a while. In reality, even in fairly stable markets, consumers expect you to wow them with fresh content regularly. That's the second key reason that metrics cannot be your sole guide in campaign planning. Metrics-only planning can lead to repetition, which is a quick way to get consumers tuning out.

Take, for instance, the rapid growth of TikTok. While it is a part of the social media "channel," the platform's dynamics are very different from Instagram's or Twitter's. Optimizing for TikTok based on metrics derived from past successes on Twitter, for instance, would be a rapid path to low engagement. TikTok's algorithm, for instance, narrowly focuses users' feeds on topics with which they have recently engaged. More to the point, TikTok's users are well aware of this action of the algorithm, adjusting their brand interactions to ensure a content feed of interest to them. For example, when consumers see content that they like on the channel, they often comment on a video, "commenting to stay on this side of TikTok." The platform is filled with this self-conscious engagement specifically to trigger desired algorithmic actions. This is a very different dynamic to what brands see on Twitter, necessitating a much different channel strategy. TikTok's users are "in on it," interacting with creators in collaborative ways designed to make the algorithm work for them.

Thus, your own data can only accomplish so much as a planning tool. You also need to gather data from outside your organization, from analyst reports to your own industry research, in order to fully optimize your marketing.

Data can tell you a lot in the planning stage, still. It can indicate what types of campaigns and targeting generally work for you. It's a good guide to the creative, audiences, and offers that regularly deliver great ROI.

Looking at past data can provide you with a template from which you can innovate new campaigns. It gives you a guide with signposts and boundaries. Think of using metrics for planning like using a map to plan a hike in the woods. It can tell you what paths are easy, which will be a challenge, and what areas it is best to avoid. It will not tell you the weather, how to dress, or whom to invite on your afternoon trek. But, you still would not want to head out without it. Just remember: what you will want to wear in January will be different than in August.

To use metrics effectively for planning, it must show consistent patterns. Data from a single campaign showing success with a 50 percent-off discount, for instance, does not prove that steep discounting is the key to growing sales.

MEASURE

Measurement is important in understanding how well a campaign is doing. There are many factors that go into what makes a successful marketing campaign to use when planning your next one. Use your data as a guide, but don't be afraid to experiment to find what works best for your brand and customers.

When it comes to adjusting campaigns while they are ongoing, look at results measured by engagement, CTR, conversions and leads generated, in that order. Within the first few hours, you will see results measurable in engagement. Within a day or a few days, depending on the size of your spend and audience, you will see reliable measures of CTR—don't look too soon at this metric or you will be misled by outliers. Conversion rates and leads data require a longer time horizon to stabilize. Again, depending on the scale of the campaign, you will see a picture of the campaign's effectiveness in a week or two, at most.

OPTIMIZE

Now that you have early metrics, it's time to optimize to do more of what works and less of what is not bringing you results. Optimization is a critical use for your campaign performance data. After a campaign has run for a while, analyzing the data to determine what worked and what didn't is essential in order to improve the current campaigns. In this section, you learned the formula for successful testing that you can use to improve your marketing performance.

Testing and measuring the results of your marketing campaigns is essential to optimizing their performance. By using data to guide your decisions, you can increase the chances that your next campaign will be a success.

While a campaign is ongoing, you might be tempted to focus on tactical measurement, but it is important to keep refining your strategy as well throughout the campaign. One of the biggest mistakes I see managers make is mistaking signal for noise. In an agile environment, there is a temptation to look at the most recent sprint's metrics as an indicator of the overall performance of an entire campaign. Sometimes, it can be. If the metrics are off the charts amazing, then your campaign is likely to be a success, if it keeps delivering, sprint after sprint. By the same logic, metrics that show an entire campaign is struggling are a sign to take action to save the campaign— or shut it down before more damage is done. However, in most cases, campaign metrics are subtle signals, mandating small optimizations.

This is not news most managers want to hear. We have all attended those workshops where the speaker shows how a small campaign tweak led to amazing results—they changed the color of this one button by half a shade, and sales grew by 18,000 percent! The reality is, most mid-campaign performance metrics are not that dramatic. Instead, A/B tests and multivariate tests usually show a few percentage point changes in key conversion rates.

When you are looking at metrics to make decisions about your campaign, it is important to remember that the signal is usually very subtle. A 2 percent increase in click-through rate may not seem like much, but if your goal is to get 100,000 clicks, then that two percent increase means 2,000 more people clicking through to your landing page.

PREDICT

The value of predictive analytics is that it helps you estimate how a change in one part of your campaign (e.g. increasing the budget by 25 percent) might impact other aspects of the campaign (e.g. impressions, clicks, conversion rate). The predictions are based on what has happened in the past when you made similar changes. You can also use predictive analytics to estimate how future changes will impact your campaigns.

In order to make data-driven decisions, it is essential to use predictive analytics. This type of analytics uses historical data to make predictions about future outcomes. Doing so allows you to plan strategically and avoid potential pitfalls. Predictive analytics can help you to answer important questions, such as:

- What is the impact of a change in budget on other aspects of the campaign?
- What is the predicted outcome of changing the target audience?
- How will increasing or decreasing the bid price for keywords affect traffic and conversions?

Campaign performance metrics are essential for testing and planning results, but should not be relied on solely. Use past data as a template while innovating new campaigns that cater to your brand and customers.

ASSESSMENT: POST-CAMPAIGN

Where metrics also really shine is in post-campaign assessment. In agile, we strive to improve each sprint, so conducting an effective sprint retrospective is the first step in that continuous improvement cycle.

Make metrics the star of your retrospectives. Scrutinize what worked and what didn't. Look at every click, share, comment, and site visit. Examine clickthroughs and audience metrics. Now is the time to get granular, dive deep into the detail screens of your dashboards, and treat nothing in your marketing as sacred.

Go beyond measuring your campaigns. Look also at how your team did. This is a chance for your team to assess themselves. Have everyone on the team give feedback on what worked and what didn't on how you worked together. Did your communication process keep processes running smoothly, or create bottlenecks? Did your team have the resources they needed to get the job done? Did someone invent a process that saved them time? Did they find a new way to QA? These wins are just as important sometimes as outcomes metrics such as CTR. Why? Because they represent investments in long-range marketing improvements. Remember, your team is not simply a conduit for your company's message. Marketing is a strategy, production, and measurement operation, and it needs its own focus on operational excellence in order to succeed. Don't just measure outputs; measure the efficiency, productivity, and quality of your team's work, as well. For too long, marketing teams have not asserted their own professionalism or made time for reflecting on their processes. That needs to change. So, use internal metrics to enact this change.

Measurement is important in understanding how well a campaign is doing, so use your data as a guide when determining what works and what doesn't. Additionally, use optimization techniques to improve current campaigns based on measurable results. Finally, rely on predictive analytics to estimate how future changes will impact your campaigns. Using this framework with agile will improve your marketing ROI while streamlining processes, to make everyone happy.

Conclusion

While it is important to rely on metrics to guide your campaigns, don't forget to use your intuition and creativity as well. Use data to plan and guide your campaigns, but be sure to use your experience as well! After all, most managers are not data scientists, and we need to rely on our experience and gut feelings to make decisions about our campaigns.

Testing is critical to campaign success. Use A/B and multivariate testing to determine what changes will have the biggest impact on your key conversion rates. Testing continuously is the reality today, so plan your campaigns accordingly.

Also, keep in mind that the signal from metrics is usually very subtle. A 2 percent increase in click-through rate may not seem like much, but if your goal is to get 100,000 clicks, then that 2 percent increase means 2,000 more people clicking through to your landing page. One of the biggest mistakes I see managers make is mistaking signal for noise. In an agile environment, there is a temptation to look at the most recent sprint's metrics as an indicator of the overall performance of an entire campaign. Sometimes, it can be. Other times, be patient and wait for statistically significant data to avoid jumping to the wrong conclusions and wasting money.

Use the information in this chapter to start planning your next online campaign and gathering the data you need to make informed decisions.

FROM THE FIELD: TAMMY WEISMAN

Tammy Weisman is Vice President of Marketing at ExploreLearning, a STEM education technology company. In her role, she is responsible for testing different marketing approaches to grow lead generation strategically. Prior to her work at ExploreLearning, Tammy headed up brand marketing at the leading publisher ProQuest, and led marketing for Bigchalk, another leading edtech firm. We interviewed her about how she tests and optimizes her marketing campaigns.

THINK BACK TO A TIME WHEN YOU LOOKED AT YOUR MARKETING METRICS AND USED THOSE METRICS TO MAKE A DECISION. IT CAN BE SOMETHING REALLY SIMPLE. DON'T WORRY IF IT'S NOT A FANCY USE OF ANALYTICS. DID YOU FIND COMPELLING DATA IN YOUR EMAIL OPEN-RATE METRICS? WHAT ACTION DID YOU TAKE UPON MAKING THIS DISCOVERY? FOR EXAMPLE, DID YOU CHANGE YOUR EMAIL SUBJECT LINE TO GET BETTER OPEN RATES? HOW DID IT IMPACT YOUR FUTURE RESULTS?

"At ExploreLearning, we offer free 30-day trials that allow educators to evaluate our products in the classrooms. After sign-up, the trial user enters a nurture campaign. Originally, the campaign featured eight messages, focused on product usage tips, sent across 30 days. We assumed many would use the trial regularly and therefore message engagement would be mostly uniform throughout the trial period.

"However, after analyzing open and click-through rates we discovered that the most significant engagement was during the first email (start of trial) and the second to last (seven days prior to end of trial). All the other emails saw decreasing open and click rates. Trial users also typically received several other non-trial emails during the same period, adding to potential message fatigue.

"Based on this, we significantly reduced the number of emails in the nurture campaign to see if a more focused message and cadence would increase engagement. We took the best-performing parts from each email and condensed the nurture to three emails: start of trial, mid-trial, and seven days prior to end of trial. After the change, the average open rate more than doubled and generated double-digit click to open rates."

WHAT ABOUT YOUR SOCIAL MEDIA METRICS? HAVE YOU DERIVED INSIGHTS FROM ENGAGEMENT RATES ON A FACEBOOK POST OR YOUR TIKTOK COMMENTS? OUR READERS WOULD LOVE TO KNOW MORE.

"We use social media primarily to build brand awareness and engage with customers. Educators are very active on social media and frequently use it to find and share ideas. This makes it a great place for us to uncover trending topics and keywords, and test and validate new content ideas quickly.

"We have found that posts with images and videos typically have the highest engagement rates on our Twitter and Facebook channels. Even including an animated gif of a product instead of a static screenshot can improve engagement. Because of this, we are starting to experiment with features that leverage this kind of content, like Instagram Stories."

WHAT METRICS DO YOU LOOK AT MOST OFTEN? (SOCIAL MEDIA, EMAIL, WEB ANALYTICS, PAID
SEARCH, SEO DATA, RANKING, POPULAR KEYWORDS, CONTENT MARKETING METRICS, BLOG
POSTS COMMENTS AND SHARES, ETC., OR OTHERS...)

"Digital marketing offers a myriad of riches when it comes to metrics! But the basics
are still standard because they are simple to use, well-defined, and easy to benchmark.
Common metrics our marketing team uses include:

- Email: open rate, click-through rate, open to click-through rate, engagement rate.
- PPC: impressions, click-through rate, cost per click.
- Social: impressions and engagement (clicks, shares, likes, etc).
- SEO: organic traffic, click-through rate, keywords, ranking, domain/page authority.
- Web analytics: visitors, sessions, page views, time on page, pages per visit,
  bounce rate, events.

"We also measure conversion rates for any campaign call to action, no matter the
channel. As a B2B business, we track that progress through the sales funnel: conversion
to a marketing qualified lead, conversion to a sales qualified lead, conversion to a sales
opportunity, conversion to a closed-won sale."

NOW, THINK ABOUT A TIME YOU LOOKED AT METRICS AND LEARNED SOMETHING
INTERESTING ABOUT HOW WELL YOUR MARKETING IS WORKING. IN TWO OR THREE
PARAGRAPHS, COULD YOU PLEASE SHARE WHAT METRICS YOU LOOKED AT, WHAT YOU
THOUGHT ABOUT THOSE METRICS, AND WHY YOU LOOKED AT THEM.

"We have a major marketing campaign that offers educator grants. This campaign runs
several times each year and generates a significant portion of leads annually via grant
applications. Because of its importance, we frequently analyze key digital and print
campaign metrics to improve performance.

"To submit for a grant, educators must fill out an application form—a short
questionnaire with several open-ended questions. As the first step to becoming a sales
qualified lead, we closely monitor the form completion rate.

"One year, website changes forced us to convert the application form from a single
page for all questions to multiple pages (one for each application question). This
created new data that allowed us to see not only the form completion rate, but also
the specific points at which applicants abandoned the form. We used the data to learn
how we could improve the form and increase completed applications."

OKAY, NOW THAT YOU'RE THINKING ABOUT THAT TIME YOU LOOKED AT SOME METRICS, WHAT ACTIONS DID YOU TAKE IMMEDIATELY AFTER SEEING THOSE METRICS? DID YOU SHOW THEM TO YOUR TEAM? DID YOU DECIDE TO CHANGE ANYTHING ABOUT YOUR MARKETING? THINK ABOUT ALL THE ACTIONS YOU TOOK IN REACTION TO SEEING THE METRICS TALKED ABOUT IN QUESTION 2.

"From the analysis of the grant application form, we discovered that we lost nearly 25 percent of applicants due to two questions in the middle that required a minimum word response. We lost another 5 percent due to two similar questions. This led us to remove the character limits and the redundant question. We also added a progress bar to help show time remaining to complete.

"After the grant application changes were put in place, form conversion increased by 8 percentage points and completion time was reduced by 7.5 minutes. Had these changes been in place during the prior campaign period, it would have generated 2,400 additional applications."

YOU TOOK SOME ACTIONS BASED ON THE METRICS YOU SAW. WHAT HAPPENED AS A RESULT OF THOSE ACTIONS? FOR EXAMPLE, LET'S SAY YOU SAW THAT ENGAGEMENTS ON YOUR FACEBOOK POSTS WERE LOW, SO YOU DECIDED TO POST MORE VIDEOS, BECAUSE YOU THOUGHT VIDEO DRIVES ENGAGEMENT—SOMETHING LIKE THAT. DESCRIBE THE RESULTS OF YOUR ACTIONS (BOTH POSITIVE AND NEGATIVE RESULTS ARE ACCEPTABLE!).

"One of our Facebook pages focuses on a product for K-2 educators. Followers especially engage with posts that share free teaching resources, and like all of our Facebook pages, the more visual the post the better.

"That product features hands-on science experiments using everyday household items. This seemed like the perfect concept for some fun step-by-step videos that would appeal and inform. We made one video to test out the idea, which quickly gained several hundred views, so we made another. The second video got even more engagement, eventually leading us to create a video collection and develop a bigger campaign around it featuring a landing page where educators could get a free trial.

"The videos were a big success in creating impressions, engagement, and drawing in new followers on social media. Yet the campaign landing-page metrics showed a much lower conversion rate to trial compared to other more static campaigns. Further review revealed that other posts focused on non-video free teaching resources had a similar pattern—high engagement, but lower conversion to trial. That meant if engagement was high enough then free resources—like the science experiment videos—could still generate more trial volume despite a lower conversion rate."

IF POSSIBLE, COULD YOU PLEASE SHARE SPECIFIC BEFORE AND AFTER METRICS. WHAT WAS THE METRIC BEFORE YOU DID THESE ACTIONS AND WHAT WERE THE METRICS AFTER YOU DID THE ACTIONS DESCRIBED ABOVE?

"The hands-on experiment videos generated tens of thousands of views, thousands of likes and shares, and hundreds of comments—significantly more engagement than any previous posts or content assets on that Facebook channel. The trial conversion rates were, at minimum, half those of other more static campaigns for the product."

DO YOU HAVE ANY ADVICE YOU WOULD LIKE TO SHARE WITH OTHER MARKETERS, BASED ON YOUR EXPERIENCE LOOKING AT METRICS AND MAKING DECISIONS?

"Metrics are powerful but they can also lead to wild goose chases or analysis paralysis. Try to keep things as simple and repeatable as possible so it's easy to monitor, compare, and benchmark programs. Focus on the areas that have the greatest impact or largest investment. Not every program or campaign needs deep analysis either—often only a few metrics are necessary to make decisions. And always keep in mind that any metric should support your key goals, inform common business questions, or drive action. If it doesn't, then stop using it or find a better metric—especially if it isn't automated."

11

Data governance and the new privacy laws

The first of the significant data privacy laws that many marketers think about is the General Data Protection Regulation (GDPR). However, we live in an age of consumer concern about privacy. From the end of many third-party cookies to an expanding array of privacy laws, people are paying more attention to how their data is being used.

This is a challenge for businesses, which need to collect and use data in order to operate effectively. But it is also an opportunity, as businesses that can demonstrate they take privacy seriously can build trust with their customers.

Data governance is the key to managing this risk and opportunity. By establishing a clear framework for data management, businesses can ensure that they are collecting and using data in a way that respects customer privacy.

The first step in data governance is understanding what data your business has and where it came from. You need to know what data you have, where it is stored, and who has access to it. This data inventory can help you identify any potential privacy risks and take steps to mitigate them.

Once you have an understanding of your data, you need to create a policy for how it will be used. This policy should include clear rules for who can access the data, how it can be used, and how it must be protected. It should also outline your company's commitments to privacy and data protection.

Ensuring that your data governance policy is followed is critical to protecting your customers' privacy. You need to have systems in place to track who is accessing the data, what they are doing with it, and how it is being protected. Doing so will help you ensure that your data is being used safely and responsibly.

The current privacy regulation landscape

As already stated above, the first of the significant data privacy laws that many marketers think about is GDPR. However, several data protection laws actually predate it. Though more limited in scope, they are relevant in many marketing scenarios. Here's a breakdown of the current privacy law landscape:

GDPR

The GDPR is the most stringent of the current European privacy laws. With an enforcement date of May 25, 2018, it applies to all companies processing data about citizens in the European Union (EU) (regardless of where the company is based), and has some very specific requirements for what needs to be documented (Article 30). Under GDPR, companies are obliged to keep records of all data processing activities, for instance. The regulation does not define what needs to be in all records, but the Article 29 Working Party has issued guidelines on this. GDPR also requires that you have a designated Data Protection Officer if your company regularly monitors citizens in the EU.

For companies with 250 employees or more, GDPR requires public disclosure of data breaches within 72 hours. If the information is likely to result in a high risk to your consumers, you must notify them directly, rather than simply issue a public notice, also within that 72 hours. No other reporting time constraints are listed in the text, but if breach notification deadlines are not met, a company can be fined up to 2 percent of its annual global revenue for failing to comply with this disclosure timeframe.

GDPR expanded the rights of individuals in regards to their data, allowing them to not only request information about what information is stored on them, but also restrict or limit access to this data or even have it erased completely upon request. In many ways, it transformed attitudes toward consumer data, well beyond the borders of the EU and well beyond the specific requirements of the law.

FERPA

FERPA, or the Federal Educational Rights and Privacy Act, is a law that protects the privacy of educational records. If you are marketing to students, you should be keenly aware of what this entails.

The law covers information about students in all stages of education—from preschool through college, professional schools, and post-graduate programs. There are some exceptions for student workers involved in work-study programs, for students over the age of 18 who are dependants, and for former students.

FERPA limits the data that can be released about students. It prohibits sharing:

- grades and marks, both for individual classes and programs overall
- disciplinary actions against the student, unless serious crimes were involved
- papers, exams, and other course materials completed by the student
- educational records kept by instructors and school officials about the student

FERPA does allow the publication of "directory information." This is defined under FERPA as courses taken, fields of study or majors selected, degrees earned, and similar information. It can also include any honors received, membership in student organizations, and scholarships or fellowships won. Schools must notify students, and if they are under 18, their parents or guardians, of what information they disclose.

For marketers, FERPA forbids very few activities. If you are trying to market to people with .edu email addresses, FERPA does include email addresses under its definition of "directory information." However, many institutions interpret student records broadly; they release little directory information. In general, it is best to avoid seeking out directory information of students in order to market to them.

When it comes to FERPA, most marketers are focused on the question of whether they can email student email addresses. However, since many schools don't publish directory information online, learning only that an email address ends in .edu is not enough.

HIPAA

HIPAA, or the Health Insurance Portability and Accountability Act, is another major data protection law. This law spells out how medical information can be shared within a healthcare organization and between organizations.

If you are marketing healthcare-related goods and services, HIPAA's impact on your marketing is twofold. First, if you are a healthcare organization and you share information with others (such as for digital health), you must follow HIPAA's data security standards. Let's say, for instance, you're a medical spa, providing skin treatments that are classified as medical procedures, such as fillers, peels, and botox. Your customers are considered patients, protected by HIPAA. You couldn't, for example, share patient data with a makeup company, so that they can collaborate with you on marketing their products to your clientele.

Second, HIPAA impacts how your data can be used. While HIPAA itself does not spell out what kind of data you can share, it does state that users must have a "need to know." The privacy regulations laid out by HIPAA include data from customers who are also healthcare patients. This makes it illegal for marketers to collect and use patient data when the only purpose of the contact is marketing.

However, in certain circumstances, HIPAA allows medical facilities to share data with companies who can aid in healthcare operations, for example, if you wanted to advertise a weight-loss service to your patients.

In both cases, HIPAA allows medical facilities and providers to share patient data only in the context of "healthcare," and it outlaws sharing that data for anything other than healthcare purposes. Thus, while you could collaborate with a weight-loss program, that weight-loss program could not turn around and share data with, say, a sports clothing or bicycle company. When marketing to healthcare sectors, you should also keep HIPAA in mind.

COPPA

The Children's Online Privacy Protection Act (COPPA) was passed with the intent to protect children younger than 13 from unintended data sharing and solicitation. If you market to children 13 and under, COPPA prohibits collecting, using, or disclosing personal information from those younger than 13 without parental permission. The rule applies to websites and apps directed at kids (under 13), but also to any service that knowingly collects data from a child under 13. It has several implications for marketers.

First, the rules on how and when to ask permission about sharing data apply if your website or app uses web tracking tools such as cookies, clear gifs, HTML 5, and local storage. The rules about how and when to ask permission also apply if a website uses behavioral targeting.

Second, the rules on how and when to ask permission about sharing data also apply to kids under 13 even if your site doesn't use tracking tools such as cookies and clear gifs. For instance, if you register a child's IP address or mobile device ID, you must get verifiable consent from parents before collecting, using, or sharing personal information from any child under 13.

If you are marketing toys, activities, or other goods aimed at children under 13, it is important to understand COPPA requirements. You must get verifiable parental consent before collecting or sharing any child data.

For digital marketers, COPPA applies any time an ad network segment is targeted using data from a child younger than 13. The rules around not sharing information with third parties without parental consent apply to behavioral targeting.

HIPAA and COPPA are two important laws that impact digital marketers. HIPAA regulates how healthcare data can be used, and prohibits sharing patient data for anything other than healthcare purposes. COPPA regulates how data from children younger than 13 can be collected, used, and shared. If you are marketing to kids or healthcare audiences, it is important to be aware of these laws and how they impact your campaigns.

Other data privacy laws

There are other US laws that protect data privacy beyond FERPA, HIPAA, and COPPA.

The Fair Credit Reporting Act (FCRA) governs how consumer reporting agencies can share credit data with third parties. It also specifies how consumer reporting agencies must share that data. One important stipulation is that the consent of the person the data is about must be obtained before sharing credit information.

Marketing to consumers using illegally obtained personal information, such as via phishing scams, constitutes mail fraud under 18 U.S. Code § 1341. This means it is critical to avoid purchasing email or other direct marketing lists. While reputable data vendors are unlikely to have acquired their lists through illegal means, it is still a good idea to avoid using lists that were not collected by you.

If your company is affected by a data security breach, be sure you understand what procedures are required of you under the law. In the United States 47 states have data breach notification laws, which require companies that experience a data breach to notify affected individuals and state authorities. There are also several federal data breach notification laws, such as the Graham-Leach-Bliley Act and HIPAA.

US state regulations

Perhaps the most famous state law in the United States governing privacy is CCPA. As of June 28, 2018 the California Consumer Privacy Act (CCPA) is effective. The CCPA has been designed to give Californian citizens control over their personal data and how it is being used by private companies. However, this is not just restricted to those based in California but also anyone that holds a California consumer's personal data. The measures contained within this new legislation are designed to protect personal information online, giving users control over their private data and how it is being used.

Under CCPA, consumers have the right to:

- know the data being collected about them
- opt out of data collection
- delete information held regarding them

In addition, if a consumer is under age 16, they or a guardian must explicitly opt in to data collection, rather than just be given the option to opt out. Consumers who exercise their CCPA rights cannot face discrimination for doing so. If affected by a data breach, consumers can privately sue the company that held the data in the breach.

CPRA

An amendment to CCPA passed in 2020, CPRA adds two additional legal protections. Consumers in California, as of 2020, can:

- correct inaccurate information about them
- limit the disclosure and use of sensitive information

CPRA offers more specific rights around data deletion, and it defines "sensitive information" to include:

- race or ethnicity
- religion
- health information
- precise geolocation
- contents of their texts, emails, and other communications

CPRA also expands obligations from businesses themselves to contractors acting on behalf of business.

Together, CCPA and CPRA represent significant changes in US privacy laws, which could impact future federal laws. The law recognizes that "online personal information" includes more than just the traditional definition of personal data, which covers first and last names, email addresses, social security number etc, but also explicitly covers "an individual's first name or first initial and last name in combination with any one or more of the following data elements for that individual: 1) social security number; 2) driver's license number or California Identification Card number; 3) account number, credit or debit card number, in combination with any required security code, access code, or password that would permit access to an individual's financial account."

The passage of the California Consumer Privacy Act (CCPA) in 2018 was a major milestone for online privacy in the United States.

State regulations of student data

While FERPA is a federal law, some states also have their own laws governing student data privacy. For example, California's Student Online Personal Information Protection Act (SOPIPA) limits how K-12 schools can collect or share personally identifying information for students under 18 years of age. Other states, such as Connecticut, have laws that specifically require school districts to protect student data from unauthorized access.

Privacy Act (Australia)

As of this writing, digital media privacy for businesses doing business in Australia is governed by the nation's Privacy Act. Under this act, personal data can only be used for the specific purposes stated at the time of collection. Businesses must also take "reasonable steps" to protect personal data from unauthorized access, use, or disclosure. If a data breach occurs, the business must notify both the individual and the Office of the Australian Information Commissioner (OAIC) within 30 days.

PIPEDA: Canada's Personal Information Protection and Electronic Documents Act

Canada's PIPEDA is a national law that sets out specific rules for the collection, use, and disclosure of personal information by organizations. PIPEDA covers any type of personal information, including digital media. The definition of protected personal data is very broad under PIPEDA and includes:

> Any factual or subjective information, recorded or not, about an identifiable individual. This includes information in any form, such as:

- age, name, ID numbers, income, ethnic origin, or blood type
- opinions, evaluations, comments, social status, or disciplinary actions
- employee files, credit records, loan records, medical records, existence of a dispute between a consumer and a merchant, intentions (for example, to acquire goods or services, or change jobs)

As you can see, the definition of personal data is quite broad and can cover a wide range of information. It is, indeed, one of the widest definitions of any legal regulations to date. Under PIPEDA, businesses must take steps to protect personal information from unauthorized access, use, or disclosure. They must also ensure that the individuals they collect personal information from have given their consent for the information to be collected and used. If a data breach occurs, the business must notify both the individual and the Office of the Privacy Commissioner of Canada within 72 hours.

Platform-based requirements and restrictions

In addition to regional laws, many advertising platforms have their own standards of what constitutes ethical use of data. Knowing these requirements and restrictions is important for understanding what businesses can and cannot do with the data they collect.

Targeting consumers based on restricted categories

For example, Google Ads prohibit targeting consumers on the basis of race, age, or gender for job ads, or promotions for housing or credit. In addition, targeting consumers with personalized ads based on their hardships is banned. Hardships are defined as any mental or physical health condition, relationship problems such as divorce, financial struggles such as debt, and issues related to bereavement, grief, or trauma. Finally, ads that imply a negative body image or engage in body-shaming are among those prohibited. This doesn't mean that you cannot advertise legal services, counseling, or healthy-living activities. However, such advertising has to have its targeting set in such a way that it does not exploit personal misfortunes. Its language must also avoid referencing the personal hardships of users.

Google also prohibits targeting based on what it calls "sensitive" categories. These include users' religious beliefs, political affiliations, and sexual orientation. Ads that are deemed harmful are prohibited by the Terms of Service for Google Ads. This includes ads that incite hatred. Google Ads also forbids ads that target users based on membership in unions, which can present challenges if recruiting within a unionized workforce, such as schoolteachers.

LinkedIn also prohibits the targeting of job ads in ways that exclude age groups, ethnicities, or genders. Similar prohibitions are in place on most social media platforms. For more information, see the LinkedIn Help Center or Facebook's Ads help. These rules change, so ensure that you are on top of them.

Prohibited products in advertising

Another platform-based restriction is on the types of products you can advertise. Google bans ads for a range of products, including:

- tobacco
- firearms, ammunition, or weapons
- non-recreational drugs and drug-related products such as medical marijuana
- adult products and services such as strip clubs and escort services
- adult toys (in most countries)
- investment opportunities or financial products such as credit cards or interest-rate reduction plans
- gambling, including online casinos, sports betting, lotteries, and games of skill that offer prizes of cash or other value

Other platforms may also prohibit some types of ads.

Google Ads also has a specific ban on ads for payday loans.

Facebook has a similar ban on ads for firearms, prescription drugs, alcohol, adult products and services, over-the-counter medical drugs claiming to help users lose weight fast, weapons of any kind (including toy guns), ammunition of all types, payday loans, gambling of any kind (including online casinos, sports betting, lotteries, or games of skill), and services that are false or misleading.

Strictly speaking, the prohibition on ads for specific products may not seem like a metrics issue. However, when you have a product range that you advertise, with some in prohibited ad categories and some not, you need to adjust your campaign performance metrics—KPIs—accordingly.

Targeting users based on personal data

Just as platform-based targeting is covered by the Terms of Service agreements mentioned above, targeting consumers based on their personal data is similarly restricted.

With this list of prohibited categories, you may wonder how you might promote, say, a gay retirees group, based in a church, that goes to casinos—not a terribly unlikely ad. Targeting restrictions might prohibit you from targeting the very consumers most interested in joining your program. However, there are ways to manage such targeting as long as you follow Google's rules around personalization features. To learn more, see Google's help documentation.

Targeting by age-related demographics

No matter your advertising goals, you will often want to consider age demographics in your targeting. That, too, can present ethical, legal, and platform-restriction-based challenges. We have already learned that targeting job ads by age groups is strictly prohibited on most platforms. Under US law, it might also violate discrimination statutes if the goal is to exclude workers over age 40.

Targeting young consumers raises issues related to COPPA, which we learned about earlier in the chapter. Since laws in the EU, the United States, and globally restrict the collection or sharing of personal information for children under 13 without parental consent, advertising to children is best not age-targeted. If your targeting strategy includes users under age 13, you must be aware of COPPA and laws around the globe related to advertising to children, before you start any campaigns. Seek legal counsel, as well as conducting appropriate consumer research with parents and children, to ensure your messaging is also appropriate to young viewers.

On Google Ads, excluding specific groups is also limited by the Terms of Service agreement and platform prohibitions on sensitive categories.

Although age-related targeting has its restrictions, it can be used in many contexts. Facebook has a number of ad targeting options that allow advertisers to select the age group they want to see their ads, as do TikTok, Pinterest, Twitter, LinkedIn, and most other advertising channels.

The US Federal Trade Commission regulations

In the United States, the Federal Trade Commission (FTC) has broad powers to protect consumers from unfair and deceptive practices. FTC regulations traditionally have been aimed at clear missteps by companies, such as making demonstrably untrue claims about a product or service. This purview has expanded into the regulation of digital advertising when such advertising involves deceptive advertising. In general, FTC regulation only comes into play with regards to consumer data if fraud is likely.

Data governance and ethics frameworks

Various data ethics frameworks have been proposed in response to the increasing concerns around data privacy and consumer protection. Among the most useful are the Fair Information Practices Principles (FIPPs), the United States Federal Data Ethics Framework, and Kord Davis's Big Data Ethics.

A general data governance framework

There are many data governance frameworks. As you develop your own data governance framework, it will be important to consider the ethical principles that are most relevant to your company and your industry.

The data company Imperva shares an especially useful one. Based on the core pillars of technology, people, and process, it breaks down governance into:

- **Ownership:** managing who owns the data, and how it is maintained.

- **Accessibility:** restricting access to data, both internally and externally, and regulating how data is used, including for marketing and research purposes.
- **Security:** establishing and enforcing policies and procedures to protect data from accidental or unauthorized access, alteration, or destruction.
- **Quality:** managing the quality of data, including accuracy, timeliness, and completeness.
- **Knowledge:** maintaining the skills of data stewards and making sure they understand the ethical implications of their work. In order to make data governance effective, it is important that all stakeholders within an organization—including those in marketing, research, technology, and operations—understand and agree to the framework's principles.

When it comes to digital advertising, data governance should include a consideration of the ethical principles of data privacy and consumer protection. Advertisers should ensure that their targeting strategies do not inadvertently violate these principles, and they should have a process in place for assessing potential violations. Having many of the provisions of a data governance framework in place is important under GDPR, and, for all marketers, it is a way to ensure that responsible and ethical data management is a core part of your business.

Privacy by design

Privacy by design is an approach to information and communication technology (ICT) development that embeds data privacy and protection into the initial design stages of products and services. Articulated by Dr Ann Cavoukian, it is a framework that can be used to ensure that privacy is an integral part of the design process, rather than an afterthought.

Under privacy by design, all aspects of a product or service are designed with data privacy in mind. This includes the collection of data, its use, retention, and destruction. It also includes the security of data, both during transit and storage.

It is based on seven principles, which we can apply to marketing metrics as follows:

1 **Proactive, not reactive; preventative, not remedial:** privacy by design should be proactive, not reactive. It should anticipate potential problems and address them proactively.

2 **Privacy by default:** consumers should not have to make efforts to protect their privacy; it should be the default.

3 **Privacy embedded into design:** privacy should be embedded into the design of products and services, not tacked on as an afterthought.

4 **Full functionality, positive-sum, not zero-sum:** privacy does not have to come at the expense of functionality. In fact, privacy can enhance functionality by protecting against misuse.

5 **End-to-end security:** security should be comprehensive, from the data's inception to its destruction.

6 **Visibility and transparency:** consumers should be able to understand how their data is being used and why.

7 **User-centric:** the focus should be on the user, their needs, and what they want you to be doing with data to help them.

When it comes to digital advertising, privacy by design allows you to build a digital marketing infrastructure that works to protect the privacy of your customers. It helps you to anticipate and avoid potential privacy problems, ensuring that your data collection, use, and retention practices are what your consumers need. From your website to your CRM, it can future-proof your technology against new regulations.

Digital marketing is evolving all the time. As new technologies are developed, and as more data is collected, it becomes increasingly important to build our tech for privacy.

FIPPs

The FIPPs were developed in the late 1970s and published in 1980, in response to the increasing concerns around data privacy and consumer protection. The principles were later updated to reflect the changes brought about by the digital age. The FIPPs are a set of guidelines that organizations can use to assess their data practices and ensure that they are protecting the privacy of their customers.

There are seven FIPPs:

1 **Data quality:** information should be accurate, timely, and complete.

2 **Collection limitation:** personal data should be collected only for specific, legitimate purposes.

3 **Use limitation:** personal data should not be used in a way that is incompatible with the purpose for which it was collected.

4 Individual participation: individuals should be able to find out what personal data is being collected about them, how it is being used, and who is allowed to see it. They should also be able to address inaccuracies and access their data easily.

5 Purpose specification: personal data should be collected for a specific purpose and not used for any other purpose without the consent of the individual.

6 Security safeguards: personal data should be protected from unauthorized access, alteration, or destruction.

7 Accountability: organizations that collect, use, or disclose personal data should be accountable for their actions.

The FIPPs are a good starting point for data governance, but they are not legally binding. They also do not take into account the unique challenges of the digital age, such as big data and data analytics. Nonetheless, they provide a framework for responsible and ethical data management.

Davis's data ethics

When it comes to digital advertising, data governance should include a consideration of the ethical principles of data privacy and consumer protection. Advertisers should ensure that their targeting strategies do not inadvertently violate these principles, and they should have a process in place for assessing potential violations.

Business consultant Kord Davis developed the Big Data Ethics framework to offer guidance on data ethics that goes beyond legal requirements. The framework is built on four principles:

- **Identity:** people have the right to express their identities online as they see as appropriate, to control those identities, and to be anonymous if they choose.
- **Privacy:** people have a right to privacy in their personal data and should be able to control who has access to it.
- **Ownership:** consumers should have ownership of their data, their identity, and their intellectual property, including content they create online.
- **Reputation:** individuals have the right to control and protect their online reputations.

These principles provide a framework for responsible data management in the digital age. They can help you consider the bigger picture as you work toward data protection.

The US federal data ethics framework

The United States Federal Government offers a framework for government agencies to ensure their data usage is legal and ethical. The framework is based on broad principles:

- **Uphold applicable statutes, regulations, professional practices, and ethical standards:** organizations must comply with all applicable statutes, regulations, professional practices, and ethical standards that relate to data.

- **Respect the public, individuals, and communities:** think about the impact of your data collection on both individuals and the community at large. Put the public interest first in your decision making.

- **Respect privacy and confidentiality:** be purposeful in thinking about the tradeoff between fine-detailed data and the privacy of the individual. Make privacy your primary focus. Protect personal data against unauthorized access, use, or disclosure.

- **Act with honesty, integrity, and humility:** document data usage carefully. Make it safe to admit to mistakes in order to address them quickly and avoid cover-ups.

- **Hold oneself and others accountable:** develop a culture of ethical data use. Make it easy to address breaches or policy violations. Ensure detailed, specific training that addresses how your organization uses data.

- **Promote transparency:** be transparent about how you are using data. Standardize methods and ensure everyone in your organization knows the standards.

- **Stay informed of developments in the fields of data management and data science:** avoid complacency. Laws are always changing. Subscribe to data privacy publications, attend workshops, and maintain a regular training schedule.

This framework is general enough that it can be used as a guideline for any organization, regardless of size or industry. It is important to tailor the framework to your specific needs, and to regularly revisit and update it as laws and regulations change. Using a broad, flexible framework can give you the ability to make decisions ethically in a data-driven world even as new technologies, laws, and consumer expectations emerge.

The data stewardship elements from the Information Accountability Foundation

The Information Accountability Foundation is a global think-tank that aims to inform national policies on data usage around the world. In 2009, they published a framework and set of criteria for data stewardship that is continuously updated. You can view the full framework at informationaccountability.org. The five "elements," as the foundation refers to the standards, are as follows, taken from the framework:

1 Organization commitment to accountability and adoption of internal policies consistent with external criteria.
2 Mechanisms to put privacy policies into effect, including tools, training, and education.
3 Systems for internal ongoing oversight and assurance reviews and external verification.
4 Transparency and mechanisms for individual participation.
5 Means for remediation and external enforcement.

The organization conducts research and shares its research-based recommendations with policymakers. Thus, familiarizing yourself with this framework is a good way to stay ahead of legal requirements coming in the future.

Managing privacy

To manage anything, you first need to know what it is. Many organizations of all sizes don't know all the metrics their different marketing functions collect. This can lead to substantial wasted resources. However, in this privacy-aware world, it can lead to worse, too: fines, loss of trust, a damaged reputation. Thus, every organization should routinely conduct a data audit. A data audit is a comprehensive effort to identify all of the data collected, handled, and utilized by an organization. It is the cornerstone function of managing ethically with metrics.

Knowing your metrics landscape

To keep data secure, you first need to know what data you are collecting, storing, and using. Conducting a consumer data audit is critical. Indeed, it is legally required. A big part of GDPR and privacy is knowing what data you have, who is accessing it, from where, for what purpose. Indeed, GDPR mandates that you know what personal data you hold on every consumer covered by the law.

We conduct a consumer data audit by determining the answers to these questions:

- What types of metrics are we collecting? What kinds of data do we have in our environment that is sensitive—that is, contains personally identifiable information (PII)?

- How many kinds of data do we collect? Your goal asking this question is to have a clear map of all the data you have. This is both a practical need and a legal requirement. In addition, once you map all your currently collected metrics, you may well find redundancy, so this first step will also help you to streamline processes eventually. However, right now, don't stop to analyze all the metrics you are collecting. Simply document every metrics type that your organization currently handles.

- Which of these metrics includes external stakeholders' PII? Knowing where PII is normally stored is key to knowing your data landscape. Your CRM, loyalty program, and email and marketing automation depend on PII to function. We'll look at more ways to identify the PII databases in your organization in the next section. For now, remember that identifying the PII your organization holds is key to compliance, ethics, and maintaining your organization's reputation as a customer-focused company.

- Who collects this data? Is it someone on your team? Another team outside of marketing? Or is it an external agency? A third-party data vendor? Is it automatically collected by a specific tool, such as your CRM? Who is the administrator of that tool? Do multiple entities collect the data, or is collection centralized?

- If collection is automated, what steps happen automatically to collect the data? Do you understand the exact mechanisms, such as cookies, user entry, screen recorders? In many cases, specific data collection methods are illegal, or being blocked by many users—for instance, cookies are increasingly blocked by most browsers. Knowing the data collection method can save you from unfortunate surprises such as being hit with legal action regarding data you thought was legal to collect, but is being collected by illegal means, or simply being unable to rely on data because the method is blocked by some users.

- If the data is being collected manually, do you have safeguards against human error? How are you ensuring data is correctly transcribed? What security measures are in place to ensure that data is kept secure while being collected by multiple contributors, potentially using non-secure offline methods such as paper forms?

- Where is the data stored? Is it on one team member's computer? Is all your data stored on your own servers or associated databases? Where is it stored and what infrastructure is in place to secure that data? Do you outsource any of the storage or hosting of that data? For instance, is some of it stored in an application, such as an email platform, for which you pay a subscription, and the data will be erased if you cancel your subscription and fail to save a copy? Would it be stolen if someone hacked into that subscription platform? Is it being transferred or shared with other organizations? If so, are you complying with the Data Protection Act requirements regarding transferring data to third parties?

- Are you collecting any sensitive information that could place individuals at risk of harm through data leaks, or data loss? How are you maintaining compliance in this area if required by your industry sector (for example, financial, medical)?

- Are you making use of emerging technologies such as cloud computing, virtualization, AI, big data analytics, etc, which could increase the risk of a data breach?

- Are you conducting regular penetration testing and vulnerability scans to ensure your systems are secure from attack, and that all identified problems have been addressed in a timely manner?

- Who has access to the data? How secure is that access? What are you doing to ensure that only those who have a need to know have access to data, and that the appropriate controls are in place regarding how data can be accessed? What are your criteria for allowing staff/volunteers to access the data? How do you ensure staff members and volunteers can access only the personal information they need? Do you make sure that only the minimum number of staff members/volunteers have access to specific databases that handle sensitive information?

- If your organization acquires other companies, is personal information (including contact details) of customers of the acquired company transferred as part of the acquisition?

- Do you have a data protection officer? Are their qualifications relevant to the job they are doing, or are they 'window dressing'? Do they have real power to ensure responsible data usage, or do they just advise, while departments can still risk breaking the rules?

- What are you doing to keep customers informed about data security breaches?

- What do your terms of service say about personal data? Do they allow for information to be shared with other organizations without the customer's consent?

- Do you have processes in place so that people can correct or update their personal information if it needs to be changed?

- What steps are you taking to protect personal information that could be exposed if your database was hacked? For example: are there encryption measures in place to protect the data at rest and in motion?

- How is the data processed? For example, are you using third-party storage or processing services who may not follow the same strict security policies that you do?

- How long are you keeping the data? For how long is it accessible to staff, and who has access to it? What is the process for deleting old data?

- Do you share this information with other people or organizations? Who are they and why do you share that information with them?

- How do you ensure that staff members who handle personal information understand their privacy obligations to the people whose information they are responsible for managing?

- What steps do you take to ensure that people can see what information about them is held in your systems, and correct any inaccuracies? For example: if someone requests their personal data from an organization, GDPR mandates that organizations provide a copy of that information within 30 days.

- What do you do to ensure people can report complaints or request their data is removed from your systems entirely? For example: people have the right to ask for their personal data to be removed from an organization's records, and if this happens, the organization must delete all copies of it. Who deals with these requests? How are you ensuring that they are handled in the correct timeframe?

- Have you mapped your organizational structure to identify all departments that collect data? Are there any gaps or redundancy?

- What are your procedures for disaster recovery? If you were to suffer a ransomware attack, would you be able to recover any of the data if you had no backups?

- Why is the data being collected? Is it important to delivering a service, or to understanding your customers? Or are you collecting it in case you might need it later? Believe it or not, under GDPR, collecting data without a good, immediate need can be against the law.

It is not just companies that need to be aware of these issues. Organizations' employees who handle customer information also need to be aware of their obligations to protect that data. Do your employees receive training on how to handle customer information securely and in accordance with applicable laws?

Are you using cookies on your website? If so, are you clear about how they are being used and have you got consent from the people visiting your site?

These are just a few of the many questions that organizations need to be asking themselves in order to ensure that they are compliant. These questions should be revisited periodically. Even within a single year, the way that data is collected, used, and protected can change dramatically. Thus, it is important to treat this checklist as a living document, one that you keep updated.

Creating a data governance team

Once you have a framework in place and know your metrics landscape, you need to appoint a data governance team. This team is responsible for ensuring that the data is managed in accordance with the organization's policies and procedures. You also need an advisory group, which should be made up of individuals from all areas of the business, including:

- IT
- Marketing
- Sales
- Customer Service

Representation from multiple job functions is key. However, you also want your team to be able to make decisions efficiently. A small team works best, between five and seven people.

With input from your advisory group, you also need a core team to manage day-to-day governance. Such a team typically needs these roles to be effective:

- **Chief Data Officer or Data Protection Officer:** the Chief Data Officer (CDO) or Data Protection Officer (DPO) is responsible for monitoring data protection within the company and ensuring compliance with GDPR. They should have the qualifications necessary to do their job effectively and be able to report any issues or concerns to senior management.

- **Information Security Officer:** the Information Security Officer (ISO) is responsible for ensuring that the company's data is kept safe. They will need to have a good understanding of the company's IT infrastructure and how data is processed and stored.

- **IT Manager:** the IT Manager is responsible for the company's IT infrastructure and ensuring that all systems are compliant with laws and best practices. They will need to be familiar with the company's data processing and storage methods.

- **Marketing Manager:** the Marketing Manager is responsible for the company's marketing activities. They will need to be aware of GDPR's restrictions on data collection and be able to ensure that the company is compliant with them.

- **Compliance Manager:** the Compliance Manager is responsible for ensuring that the company is compliant with all applicable regulations, including GDPR. They will need to be familiar with the relevant law and be able to implement the necessary changes within the company.

- **Legal Counsel:** the Legal Counsel is responsible for ensuring that the company is compliant with all applicable regulations, including GDPR. They will need to be familiar with the relevant law and be able to provide legal advice on how to comply with it.

These roles don't always need to be an employee's full-time job. In a small organization, it is likely that someone will wear multiple hats. For example, a compliance manager may also be the IT manager or the legal counsel. However, it is important that someone is specifically designated to these roles in order to ensure that the data is being managed effectively.

It is important that the team is able to work together effectively. The CDO or DPO should be the team's leader and be responsible for ensuring that everyone is aware of their responsibilities and is working to fulfil them. Proper data governance requires organization and structure, so having a dedicated team in place is essential.

Define the processes

Once you have your team in place, you need to define the processes they will use to govern data.

CREATING A PRIVACY-FIRST DATA PROGRAM

Now that you have your team in place, it's time to create your privacy-first data program. This is a set of guidelines and procedures that will help ensure that the company is compliant with data governance practices.

DATA RETENTION

The first step is to develop a data retention policy. This policy will outline how long the company will keep different types of data and why it is being kept. It should also include instructions for destroying data when it is no longer needed.

DATA CLASSIFICATION

The next step is to classify all of the company's data. This will help you determine which regulations apply to each type of data. You can use a variety of methods to do this, such as:

- **Hierarchical classification:** this system classifies data according to its level of sensitivity. The most sensitive data is at the top of the hierarchy and the least sensitive data is at the bottom.

- **Asset-based classification:** this system classifies data based on its value to the company. The most valuable data is at the top of the hierarchy and the least valuable data is at the bottom.

- **Functional classification:** this system classifies data according to its function within the company. The most important data is at the top of the hierarchy and the least important data is at the bottom.

DATA PROCESSING

The next step is to develop a data processing policy. This policy will outline how the company will process and store data. It should include instructions for protecting against unauthorized access, data breaches, and other security risks.

DATA USAGE

The next step is to develop a data usage policy. This policy will outline how the company will use data and who will have access to it. It should include instructions for obtaining consent from data subjects and for deleting or destroying data when it is no longer needed.

DATA TRANSFER

The next step is to develop a data transfer policy. This policy will outline how the company will transfer data between different systems and organizations. It should include instructions for protecting against unauthorized access, data breaches, and other security risks.

DATA BREACH NOTIFICATION

The final step is to develop a data breach notification policy. This policy will outline how the company will notify affected individuals and regulators in the event of a data breach. It should include instructions for notifying individuals and regulators as quickly as possible, without compromising the investigation.

Final thoughts

Implementing a privacy-first data program is not easy, but it is essential for ensuring compliance with the ever-growing landscape of data protection regulations. By following these steps, you can create a program that will help your company meet all of the legal requirements.

Blockchain and the future of trustworthy marketing metrics

No discussion of metrics today would be complete without talking about blockchain. Blockchain is a ledger system that utilizes a cryptographic security model to securely store immutable information. Once information is stored on a blockchain, it cannot be erased. Thus, it is thought to be the most trustworthy way of storing data.

We often hear the term "the" blockchain, creating the impression that blockchain is a single, official ledger being kept somewhere by a global authority. It isn't. Blockchain, despite all the mystification, is simply a system that allows people to store encrypted data securely with two key features: 1) data cannot be erased once on a blockchain; 2) data related to an entity, such as a person or piece of property, is stored in sequential order as it is created.

If you own a house, you have been exposed to feature #2. When you bought your house, you got the deed to your house. If it was not newly built, it had a prior owner. That owner had the deed when they owned it. If it's a really old house, several people have owned it, down through the years. Each time the house got a new owner, their ownership was recorded in a deed book, at the local authority. This authority is county registrar in the United States. In that deed book, there is a record of every single person who has ever owned your house. You can, if you own a very old house, go to the registrar and look up the names of all the past people who owned your house. It is an amazing experience to see the names of long-gone people, written in old-fashioned handwriting, in an old deed book, knowing they once lived in your house.

That is the principle of blockchain. It's a "track record" of every transaction related to something—every time it changed owners, or a claim was placed on it, or it otherwise was subject to new activity.

Now, think of those fragile old deed books, collecting dust in the registrar's office. Such old books have been destroyed by natural disasters or just age many times. In fact, the loss of old records creates a lot of work for archivists and genealogists. Now, imagine if a record of every transaction related to your house were not only impeccably recorded, as it is now, but protected from destruction. That is the promise of blockchain. It is a record of every transaction or activity related to a person, place, action, or thing, protected from hacking, deliberate erasure, or accidental deletion. You cannot remove information from a blockchain.

Although blockchain is most commonly associated with cryptocurrencies, it offers a unique opportunity for the secure storage of nearly any kind of data. You could store every transaction a customer does with your company on a blockchain. You can store the stops a cargo container makes on a blockchain. While it might be overdoing it right now to use an advanced, secure technology to store transactions if you sell cat food, for instance, you could use blockchain to secure and authenticate the receipts you give customers for their cat food purchases. Many industries have clearer need for this level of security. For instance, let's say you're an app that helps consumers track their prescriptions. You can store patient records on a blockchain, so that patients have complete control over who has access to their health data—and, higher security for these sensitive records. Blockchain helps marketers who need to use consumer data for personalization to provide greater safety for that data while also ensuring higher accuracy.

Blockchains can also be used to share information with trusted third-party organizations such as auditors and regulatory agencies. As a result, companies can prove that they are adhering to corporate governance practices. While you don't need blockchain to be GDPR or CCPA compliant, blockchain can help you get there.

Blockchain helps brands and consumers manage the online use of their personal data, whether that be how or why it is collected, where it goes, or what information is passed on to third parties. Blockchain gives control back to the individual about their personal data and helps them determine who they want to have access to that information while also providing more transparency on where their data is going and how each party involved is using it. Marketers are just thinking about how to use this technology.

Key blockchain concepts

So how, exactly, does blockchain work? What does it do? In this section, you will get an overview of a few key blockchain terms in context. You can skip this section if you are not into technology.

The data stored on a blockchain can be made public or private depending on the owner's preferences. A public blockchain allows anyone to see the transactions recorded on it; its value is, in part, in its transparency. A private blockchain allows only authorized users to access it, such as your own employees.

How exactly does blockchain achieve its security and integrity? At the center of blockchain's secure protocols for managing user personal data protection is cryptography, which ensures that transactions are secure and cannot be tampered with. Blockchain provides a more transparent view of who sees what and makes it possible to track the transactions that occur in the network.

Implementing blockchain technology can help organizations protect their data's reliability and integrity. Here are some of the concepts you need to know to understand blockchain.

First, let's start with the distributed ledger. A distributed ledger is a tamper-resistant, shared, and replicated ledger that records information across all the nodes or members of a network. Basically, it is a set of multiple copies of the same data, stored on several different computers that are connected to each other. If someone tries to hack into any one computer or even steal an entire database, they cannot actually change anything because they would have to change the data on all of the ledgers in the blockchain throughout the entire network. The system also prevents anyone from trying to revert back and duplicate something that was already processed because it would show up as already used.

A blockchain can be used to provide an audit trail for data integrity because changes made by authorized users are cryptographically hashed and written down in an immutable fashion. A hash is a cryptographic representation of data that is of finite length. The hash created by authorized users would be stored, then linked to all previous hashes. This makes it very difficult for unauthorized parties to tamper with data that has already been stored without making a new entry on the ledger and invalidating. For example, if someone tried to change a customer record, that record's hash would change and the new record would not match up with all of the hashes on the other copies.

The security of a blockchain is based primarily on public key cryptography and digital signatures. Public key cryptography, as the name implies, uses different keys for encrypting and decrypting data. In a nutshell, something encrypted with one key can be decrypted only with the other—they are complementary.

Digital signatures add an extra layer of security on top of public key cryptography. Digital signatures provide a way for someone to prove their identity electronically, based on something they know (e.g. password), something they have (a certificate), and something that only the originating party possesses (e.g. private key).

Blockchain has many industry applications:

- **Banking and financial services:** blockchain can help reduce the cost of banking transactions and speed up settlement times. It can also be used to create digital currencies and manage customer identities.

- **Healthcare:** blockchain can be used to create tamper-proof medical records, streamline the healthcare data transfer process, and ensure the privacy of patient data.

- **Government:** blockchain can be used to manage digital identities, record land registry information, and track the movement of government funds.

- **Retail:** blockchain can be used to reduce fraudulent activities, streamline supply chain processes, and create more secure customer interactions.

- **Enterprise:** blockchain can help enterprises reduce the cost and complexity of doing business, streamline processes, and create more secure and transparent supply chains.

- **Education:** blockchain can be used to store academic records, grant digital degrees, and manage tuition payments.

- **Nonprofit:** blockchain can be used to manage donations, track the distribution of funds, and ensure that funds are spent only on authorized activities.

- **Personal:** blockchain can be used to store personal information, such as birth certificates, passports, and social security numbers. It can also be used to manage digital assets, such as music and video files.

- **Logistics:** a recent industry report from global consulting firm Accenture noted that blockchain technology could save shipping carriers as much as US $20 billion a year by reducing by 25 percent the time it takes to track and transport goods.

Okay, the technical part is over. Now, back to why you, as a marketer, need to know about blockchain.

Marketing and blockchain

There are some who think that blockchain has no applications with marketing. There are others who see potential in the technology.

As with everything new, it is hard to tell what will emerge (if anything) with any certainty. But time has taught us one thing: when you ignore something, you tend to lose out. Right now, you may want to stay informed and then decide how this technology might fit into your marketing strategy. On the following pages I will try to help you get a better idea of what blockchain is and where it might make sense for marketers.

You can use blockchain for a lot of different things but most importantly you can use it to create trust. For example, let's say you're a retailer and you want to make sure the products you are selling are actually coming from where you say they are. With blockchain, you can create a tamper-proof ledger of product origins that your customers can trust.

You can also use blockchain technology to create transparent supply chains. This could be valuable to your customers, who would be able to see where their products are coming from and how they are being made.

Another potential use for blockchain in marketing is to create digital currencies. For example, a restaurant could create its own currency and use it to reward customers for loyalty or as a way of accepting payments.

Some other applications for blockchain include:

- **Create more efficient customer loyalty programs:** for example, customers could earn rewards points that are stored on the blockchain and can be redeemed for products or services.
- **Tracking leads:** blockchain can be used to track leads from the time they are generated to the time they are converted into customers. This would allow businesses to see which marketing campaigns are most effective.
- **Managing digital rights:** blockchain can be used to manage digital rights and track the distribution of digital assets. This could be valuable for content creators, who could use blockchain to ensure that their work is being credited and paid for properly.
- **Reducing click fraud:** blockchain can be used to reduce click fraud, which is when clicks from bots are used to overcharge advertisers for clicks that were not from humans at all.
- **Creating unique collectibles:** NFTs, or non-fungible tokens, are a type of digital asset that is unique and tracked on the blockchain. Think of it as a signed limited edition, only virtual. This could be used to create digital collectibles, such as rare paintings or pieces of music. Some brands, such as Coach, are experimenting with NFT virtual products that are only available online. Brands that are based on exclusivity can use NFTs to create non-piratable, one-of-a-kind digital media that can become collectors' items.

As you can see, there are a number of potential applications for blockchain technology in marketing. It's still early days, so it's hard to say which of these applications will take off and which will fizzle out. But it is worth keeping an eye on blockchain and seeing how it could fit into your marketing strategy.

Conclusion

A range of regulations make using marketing metrics more complex than ever. Laws such as the GDPR and California Consumer Privacy Act (CCPA) have added new requirements for how data must be collected, used, and protected. As a marketer, it is important to stay up to date on these regulations and make sure you are in compliance.

The good news is that there are a number of frameworks that can be the tools to help you do this. Frameworks such as FIPPs, the Data Stewardship Elements, and the Privacy by Design Framework can help you collect, use, and protect data in a way that meets the requirements of these laws.

It is also important to remember that compliance is not a one-time event. You need to continually review your processes and make sure you are up to date on the latest regulations. By using frameworks and following best practices, you can help make sure your marketing is compliant with the latest regulations.

When it comes to digital advertising, data governance should include a consideration of the ethical principles of data privacy and consumer protection. Advertisers should ensure that their targeting strategies do not inadvertently violate these principles, and they should also take steps to protect the privacy of data subjects.

Blockchain promises new transparency, security, and reliability of data. It is still in its early days, but marketers should keep an eye on it and explore how it could be used in their campaigns. There are a number of potential applications for blockchain technology in marketing, including transparent supply chains, digital currencies, customer loyalty programs, and reducing click fraud.

FROM THE FIELD: MARK THOMPSON

Mark is Director of Research and Insights at International Association of Privacy Professionals (IAPP). In this role, Mark is focused on providing relevant, strategic, and pragmatic research and insights to the privacy community.

Prior to joining the IAPP, Mark was Global Lead for KPMG's Privacy Advisory Practice, which specializes in providing privacy-related support to global clients and the UK Cyber Risk and Regulation Lead.

Mark has supported 100+ global organizations on their privacy journeys, from small startup-based organizations that needed pragmatic and flexible structures to support innovation and business growth, to a large selection of global 100 organizations, processing hundreds of millions of customer records.

Mark has direct experience in multiple sectors including retail, telecommunications, media, pharmaceuticals, medical devices, clinical research, biotechnology, utilities, government, health services, manufacturing, travel services, public transport, aviation and financial services.

WHAT ARE SOME OF THE BIGGER TRENDS YOU ARE SEEING IN CONSUMER PRIVACY?

"That's a really, really good question. Going back to when I was at KPMG we did a piece of research, Crossing the Line. We surveyed about 6,900 people globally, looking at where the line was when something was creepy vs cool. So an example would be, you are driving down the road one day and the billboard on the right-hand side changes and shows customized ads based on the breakfast you had this morning: 60 percent of Chinese people thought it would be cool; 88 percent of Japanese people think it is creepy. So you immediately see a huge difference across demographics.

"When you talk about trends in consumer privacy there are a number of factors that feed into them. The first is awareness and market. How aware are individuals of what is actually being done with their data by an organization? I often asked the question when I was presenting to different organizations, 'Put your hand in the air if the organization you work for knows what they are doing with your personal information.' Generally people can't; they just don't know, because of the complexity, the volumes, and variety of data, the number of products and services; the scale and number of systems is massive. The secondary point is demographics. Everyone has different expectations in different countries, in different markets, of what is reasonable and acceptable use of data. So what a Swedish consumer would consider really critical is going to be different to what a British person does, even though they are both in Europe. An example is data on how much you get paid a year. If you ask a Swedish person, they will probably tell you because it's publicly available tax information. You ask a person in the UK the same question, whom you know really well and you're having a couple of drinks in the bar, they will probably tell you. Asking a Dutch person wouldn't have a great outcome because it can be considered quite an offensive thing to ask in the Netherlands. So you've got these different dynamics playing out in different markets because of consumers' expectations.

"So when you talk about trends, this has been wrapped up into massive variance across the world. One of the challenges we are seeing is due to the nature of globalized business and how everyone is trying to push through centralization. There is a push toward a one-size-fits-all, keep it simple, do it globally at scale approach. You are eventually running into this barrier, where something in one market had been fine, but in another market is considered very much not okay. Therefore, you are seeing this backdrop of increasing consumer protection issues, even class-action lawsuits. People are getting more and more uncomfortable with what is being done around data when they are utilizing a product or service."

THIS IS A VERY LOADED QUESTION. I GET IT A LOT FROM BOTH MANAGERS AND THE PUBLIC AT LARGE. WHAT ARE THE TYPES OF CONSUMER DATA ESPECIALLY WITH WHICH WE SHOULD BE MOST CAREFUL?

"The question organizations should be asking is the right mix an organization needs to have of data to create value, to maximize shareholder return, achieve strong profitability, differentiate services, and have great customer experience, whilst not having too great a risk. Interestingly enough, it is different in every single scenario, because the context is absolutely critical. If you think about a scale, if you have one side heavily weighted it will tip over and cause a mess.

"Let's take a really severe example: if I lose 10 email addresses in a data breach, would you consider that to be significant? While the majority of the time you go, well, some email addresses, it's not the end of the world. If you have 10 email addresses of a particular kind of very sensitive health clinic being released, that potentially can have a threat to life in certain countries. So you easily have the same piece of data having very different scales of harm playing out.

"So when you talk about what is one of the riskiest types of data, the answer is the data that is highly personalized to the individual. As you get closer and closer to the individual, and get into their likes, preferences, and other data classed as sensitive information categories under the GDPR and equivalent, there is increased risk. But again, having said that, back to my email example, something fairly innocuous can have a very significant harm basis.

"That harm perspective is really important. Because you have to think: what are the consequences of using this data? We are not just collecting data to look at it and say, 'Oh, we have all of this data.' That impact is not just on the company's bottom line and our finances. It's also important to look at the impact on the consumer, as well."

DO YOU HAVE ANY EXAMPLES OF COMPANIES THAT ARE DOING A GREAT JOB OF RESPECTING
THEIR CUSTOMERS' PRIVACY? WHO IS WINNING AT THIS? WHO IS DOING A GREAT JOB?

"I can't call out companies so I'll share examples of what organizations are doing well,
and what they could be doing better. So we talked about harm. It's a fascinating topic,
because every single jurisdiction quantifies harm differently. There's also the question
of when someone is harmed mentally as a result of the data-related harm that
occurred.

"How do you quantify that and how do you measure that and is that harm covered
under any legal framework that exists?

"Financial harm can be quantified, but what about embarrassment, or other issues?
There are numerous ways individuals can be harmed, but a lot of them are quite hard
to quantify in a way that would play out in the regulatory space as something that you
could take action against.

"So that is a particular issue, which is creating a lot of challenges in a lot of markets.
We talk about organizations and what they can do to improve customer relationships.
I think transparency is number one. The clearer you are, the better it is. Here's an
example. If I were to ask you who you trust the most. You're going to say my mom, my
dad, my husband, wife, children, your best friend. Why? The reason you trust them is
because they behave like you're expected to behave in given scenarios. And the trust
of organizations is no different. You trust organizations that are going to behave in a
way you expect them to. Now, ironically, the more that you trust individuals, the more
they can behave like you, the more data they need about you. So in an organization
context, if you don't have that dataset, it's actually much harder to build that trust
environment. But transparency is really important because if you are transparent, and
you really understand who you are interacting with, and you can behave in a way that
is expected, then there is going to be increased trust toward that organization.

"And you can see some organizations really trying to be hugely transparent by
standing up at customer trust centers, really trying to tell everyone what they are
doing, giving real-time access to their data, and letting consumers delete their account
with a few clicks. Other companies, it is hard to tell what they are doing, what their
websites are saying, or what their public statements are saying. When you want to
delete your data they hold, it is very hard to find it or they make it extremely inconvenient. Some business models are built on leveraging more personal information. So
there are a wide spectrum of approaches."

WHAT IS YOUR ADVICE TO SOMEONE WHOSE JOB IT IS TO USE CUSTOMER DATA? HOW
SHOULD THEY LEARN THEIR CUSTOMERS' PREFERENCES? THE FIRST STEP TO TRANSPARENCY
IS EMPATHY AND UNDERSTANDING WHAT THE CONSUMER EXPECTATIONS ARE. AND YOU
TALKED ABOUT HOW DIVERSE THOSE EXPECTATIONS ARE. HOW DO WE BEGIN TO LEARN FOR
OUR CONSUMERS?

"This is a really good question. Let's take a tangible example. I worked for a digital
television provider, and they are gathering every single button click, tracking how long
you are fast forwarding and how long after purchasing a movie you actually watched
it. Did you watch the whole movie?

"Everything the brand wanted was captured. For some of that data, the company
had to get consent. So they wrote a consent form, put it on their platform, and then
did market research and realized that 20 percent of people would opt in and 80
percent of people would opt out.

"But we spent time with them and said, 'Look, if you're an individual who reads
that, what would you think?' It's really, really complicated legalese; you struggle to
understand what is being written. So we worked with their marketing team, their
customer team, and we wrote this really clear, very short transparent statement with
a nice green button for Yes and a red button for No. Opt-ins rose to over 90 percent.
We made the platform reliable. So there is this belief that people will say no when you
ask them for their personal data, and that is not strictly true, people will say yes, if
they understand it, and they feel it adds value, and they feel they have got the ability
to control it or turn it on and off as they want. What people struggle with is having no
control.

"Getting to that trust dynamic is a challenge. As a marketer, how do you do that?
It's really difficult. You often have very, very limited space where you can interact with
an individual, whether it's a phone screen or a PC screen. Sometimes you have literally
no ability to interact with them; they are just filling in a bit of data or actually data is
being provided passively. So, the number one thing for a marketer is to try to put
yourself in the position of the consumer. How would you feel if that was you? That
personal element is key.

"There is no quantification of data as an asset. People cannot tell you how much an
email address is worth or a postcode or zip code is worth. They can tell you a customer
record is worth X. It becomes a thing that people use, without understanding its value.
Picture a Ferrari over there. You would make sure you insure it, make sure you wash
it, make sure you put an alarm on it and a tracker, and that it's locked up at night
where there is a security guard. Brands need to understand the tangible value of
consumer data, its importance, and how critical a data asset is. If they have that
respect for data, they will protect it in the right way and use it in the right way. They
don't end up running the risk of using a Ferrari the way you would use a pushbike."

THAT IS LEADING VERY NICELY TO MY NEXT QUESTION, WHICH IS: WE ARE UNDER PRESSURE TO DELIVER MORE AND MORE ROI; MARKETERS DREAM OF CAMPAIGNS THAT ARE PRECISELY MICROTARGETED AND TRACKED TO THE NEAREST CLICK AND DOLLAR SPENT BY THE CONSUMER. WE ALSO HAVE NEW PRESSURES DUE TO THE LOSS OF THIRD-PARTY COOKIES. I KNOW COOKIELESS WORLD IS A GROSS OVERSIMPLIFICATION OF WHAT IS ACTUALLY HAPPENING. BUT WE'RE UNDER PRESSURE TO GRAB AS MUCH DATA AS WE CAN BECAUSE THERE IS THIS PERCEPTION THAT DATA IS GOING AWAY BECAUSE OF THE THIRD-PARTY COOKIE DEPRECATION. HOW CAN WE AS MARKETERS WHO ARE IN BETWEEN THIS DEBATE BETWEEN PRIVACY ON THE ONE HAND AND ROI ON THE OTHER CONTINUE TO LEVERAGE CONSUMER DATA BUT DO IT IN A PRIVACY-FRIENDLY WAY?

"I have another analogy: what's better—to have two pieces of data worth US $500 each, or 100 pieces of data worth $1 each? The first gives a better return on investment. And because organizations are not quantifying the value of the individual data assets, they are defaulting to just gathering everything. The more you gather, the more risk. There is this intrinsic belief that the more data we have, the more insight and analytics we have, but actually the more data we have, the more complexities there are to doing analytics, because there are so many different datapoints. Some data are accurate, some are inaccurate, modeling gets more complicated and bigger and bigger, and so on.

"What matters most from a data perspective are the four or five datapoints that actually are going to deliver a return on investment. An accurate email address with someone's salary information may be vital for a mobile phone company. The date when someone gets their bonus each year may be huge for an automotive dealership because they know people buy cars when bonuses are paid. You market to them at that point in time. Other data, though, like their color preferences, may not be essential.

"So focusing on what is the critical, most important data that really adds the most value is the first thing. The second way to enhance privacy becomes possible at scale. There are loads of different types of privacy-enhancing technology. There is synthetic data, which effectively takes a dataset and by complicated mathematical principles it generates a completely different dataset, but when you analyze it, it will produce the same outputs. So the utility of the data is maintained. There are other ones that will enable you to run analytics across tokenized, encrypted datasets—again, maintaining utility. There are loads of different techniques out there that can be utilized. Again, some of them are easier to implement than others. Some of them are more complex than others to manage and run at scale. But you can implement so many technologies.

"The other thing I'll say as a practical perspective, is always try to start with a smaller dataset and build up. Many brands collect a big dataset, and then try to work out what they need, rather than saying, 'What are the minimum datasets we think we need?'

"Think about what data you need and build out as you identify missing elements, rather than gathering unnecessary data. It can take longer, it can be more complicated. It can be a little bit duplicative at times, but again, that's another way you can try to enhance and manage privacy."

WONDERFUL ADVICE. IS THERE ANYTHING THAT WE'VE MISSED? FINAL ADVICE FOR MARKETERS WHO CARE ABOUT PRIVACY WHO CARE ABOUT DATA ETHICS?

"People have always tried, since the dawn of time, to sell people the right products or services to make their lives better, simpler, more efficient. It's no different today— whether you walk into a shop, go to a car sales showroom and talk to sales staff, or go to buy a phone for yourself on the internet. People are trying to understand your needs, your wants, your desires, so they can meet them with a product or service. That principle has always been there. What has fundamentally changed is the way in which we are trying to gather data.

"Talking about cookies as well, we still have so many means of tracking, from IP addresses to digital fingerprinting; there are other ways to track other than cookies, so I don't see tracking going away. What I also don't see going away is the basic need for people to understand their customers' needs and expectations so they can fulfill them in the most efficient way. So I think, again, the balance question is key. Think about how you as an organization strive to get that right balance between those two, to make sure that you are kind of maintaining the trust of the customer long-term.

"I like the idea of building on small datasets. I think it's very counterintuitive based on what I'm seeing in most organizations. But I think it's really important to start small. And you probably don't need to know what your car purchaser ate for breakfast. It doesn't have any impact on what they want to buy."

12

Building dashboards and data evangelism

The importance of data evangelism

Organizations are increasingly looking to data-driven decision making to help them stay competitive. However, many of these organizations do not have the right tools or skills in place to make the most of their data. This is where data evangelism comes in.

Data evangelism is the process of teaching people how to use data effectively, leadership in data-driven decision making, and creating a data-driven culture within an organization. This is important because data can be overwhelming if you don't know how to use it. Data evangelism can help people make the most of their data by teaching them how to ask the right questions, find the right data, and use that data to make daily improvements in both business operations and strategy.

Why do it? There are many reasons to engage in data evangelism, but some of the most common include:

- to help people make better decisions
- to improve business processes or operations
- to enable innovation

An organization with a data evangelist is one that has leaders who can make data-driven decisions, employees who are able to use data to improve their work, and a corporate culture that values data-driven decision making. This can be a powerful tool for organizations looking to stay competitive in the modern business world.

As a marketer, you are in a uniquely strong position to become that data evangelist. Why? Because you understand the business value of data and you have the skills to turn data into insights. You also have a good understanding of how data can be used to improve marketing efforts. You have your finger on the pulse of most of the metrics your organization needs to grow: the voice of the customer, the competitive landscape, and the newest industry trends. You are also best placed to disseminate this data across the organization, since internal communications can fall under your purview. Finally, you are able to synthesize data on finance, UX, product R&D, and other vital data types across your organization.

So, don't be afraid to evangelize data within your organization. It can make a big difference in the way your company operates and the decisions it makes. In this chapter, we learn the leadership tactics that will transform your organization into a metrics-driven one.

Democratizing data

The first step in building a data culture is democratizing your data. What does that mean? It means that metrics are broken out of their silos and that everyone in your organization has at least some access to quality data in their daily jobs. Why is this important? For one thing, you cannot use metrics to drive your organization forward if you are the only person or your department is the only group that believes in them. You also cannot communicate metrics-informed decisions to stakeholders who don't understand the metrics underlying those decisions. Without everyone on board with metrics in your organization, data becomes just another opaque driver of management decisions. In today's transparent workplace, that just won't do.

On the flipside, everyone in your organization can do their jobs better with data. Giving people access to data means they can answer questions about their work, improve their processes, and even find new opportunities for innovation. When everyone has access to data, the organization becomes more nimble and can quickly adapt to changes in the market. Analytical skills are also among the top in-demand abilities for workers today. According to research from Indeed.com, analytical skills rank near the top of the 15 most in-demand skills for the decade. Democratizing data ensures that your workforce learns these essential skills across any job function. Finally, data is cool. People get excited when empowered with numbers that show the impact of their work. It motivates them. It gives their work meaning. Data democracy is more than just a driver of efficiency—it's a way to build a smarter, empowered workforce.

Data democracy is built on three pillars:

- self-service metrics
- functional dashboards
- training for success

Let's explore each of those pillars in detail.

Self-service metrics and data discovery: everyone an analyst?

Counterintuitively, the first step in leading your organization's metrics transformation is to let go of your department's centralized role in some ways. This is because successful data-driven cultures rely on the democratization of data access and analysis. In order to achieve this, self-service metrics and data discovery tools must be widely adopted.

This doesn't mean that you have to step back; it is still important to act as a steward for your organization's data and analytics infrastructure. But by empowering business users to take control of their data and analysis, you will create a culture of data-driven decision making that permeates every corner of your organization. Your role should be to guide the data strategy, not be your organization's "numbers cruncher," or "chart maker."

The benefits of data democratization are clear. When everyone has access to data, they can identify new opportunities and problems and propose solutions. This type of thinking is essential for organizations looking to be truly metrics-driven. The first step in data democratization is setting up self-service data programs.

Why self-service data is important

Teaching your teams to be more independent in sourcing data is critical. Not only will they feel more ownership over their metrics, but they will also be able to ask more informed questions of the data and the business intelligence (BI) team. As datasets grow, it becomes ever more important for business users to have some ability to explore that data on their own.

One of the biggest benefits of self-service data is that it can help to shift the focus of decision making away from gut feel and toward actual data. One of the things we have noticed is that, if users only see data in dashboards or presentations, they often make note of it, but continue to make decisions without it. Data becomes just another meeting with pretty pictures, rather than a true source of insight.

With good data at their fingertips, business users also have more trust in metrics. They can see that the numbers are coming from somewhere and that they are not being manipulated. This increased trust can help to make BI teams more influential within the company.

They are also able to more easily identify correlations and trends in the data, which can lead to better business decisions. They can look back as far as they need to, examine the data through different filters and views, and see patterns through the lens of their own expertise. That's the final and most important reason self-serve data is critical. It brings more perspectives from different departments to data interpretation, which leads to better decision making.

In short, implementing self-serve data is the first step in leading your organization to a data-driven culture. Creating a data-driven culture within your company is critical for success with BI and analytics. It is not enough to simply have the technology and the data; you also need people who are comfortable working with that data and exploring it for insights.

All of these benefits are why self-service data is so important. So how do you implement it?

- **Identify self-service tools:** the first step is to identify which tools are available for business users to explore data on their own. Chances are, your team is already using a variety of tools such as Tableau, Qlik, and Spotfire. However, you may need to adapt your toolset to the needs of users with differing skills. Many of these tools allow you to create views of varying complexity, so you can probably use the same toolset. It is best to limit self-service to a single tool for most users, with user roles defined to view-only in some cases. You are providing informational access but not necessarily giving everyone full access to all data.

- **Train users on how to use the tools:** once you have identified the tools it is important to train users on how to use them. This includes both basic training on how to navigate the tool and more in-depth training on how to find insights in the data. We will talk about tactics for doing this later in the chapter.

- **Create datasets that business users can explore:** the final step is to create datasets that business users can explore. This may include data from your internal systems as well as data from external sources. You will want to make sure that the data is accessible and easy to use, so business users can get started right away.

- **Maintain an open door:** one of the most important things to keep in mind is that self-service data is a continuous process. You will need to be constantly adding new datasets and training users on how to use the tools. It is also important to maintain an open-door policy, so business users can come to you with any questions or problems they encounter.

- **Keep the training going:** training is not a "one and done" affair. As your company's data and BI tools evolve, so too will the training required to use them. Make sure you have a plan in place to keep training up to date.

Making data available to business users is the first step in creating a data-driven culture within your company. However, simply giving users access to data is not enough. You also need to provide training on how to use the tools and create a mindset of data-driven thinking. With a solid foundation, your company stands a greater chance of success in transitioning to a metrics-focused way of doing things.

Dashboarding

Now that we are on the path to a democratized, evangelized data culture, we need to get smart about tactics. Central to the ways in which organizations consume metrics are dashboards. They can be the critical entry point to self-service data; they are also the primary way that teams communicate their data to stakeholders across the organization.

Organizations are data-rich but time-poor. The pressure is on to make data digestible and actionable without sacrificing detail. This is the challenge that marketing metrics teams face when it comes to dashboard design. It's not simply a matter of displaying metrics in an easy-to-read format; it's also about telling a story with data. It's mostly about translating business goals into metrics. Throughout the book, we have talked about just that. For instance, let's say you work for a chain of car washes. The company's goal is to "be the most trusted carwash brand in the northeast." What does that mean in terms of metrics?

When it comes to data evangelism, dashboards are essential. They provide an easy way for business users to explore data and find insights. When done correctly, they can be a powerful communication tool for stakeholders across the organization.

Types of dashboards

There are different types of dashboards for different types of people. In our practice, we divide dashboards into two main kinds: strategic and operational.

Strategic dashboards are used by executives and other leaders to understand how the organization is performing overall. They typically contain high-level metrics and trends, as well as information about specific business areas or initiatives.

Operational dashboards are used by managers and team members to track the progress of specific tasks or projects. They typically contain data about individual goals, objectives, and tasks, as well as information about the team or organization as a whole. Since operational dashboards are for people who need to stay on top of day-to-day operations, they are equally about managing access to data as they are for presenting key metrics.

Both types of dashboards are important, and each has its own set of best practices.

Best practices for strategic dashboards

The strategic dashboard is the high-level single version of the truth. It is the common ground on which the teams doing the frontline work and executives meet to know the status and impact of your marketing initiatives. When creating a strategic dashboard, there are a few key best practices to keep in mind:

- **Keep it simple:** the goal of a strategic dashboard is to provide a high-level overview of the organization's performance. So, keep it simple and avoid cluttering the dashboard with too much information.

- **Focus on the key metrics:** there are certain key metrics that executives and other leaders need to track in order to understand how the organization is performing. Make sure that you have complete agreement on the KPIs that your leadership or clients want to track, and focus in on them.

- **Use top-notch visuals:** a picture is worth a thousand words, and the same is true for dashboards. Make sure to use visuals to help explain the data and make it easy to understand. Keep charts simple, with limited but clear labels, broad categories, and on-brand colors. You want your visual to be reflective of your organization's brand in order to signal alignment with its goals.

- **Tell a story:** the data on your dashboard should tell a story about how the organization is performing. Think about how you can use the data to create a narrative about how the organization is doing.

- **Deep-dives:** occasionally, you will want to dive deeper into a particular metric. For example, you might want to look at the performance of a specific campaign over time. Having a deep-dive section on your dashboard allows you to do just that.

- **Keep it up to date:** as the organization changes, so too will the data on the dashboard. Make sure to update the dashboard regularly to reflect the latest information.

A strategic dashboard should be one of the main ways you communicate data to external stakeholders. While informal conversations, Excel sheets, and emails are good for quick feedback, you want to have a clear, consistent, substantive ground truth for major metrics conversations. Image is part of data evangelism. So, too, is signaling a professional approach to your metrics. Dashboards ensure a consistent view of the data, which reduces uncertainty. That in turn keeps the focus where it should be: on making decisions based on what the metrics say.

Best practices for operational dashboards

An operational dashboard is a quick view into the data that marketing teams need to know on a day-to-day basis. It should be task-based, use real-time data, be concise, and easy to navigate. When creating an operational dashboard, remember to make it easy to access the data sources you are using. When creating an operational dashboard, keep in mind:

- **Make it task-based:** the goal of an operational dashboard is to help managers and team members track the progress of specific tasks or projects. So, make sure to organize the dashboard by task or project, and use clear visuals to help explain the data.

- **Use real-time data:** operational dashboards should always use up-to-date data so that managers can make timely decisions. Most tools today, such as Data Studio, make it easy to connect "live" data to a dashboarding tool, ensuring that the data you see is mere seconds or minutes old.

- **Keep it concise:** managers need to be able to quickly scan the dashboard and get a sense of how a campaign is progressing. So, keep the dashboard concise and avoid cluttering it with too much information.

- **Link to tools:** when it comes to taking a deep dive into the metrics, most employees responsible for day-to-day marketing prefer to go to the source. A strategic dashboard should filter even the deep-dive data; in an operational dashboard, there is no need to pull in deep-dive metrics at all. Instead, make it quick to go straight to the source data from within the dashboard. For instance, web analytics data in the dashboard should have a quick link taking users straight to Google Analytics.

- **Design for quick thinking:** reduce cognitive load by making it easy to see actionable data at a glance. This can reduce potential errors, while speeding up time-to-decision. Use color to highlight important data on a dashboard. Use colors that are easy to see and that make sense for the data you are displaying. Make important data larger. Place labels above or to the side of data visuals, rather than below them.

Operational dashboards are an easy way to glimpse the key metrics you're monitoring all in one place, for faster decision making. The goal is to make it easy to see how tasks are progressing and where potential bottlenecks may appear. The dashboard should be tailored to your needs, use real-time data, and be concise and easy to navigate. It is not meant to replace your channel data tools. Rather, it is an efficient way into your channel and campaign data.

You should plan on several operational dashboards. For example, one dashboard per social media platform, one for email marketing, and one for website analytics. This will keep the data easy to digest and help you make decisions quickly. It also gives people just the data they need. If you are running a multi-channel campaign, create a dashboard to track it, too. Pulling in data from all the channels on which the campaign is running, it gives you all your campaign metrics, from clickthroughs to qualified leads, all in one place. Once the campaign is done, reports can be pulled easily from the dashboard tool for a campaign retrospective report.

Creating a library of past campaign reports can, in turn, be a great tool for organizational learning. You can create trainings around what campaigns generated the best results, look at pitfalls to avoid, and have a cookbook of tactics with the data to back them up from past successes. If you know that a particular strategy delivers high ROI, you can use that data to duplicate your earlier success for your next campaign.

For instance, let's say you're building a virtual reality campaign for SandWish; customers will be able to hold their phones in front of any food and get a sandwich recipe that includes that food. You already know from your past campaign reports that Keto, gluten-free, and vegan recipes convert the highest on other channels, such as social media. With this information from your past campaign reports, which are all built from your campaign dashboards, you prioritize these types of recipes. The augmented reality (AR) application is a hit, increasing new subscriptions by 10 percent. Creating campaign dashboards streamlines not only campaign management, but also accelerates identification of your best messages, calls to action, content themes, creative, and other campaign elements.

Marketing management dashboards

One operational dashboard that you must have is the marketing management dashboard. It's a high-level view of all your marketing activities and performance. The goal of this dashboard is to help you quickly answer questions such as:

- How are our overall marketing efforts performing?
- Which channels are generating the most leads?
- What content is being shared the most?

The marketing management dashboard should be tailored to your needs, providing a high-level operational "command center" from which to manage daily marketing activities. It's not a strategic dashboard, but it's more high-level than a campaign-focused or channel-focused operational dashboard.

There are endless possibilities for what a marketing management dashboard could look like. However, let's outline some of the more essential components that should be included in any marketing dashboard:

- **Topline data story:** the top metrics that you want to look at every day. They could be anything from website visits, to newsletter signups, or even sales revenue.

- **Marketing funnel:** this should give you a visual representation of how leads are moving through your marketing funnel. It is essential to have a good understanding of where your leads are coming from, and where they are flowing.

- **Campaign performance:** this is data on how your marketing campaigns are performing. This could include data on website visits, email opens and clicks, social media engagement, and other campaign measurements.

- **Organizational performance:** this is data on how the entirety of your organization is performing. For example, you might track revenue, market share, or customer satisfaction against company KPI targets.

In building your marketing management dashboard, think about what you need to see first thing Monday morning when you plan your week. What are the topline metrics that you need to act on? What campaigns need more attention? What channels are falling short?

The marketing management dashboard is a critical tool for any marketer. It gives you a high-level overview of your marketing performance, so you can quickly identify and address any issues.

Building your dashboards: tips for success

Now that you know the basic language of dashboards, it is time to learn how to build them. Having a repeatable system in place for dashboard building ensures the consistency that builds trust. It also allows you to build more in less time.

Here are some key points to remember when creating any dashboard:

- **The first step is understanding your data.** What are the key metrics you want to track? Once you have a list of metrics, you can begin to design your dashboard.

- **Articulate your goals.** What are the key performance indicators (KPIs) that you want to track? What questions do you need answered?

- **Identify the data sources you need.** In order to track your data, you need to know where it comes from. This might include data from your website analytics, marketing automation platform, social media listening tool, or CRM.

- **Describe the target audience.** Is this a dashboard for executive management, marketing staff, or other stakeholders?

- **Consider how you want to organize your data.** Most dashboards are organized by time, so you can see how metrics change over different periods of time. You can also organize data by category, so you can see all the metrics for a particular campaign or social media platform together.

- **Design your dashboard layout.** Once you have your data sources identified, it's time to start designing the look and feel of your dashboard.

- **Dashboards should be easy to read and understand at a glance.** Try not to include too much data on one dashboard. If you have too much data, it will be difficult to see relationships and trends. Less is more.

- **Make sure you test your dashboard before rolling it out to everyone.** Get feedback from colleagues and make sure the dashboard is easy to use and understand.

The flowchart in Figure 12.1 is a guide to crafting dashboards. Use it to create a repeatable process for yourself, so you can build high-quality dashboards in less time. Remember, this is just a guide. You can add steps, combine them, or remove the ones that don't resonate. For instance, if right now you are only building dashboards for your own team, you already know the target audience. It is important to have a system that works for you. You can always change it later.

FIGURE 12.1   Creating the right dashboards

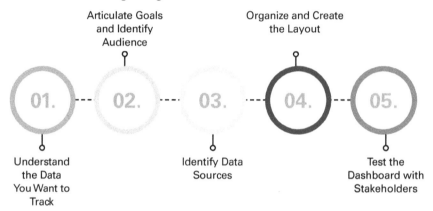

The importance of context

One of the biggest problems with dashboards is that they can be very easy to misinterpret without proper context. They can be especially challenging when presenting to stakeholders outside your program, as they can easily lead to wrong conclusions. For example, take a metric like customer churn. If you only have the churn rate, you might not know if it's good or bad. However, if you have historical data on churn going back, say, 18 months, you can see if the churn rate is getting better or worse.

In order to avoid misinterpretations, always provide context for your data. This could be anything from data on historical performance, to comparisons against industry benchmarks or company targets.

Another way to mitigate misunderstanding is to always include a narrative with your dashboards. This will help explain the data in context and provide additional insights that might not be apparent from the dashboard itself. For example, you could include a sentence or two beside each metric that explains what it means and why it is important.

You can also provide context by including more detailed explanatory notes directly on the dashboard. This can be especially helpful when you have a lot of data to present. It is also a good way to prevent stakeholders from misinterpreting your data.

A really effective way to add context is by including charts and graphs that compare your data against past performance or industry benchmarks. This can help provide a more complete understanding of how your organization is performing. Indeed, benchmarking has been the best way to contextualize data in most of our work at Thoughtlight. For instance, we were working with a university on their email outreach to their stakeholders. We built their email list from 100 subscribers to several thousand, which can often drive down open rates. We stayed vigilant, however, using metrics to maintain high performance of the email program. Our tactics were strict hygiene, A/B subject line testing, and weekly click metrics reviews. Open rate percentages remained in the 40s, garnering us an award and the client record-breaking event attendance. They were pleased, of course. But when we shared that typical open rate percentages in education are in the 20s, they realized both the true value of the services we were providing and the deep regard with which their stakeholders viewed them.

Bringing in benchmarks can show not just how you are doing, but how you compare to the rest of your industry. They mean the difference between guessing what your metrics mean to knowing the full picture, including what actions are indicated by the data. For instance, if we see open rates drop on a single email, we know to keep an eye on opens, but that taking dramatic action may be harmful, since opens are still extremely high. We can protect our success through continued testing, list hygiene, and click analysis, while avoiding changing course too much or too soon. Knowing our benchmarks is key to this analysis.

The dashboard dilemma: too much data or not enough?

When it comes to dashboards, there is often too much data or not enough. On one hand, you want to include all of the relevant data in order to give a complete picture. On the other hand, if you include too much data, it can be difficult to understand and can obscure the most important metrics.

The key is to find the right balance. You don't want to include so much data that it is difficult to understand or provide so little that meetings get derailed by teams scrambling to pull data that is needed for a discussion in the middle of the meeting.

This dilemma can be solved in a few ways:

- Ask what actions each metric informs. Does it tell us whether or not we're on track to achieve our goal? Does it look backwards, telling us about past performance, or can it contribute to learning what we need to do moving forward? For example, is open rate a good metric to look at if we want to know how successful our email program is?

- For strategic dashboards, focus on metrics closest to long-term company-wide goals. This can be done by focusing on KPIs or by selecting a limited number of metrics to track over time. This will help you focus on the most important information.

- Include trend data whenever possible. This will help give a more complete picture and show how the organization is performing over time.

- Prioritize data for which you have benchmarks. Whether internal or external, benchmarks help you contextualize your data, which in turn lets you understand what actions to take next. Internal benchmarks can be data on past performance, while external ones come from industry reports, analyst content, and other larger studies.

- Look for redundancy when measuring a single KPI. For instance, you may not need to measure conversions and bounce rates in a single dashboard to track customer acquisition. Conversions may be enough.

- Provide those deep-dive tabs. When in doubt whether data is needed, you can provide it on a secondary tab to which you can refer as needed.

When designing a dashboard, make sure you focus on the most important metrics and avoid cluttering the screen with too much information. By following these tips, you can create a dashboard that is both informative and easy to understand.

How to create your own dashboard

Okay, so you have created a comprehensive set of dashboards for operational excellence. Your strategic dashboard has your C suite excited about metrics. Yet, you have your own unique metrics that are important to just your job. For instance, say that you are the influencer marketing manager at SandWish. You alone need to track the results from each individual influencer partnership, including reach, sentiment, and revenue. This data currently lives in your influencer marketing platform, social media tool, and CRM. While you can certainly go straight to each source, it would be ideal to have all your metrics handy. Can you create a dashboard just for yourself? Of course! Creating your own dashboard is a great way to get more out of your data. Not only will it help you understand your data better, but it can also help you track important metrics over time.

Using dashboards to drive business results

Many organizations use dashboards to track business results. This could include anything from sales data to customer satisfaction metrics. By tracking these metrics over time, you can see how your organization is performing and identify areas where you need to make changes. The key to making dashboards work is to stay focused on goals for each dashboard.

Focus on the most important metrics. This is especially the case when it comes to making strategic decisions about the bigger picture—how to grow and improve your business. Indeed, I would argue that C suite management should not be looking at operational data on the campaign and channel level daily, or even weekly. That is a sure sign of micromanagement, an indicator that marketing is not viewed as a strategic initiative, but rather a mere set of tactics, not led by marketing professionals but under the daily management of those outside marketing—and marketing decisions made by amateurs in marketing are a recipe for disaster. In a healthy organization, teams are trusted to do their work within their areas of expertise, and are measured on results, not micromanaged at the task level.

Don't go dashboard-crazy. Teams can spend more time on dashboards than on acting on them. Dashboards can become "kid in a candy store" exercises and lead to data overload.

Training for metrics success

Every metrics success story starts with building the skills your team needs. You need the data literacy to be able to use the dashboard, as well as understand what it is telling you. But even if your team has these skills, that doesn't mean they know how to use the data to improve their work. That's where training comes in:

- Make it relevant. Adults learn best when a skill being taught is relevant to their work. So, when teaching people how to use data, make sure the examples you use are relevant to their work. This may mean you have to give customized sessions to different departments at times. This can be done efficiently. For example, your UX team may care most about how to access consumer sentiment data, while finance may need to know how to track ROAS. Look for what information all teams need, focusing most of your training on it. Then, host short sessions with specific teams to connect organizational data to what is relevant to them.

- Get practical quickly. Adults also learn best when they are able to practice what they have learned. So, make sure your training includes plenty of opportunities for people to try out what they have learned.

- Scaffold. In education, we use the term scaffolding to refer to the support we give learners as they develop new skills. This support might include providing a model for the skill, doing a skill partially and then handing it to the learner to complete with your help, and doing skills together at first. For instance, you might show a group how to create a pivot table, then start one, select the first field and have the students select the rest and finish the table, and finally, stand by to help as they create one themselves from start to finish. That builds confidence, speeding the time to learn a task.

- Make it fun. Adults learn best when they are enjoying themselves. So, make sure your training is enjoyable and engaging.

- Determine the balance of technical and business skills needed. For example, finance already understands spreadsheets, statistical analysis, and other technical skills. What they may need help learning is how marketing data provides them with strategic insights into revenue forecasts. So, when training this team, focus on teaching them business skills that they need.

- Train on problem-solving rather than button-pushing. Tools change all the time. If your team only knows how to use a platform by rote, they will not be able to use the tools after inevitable updates. Teach them how to try different features, assess results, and use documentation.

- Teach your team how to ask the right questions and use data to answer them.

- Finally, make sure you include everyone who needs to be part of the learning process. This might include people in different roles or at different levels within the organization. It can be difficult to find time for everyone on a regular basis, but periodic sessions can help everyone stay up to date. Asynchronous learning, like short videos, job aids, and simulations are also a good way to get training to more colleagues. If you do use videos, make them under seven minutes, focused on a single concept. Research has shown this length to be ideal for memory retention. Shorter is better.

The goal is to make sure everyone has the skills they need to use data effectively to improve their work. And, importantly, that everyone enjoys learning and using data!

Conclusion

One of the best ways to get buy-in for data-driven decision making is to evangelize data within your organization. This means going beyond simply collecting and reporting data; you need to make data a fundamental part of your organization's culture. Data evangelism is essential for any company looking to become more data-driven. Marketers are well-positioned as evangelists because they touch on all of an organization's growth-leading data. They need to be able to use data to inform their decisions, understand how data can be used to improve the customer experience, and know how to use data to measure the effectiveness of their campaigns. To bridge these skills into a role as your organization's data evangelist, you need to democratize the use of data, create data-driven dashboards that are easy to understand and make use of, and be able to translate business needs into data requirements.

This involves building data literacy within your team, making sure everyone has the skills they need to use data effectively. It also means making training enjoyable and engaging, so people will want to learn. Finally, it is important to include everyone in the metrics process, to maintain trust in the metrics.

With these skills in place, you will be well on your way to evangelizing data within your company and making data-driven decisions the new norm.

Finally, make sure you enjoy learning and using data yourself! This will ensure that you are an effective evangelist for data within your organization.

FROM THE FIELD: JULIE PREISS

Julie Preiss is a renowned full-stack marketing leader with extensive B2B experience. Currently Chief Marketing Officer at Appgate, she shared with us how she consolidates data to make metrics-driven decisions, evangelizes data, and uses cross-functional data. Her experience provides guidance for anyone looking to become a data evangelist.

WHAT METRICS DO YOU LOOK AT MOST OFTEN? (SOCIAL MEDIA, EMAIL, WEB ANALYTICS, PAID SEARCH, SEO DATA, RANKING, POPULAR KEYWORDS, CONTENT MARKETING METRICS, BLOG POSTS COMMENTS AND SHARES ETC., OR OTHERS...)

"Marketing metrics are tricky—part art, part science, and always changing. I think it is important to tell a story through your metrics to help stakeholders see the big picture.

"I look at many traditional metrics monthly, including top organic and paid keyword search, website traffic trends, email click-through rate (CTR) and click to open rate (CTOR), video view-through rate (VTR), social media followers/shares, conversion rates for chatbot conversations, demos, campaign calls to action (CTAs), and landing pages. Of course, I also track marketing qualified leads (MQLs), sales accepted leads (SALs), sales qualified leads (SQLs), and opportunities created and won/lost. These provide perspective on the impact of daily, always-on activities on individual leads. However, they don't provide insight into account-level activity, which is important in B2B high-tech marketing where most buying is done by committee. A buying committee includes multiple people who have different roles in the decision process. Isolating a single person's activity is not as meaningful as understanding what the entire buying team is doing. This is why I leverage rich data from our account-based marketing (ABM) platform to understand engagement with our target accounts. Important metrics include account CTR and account VTR for targeted campaigns, newly engaged accounts, accounts with increased engagement, accounts engaged by sales, accounts reached by sales, and opportunities created and won/lost.

"With so much data available, it can become overwhelming. At the end of the day, what matters most is understanding how and why a prospect becomes an opportunity, what interactions progress them through the funnel, and what percentage ultimately buy from you. Metrics are critical to the process and need to provide a holistic view or we risk making decisions based on incomplete or irrelevant data."

WHAT ABOUT A TIME YOU LOOKED AT METRICS AND LEARNED SOMETHING INTERESTING ABOUT HOW WELL YOUR MARKETING IS WORKING. IN TWO OR THREE PARAGRAPHS, COULD YOU PLEASE SHARE WHAT METRICS YOU LOOKED AT, WHAT YOU THOUGHT ABOUT THOSE METRICS, AND WHY YOU LOOKED AT THEM.

"With so many metrics to consider, isolating an 'ah-ha' moment is tough but one comes to mind. In the middle of the Covid pandemic, we noticed an important trend when it came to video content consumption. We had much better engagement and conversions on social media posts and campaigns that included video, which isn't surprising given the environment, for a couple of reasons.

"First, face-to-face selling disappeared overnight so people turned to video, whether live or on-demand, for that human interaction. Second, B2B buyers were already moving toward a self-serve model, consuming vast amounts of content before ever engaging with sales. Rich video content makes it even easier to educate yourself about a company and its products before taking the next step. Watching a video is 'low risk' and allows the buyer to pre-qualify themselves."

OKAY, NOW THAT YOU'RE THINKING ABOUT THAT TIME YOU LOOKED AT SOME METRICS, WHAT ACTIONS DID YOU TAKE IMMEDIATELY AFTER SEEING THOSE METRICS? DID YOU SHOW THEM TO YOUR TEAM? DID YOU DECIDE TO CHANGE ANYTHING ABOUT YOUR MARKETING? THINK ABOUT ALL THE ACTIONS YOU TOOK IN REACTION TO SEEING THE METRICS TALKED ABOUT IN QUESTION 2.

"After noticing this trend, the marketing team dug into which videos had the best VTRs and what the viewer did next. We noted that views of a two-minute product demo video increased significantly vs the prior year. We saw increased viewership in other videos showing how to use the product to solve for a specific problem. There was also an uptick in viewership of videos that were not thought-leadership-oriented and focusing on discussing common issues and trends."

YOU TOOK SOME ACTIONS BASED ON THE METRICS YOU SAW. WHAT HAPPENED AS A RESULT OF THOSE ACTIONS? FOR EXAMPLE, LET'S SAY YOU SAW THAT ENGAGEMENTS ON YOUR FACEBOOK POSTS WERE LOW, SO YOU DECIDED TO POST MORE VIDEOS, BECAUSE YOU THOUGHT VIDEO DRIVES ENGAGEMENT—SOMETHING LIKE THAT. DESCRIBE THE RESULTS OF YOUR ACTIONS (BOTH POSITIVE AND NEGATIVE RESULTS ARE ACCEPTABLE!).

"We amped up video production to provide more opportunities for buyers to engage with us via what was quickly becoming their preferred medium. For example, we created short-form videos (15–20 seconds) to include in social posts. We also integrated videos into our digital ad campaigns, replacing or supplementing static banners.

"Short-form videos are wildly popular thanks to apps like TikTok and Instagram. As people's attention spans—and spare time—are decreasing, the desire for short-form videos in the B2B world is rising. There is a rise in views and clicks on social media posts when you drop a short video into it."

IF POSSIBLE, COULD YOU PLEASE SHARE SPECIFIC BEFORE AND AFTER METRICS. WHAT WAS THE METRIC BEFORE YOU DID THESE ACTIONS AND WHAT WERE THE METRICS AFTER YOU DID THE ACTIONS DESCRIBED IN THE QUESTION ABOVE?

"When we promoted our two-minute demo video beyond the confines of the website, viewership increased more than 40 percent during the first 10 months of 2021 vs the entire prior year. Social media followers increased by 76 percent in the year since video became part of our social strategy."

"With so many technology tools available, metrics are easier and harder than ever. There is so much data to consume you must stay focused on the end goal, which is to understand who eventually buys your product and what helped to move them through the journey. With this type of introspection, you can uncover and close gaps. Data integrity and integration across systems is essential."

CHECKLIST: DASHBOARD MAKING

Now that you are ready to create your first (or next) dashboard, keep this checklist in mind:

The dashboard development framework

- Make sure you understand the business question you are trying to answer.
- Determine the data you need to answer the question.
- Identify the right data visualization for the data and question.
- Collect and cleanse the data.

Questions to ask when creating new dashboards:

- Identify data sources.
- Ensure access to data source.
- Understand how data will be connected to the dashboard. Built-in integration, as between Google products and Data Studio? An API? A connector tool such as SuperMetrics?
- Who is the target audience for the dashboard?
- What users need what levels of access: view only, edit, admin?
- How often will they view the data?
- Will the dashboard be used in meetings and planning sessions?
- What graphics and data visualizations will be used?
- Will it be a single screen, multiple screens, or tabs?

- Do you need to account for different screen sizes or mobile devices?
- Can you embed the dashboard in another application, such as a website or blog?
- Do you need to develop custom calculations or algorithms?
- What data cleansing and preparation is required?
- Are there any existing reports or data visualizations that can be reused?
- What filters, deep dives, and sorting will be available?
- What formulas, if any, will be needed?
- Is the dashboard for long-term use or is it for a specific campaign or initiative?
- If the dashboard is to be retired after a specific milestone, such as the end of the campaign, will it be archived? If so, where?
- Who else needs to see a "draft" of the dashboard before it is finalized?
- Steps in designing user-friendly, great-looking dashboards:
  - Create a style guide.
  - Plan the layout and design.
  - Define the colors, fonts, and styles.
  - Create a storyboard or wireframe.
  - Design the dashboard's navigation.
  - Label all data visualizations, buttons, and other elements.
  - Ensure that the layout is visually appealing.
  - Check for errors, both logical and factual.
  - Check for usability and clarity.
  - Test the dashboard with a limited set of users.
  - Launch! And continuously improve.

13

What are the skills of a metrics-driven marketer?

Throughout this book, you have learned strategies for becoming a metrics-driven marketer. Knowing these strategies is the first step in becoming the kind of marketer most sought-after in a range of roles, from analyst to CMO. According to a survey published by the respected data firm eMarketer, data science and analysis was cited as the top skill in demand.[1] This demand has only grown, with no signs of abating anytime soon.

People often ask "Do I need to be able to code to succeed in digital marketing?" or "How much advanced mathematics is involved in using marketing metrics?" The answer is "It depends." The focus in this book is how to manage marketing campaigns and programs on the ground level. Being successful in applying metrics to your campaigns does not, as we have seen, require coding skills or advanced calculations. However, if you are mathematically inclined, opportunities abound to take your marketing skills and translate them into a data analytics role. Such roles typically do involve both the use of advanced mathematical skills and coding in languages such as Python. On the other hand, demand is vast for professionals who have no coding knowledge, yet can apply metrics to campaign planning, ad buying, content marketing, social media, and program optimization. For such marketers, being an effective communicator, possessing analytical skills, and being highly organized and tech-savvy are more likely to boost your career. The reality is, there are roles for employees with many different strengths in the modern, metrics-driven marketing department.

Nor are opportunities limited to specific types of work. Interdisciplinary thinking is, in fact, essential to growing in your marketing career, including a metrics-focused career. To be a leader at any level, marketers need to have a varied skillset that allows them to work with data. In this chapter, we learn about the comprehensive set of skills that place a marketer in demand as a data-savvy creative business professional. We will break down those skills most in demand within marketing analytics.

Critical skill types

During my 20 years in communications I have learned one thing: the tools that are today's must-haves will be tomorrow's forgotten technologies, and the platforms to which we rush today may not be around in five years. While technical skills are important, what makes for longevity in marketing are core skill types that resist changing times. These include communication, synthesis and analysis, numerical literacy, systems thinking, ethics, and empathy.

Communication

Presenting data requires comprehensive communication skills. Marketers who work with data should have strong logical reasoning, fluent writing and speaking abilities, and the ability to communicate visually. Communication is what distinguishes a leader. Once you understand what needs to be done after looking at the data, you need to inspire your team to actually do the work. Since many people find metrics intimidating, being that communicator makes you the vital bridge between the metrics and what they mean. Communicating about data makes you the go-to person in your organization for all things metrics-related.

Writing clearly is the first step in being a strong communicator. Learn to write simply. Use direct language, avoiding jargon. Nearly half the US population is most comfortable reading at sixth-grade level, so use tools such as Grammarly to assess the reading level of your written communications. Even when communicating to highly educated colleagues, remember that complex topics such as metrics impose what psychologists call cognitive load—in plain language, they tax our mental processing capacity. Using simple sentence structure takes away another factor in cognitive load: decoding language itself. By keeping your metrics-focused writing simple, you help others understand data more readily.

It's not enough to write well; the key skill is the ability to convey complex numbers with the meaning behind them. Also vital is the ability to help an audience see connections, as well as provide realistic next steps. Put yourself in your audience's shoes: what do they already know? What questions might they have and can you answer them before they are even asked? Will they want to know the next steps? Are there any terms you use that need definition? At its heart, communication starts with empathy, another core skill.

In addition to words, you also need to have a good sense of the visual. Know when an image will help your audience grasp a concept. Understand what specific type of visual will be most illuminating. You don't have to be a graphic designer. Many tools exist, from Piktochart (https://piktochart. com), LucidChart (https://lucidchart.com), and even Canva (https://canva. com), loaded with outstanding templates that will inspire your visual communication. The key again is to know what your readers or presentation audience will need from you, and learn to provide that content. This skill alone can make you a recognized leader in your organization.

Synthesis and analysis

It is critical for data-driven marketers to be effective at synthesizing different types of information, as well as analyzing data. Data on its own, as we learned, is simply descriptive. It can tell marketers the state of affairs. Effective data-driven marketers are those who can take that information on the state of affairs and transform it into a plan for what needs to happen, based on that information.

Data is seldom all of one type, nor is it all from one source, despite our efforts to break down silos in the modern organization. Thus, synthesizing metrics from different channels, tools, and even domains remains critical. If you can see across your own departmental silos, understanding the uses of metrics from sources across your organization, you are good at synthesis.

If you can then use that data to assess campaign performance and create new recommendations, you're a top-notch analyst. As you have probably guessed, you need first to synthesize a range of data before you embark on analysis. Otherwise, you are missing vital data. Marketers who can see the big metrics picture, then turn that picture into insights, optimized campaign plans, and program improvements are highly valuable to their organizations.

Numerical literacy

Numerical literacy, or numeracy, is the basic understanding of math concepts. Marketers should be confident in doing basic calculations, including calculating the mean averages of numbers. More importantly, they should feel comfortable with basic business financial concepts, such as profit margins, gross and net sales calculations, and understanding balance sheets and profit and loss statements. A managerial finance course for non-finance majors, as well as online resources such as the website Alison.com (https://alison.com/courses/finance) can help you learn these core topics confidently. Marketing is critical to a company's bottom line. Being able to demonstrate clearly how your efforts contribute to a brand's profitability can ensure that your work is recognized, advancing your career.

The big picture: empathy, future thinking, organization, and systems thinking

While being a clear communicator, understanding numbers, and thinking analytically will help you do your work well, being a metrics-driven leader means going beyond the immediate to seeing the long-term organizational impacts of data. For marketers, it also means retaining that critical customer focus that is the heart of modern marketing. This is also why empathy, future thinking, and organization are key to effective marketing. These three factors are critical for managerial success. If you aspire to be a manager, read on for how to develop your leadership abilities.

Empathy

Empathy is the ability to see what others see, and know how they feel. It has always been vital to be able to understand precisely what customers will need. Note that empathy is not the same as sympathy. Feeling badly for a customer who had a poor experience is sympathy. Understanding the customer journey and knowing that it's confusing to assemble furniture, so you might need more accurate directions, is empathy. It's putting yourself in the customers' shoes, rather than just having a positive attitude.

Empathy is critical to leading with data. It allows us to anticipate what others will do, know what our teams need to act on metrics, and interpret data on consumers effectively. An empathetic marketer is a successful marketer.

Future thinking

Future thinking is more a mindset than a tactic. In marketing, it is to anticipate the needs that consumers and your market will have. You need to keep an eye on what your customers are saying, and what those in your market are seeking. That will help you predict issues and needs before they occur.

How do you develop your capacity for future thinking? One way, ironically, is to look to the past.

- Analyze metrics on how campaigns have succeeded—or not.

- Look at the factors that led to success, and do a post-mortem. What worked outstandingly well? How could the process have been improved? What creative could we have used that was even more effective?

- Exercise empathy. There's that word again. Research has shown that workers become more mindful of their retirement savings when shown a digitally aged photo of themselves. The photo increased their empathy for their future selves. Think about your future self, your future customers, employees, company, and community. Based on current metrics, what will they need in one month, one year, five years? What will the metrics of their success be? What will they want you to have done today?

Seeing the future is impossible. What we can do is seek patterns, using them to develop a mental map of what happens in specific circumstances. Over time, we become better at predicting outcomes based on patterns.

True leaders look beyond their organizations to see how their firm fits into larger social, cultural, and economic trends. Future thinking in marketing metrics means using the numbers from the past to understand where you are headed in the future—a key planning step.

Organization

Knowing that your customers may need better directions is one thing; having those better directions at your fingertips is another. This is where many brands struggle. They understand what their customers need, but they struggle to create the right processes and infrastructure to deliver every time on those needs.

Organizational excellence ranks high on the list of factors in marketing campaign success. It is especially important for metrics-driven agile marketing. To plan for your next sprint, you need ready access to the right metrics, distributed to the team at the right time. This is not a one-time need, but an ongoing effort to keep the flow of metrics steady into the decision-making process. Only the organized team succeeds.

As a leader, whether scrum master or product owner, your role is to facilitate that success by providing needed resources. Having an organized process to collect, analyze, and communicate metrics in a timely way is core to that responsibility. Without it, you will struggle each sprint with gathering data, putting it into the right formats, and communicating the metrics-informed strategy to your team. With good organization, you can relax knowing that data is reliably available for all steps in the campaign process, from spring planning to retrospectives.

How do you become organized? It's a talent we all can learn. It starts with systems thinking.

Systems thinking

At the heart of organization is systems thinking. Systems thinkers do more than simply label information or create processes. They look at entire systems as a whole, whether that's a company's industry or their marketing infrastructure. They understand how different aspects of a system interact to deliver results. For example, think about getting the dishes done after dinner. The system for cleaning dishes includes your sink, towels, soap, dishrags, and dishwasher. It also includes the time it's right to clear the dishes (after everyone eats), who clears the dishes (each person at the table), and what happens after the dishes are clean (they are put away to be used again). Think about how these elements interact. What happens if your family doesn't clear their dishes? How would changing your dish soap or dish-washer alter the process? If a new housemate joined your household, how would you integrate them into the process smoothly? We engage in systems thinking all the time. Modern work styles often encourage us to "stick to our knitting," focusing on our official job responsibilities. That can impede systems thinking. Even in your own role, however, you likely have thought about:

- How your role fits into the bigger picture of your company's success.
- What the different responsibilities of your role are.

- How those responsibilities work together to create impactful results.

- What can be done better to achieve efficiency as you work through different tasks.

This is systems thinking. The key to improving your capacity for this kind of thinking is threefold:

- Consciously look for patterns. Ask yourself what types of data seem to repeat, how often they repeat, and at what intervals.

- Put things into context: how does one activity integrate with others? What are its dependencies? What actions does it influence? How vital is it in comparison to other things and actions that exist alongside it? For example, what role does dish soap play in cleaning dishes? You would say it's essential. You'd note you use it after dishes have been cleared but before you dry them. You'd note that it works along with water to get dishes clean. That's the context in which the soap exists. Everything in marketing can be put into context. You can understand a campaign in the context of your larger marketing programs, a consumer segment in the context of their lifestyles, a competitor in the context of your industry. The more you see patterns like this, the better you become at contextualization.

- Imagine new relationships: how could the interactions among different aspects of a system change? What if, for instance, one person at your table was tasked with clearing all the dishes? Envision how that would impact the entire process. Would it be faster? More equitable? Slower? Would it reduce breakage? Think through new ways of configuring the parts of a system. That will help you re-engineer the system to work better. Don't be afraid of making mistakes—remember, part of using metrics effectively is through experimentation. Map out new systems to solve existing problems in completely different ways. When you progress from thinking about systems to designing them, you are becoming a true systems thinker.

Systems thinking is critical for moving from descriptive and predictive analytics to prescriptive analytics—metrics that point the way toward new actions, rather than just assessing what happened before. Those kinds of prescriptive metrics help optimize marketing continuously, providing a vital competitive advantage. Becoming the engineer of that advantage makes you critical to any organization.

Ethics

According to a study published in Forbes, 69 percent of consumers are concerned about the way in which companies use their personal data. As metrics-focused marketers, we collect millions of datapoints about consumers every day. Handling this data ethically is a core competency of today's marketers. Honing an ethical vision for your metrics-focused marketing programs is not a nice to have—it's vital for maintaining customer trust. In an increasing number of cases, it will keep your company out of legal trouble. Laws such as GDPR, CCPA, and other regulations provide for heavy fines on companies that violate consumers' privacy, security, and "right to be forgotten" by the organizations with which they do business. Not having strong ethics can break customer trust while also costing a company millions of dollars.

Ethics becomes action through a management process called data governance. Data governance is the work of evaluating, documenting, optimizing, and controlling data within an organization. It can include documenting where data is stored throughout the organization, controlling access to information to reduce security risk, ensuring proper cybersecurity, and establishing protocols for handling different types of information. Data governance is an interdisciplinary field that encompasses a range of systems, stakeholders, and regulations. It is a perfect way to put that systems thinking into action.

To realize the benefits of digital marketing, brands have to do more than install software. They need that human touch, as well as a well-structured marketing operation. It's complex. This is why brands that do it well stand out.

Hard skills: technologies and tools

We have talked about the strategic skills that you need to be a metrics-focused marketer. Often, such mental abilities are called "soft" skills in HR parlance. When people ask about what they need to know to succeed in today's metrics-focused world, however, they often mean hands-on technical abilities, which fall into the category of "hard" skills—those that are the result of practical training, rather than of personal development. While there is no doubt that soft skills are those most creative marketers will rely on, especially in managerial roles, hard skills are important on many career tracks. Those who wish to work more directly with measurement need particular abilities in math, technology, and data visualization, as well as other tools. Let's take a deep look at what these skills are—and how to learn them for free, at your own pace.

Quantitative skills

Strong quantitative skills are essential in today's marketing. However, even a "math-phobic" creative marketer can develop the skills needed to be a strong analyst of data. Many of the calculations for basic marketing metrics are done by software. The real skill lies in being able to reason through data—the analysis and synthesis of data.

That said, it is essential to be able to understand the calculations that underlie metrics such as customer lifetime value, as well as know the basics of how statistical methods such as linear regression and confidence intervals work. In addition, fundamental skills with spreadsheet software are a critical business skill, as relevant to marketers as to other business professionals.

Spreadsheet applications

Knowing how to use spreadsheet software such as Excel or Google Sheets is basic to many business roles. While we have learned about a wealth of tools, it is surprising to many new data-driven marketers how much work is performed using spreadsheets, including turning data into simple charts and tables. The current author once managed an entire campaign quite recently by organizing all creative, test variations, and tagged URLs in a spreadsheet with dozens of rows at a client's request—it was simply the easiest way for such a small amount of data. Many businesses are reliant on spreadsheets for tracking small to mid-size quantities of information.

It is a standard, useful tool, even with the wealth of other options. Used in conjunction with other applications, comma-separated value (CSV) files, a standard file type associated with spreadsheet applications, are also the backbone of other, more sophisticated methods. For example, data from other applications for which there is no current connector available can be readily moved to Google Data Studio as a CSV file. Most programs that generate data, such as e-commerce systems or CRMs, allow the export of the data generated as a CSV by default, with CSV often being the only option.

In addition, Excel can be used to perform basic analysis, including calculating CLV for a modest number of customers, or averaging sales over a week or month. It can also be used for statistical work, including regression analysis, calculating averages, and even probability analysis.

Statistics

Statistics are at the heart of how marketing metrics are turned into useful insights. Statistics, or statistical analysis, is the practice of using mathematical equations to understand datasets. Think about the last time you heard on the news about a study that found, for example, that people who exercised were a certain percentage "more likely" to live longer. That percentage was arrived at by examining data on exercise and longevity using statistical analysis. Statistics are a big part of everyday life. Even the term we often use to mean that two things seem to go together, *correlation*, is the same as the word for a specific type of statistical analysis used to find whether two phenomena go together. A basic understanding of statistics is useful for interpreting marketing data that uses statistical modeling to describe or predict, as we have seen in this chapter. Core concepts such as regression modeling, Bayesian inference, the calculation of confidence intervals and margins of error, and other descriptive and predictive methods are useful, and often required in MBA programs.

The good news is, you don't need to be a genius to learn statistics. Since much of it is applicable to everyday life, many marketers find it more intuitive than calculus or other math disciplines. You can also learn it on your own, at home.

Many excellent texts on statistics are available, and most colleges offer statistics courses at undergraduate and graduate levels. One place to start developing a core understanding of statistics is through the free online tutorials of Khan Academy (https://www.khanacademy.org), Brown University's Seeing Theory interactive statistics demonstrations (https://seeing-theory.brown.edu), or the free ebook, *Statistics at Square One* (https://www.bmj.com/about-bmj/resources-readers/publications/statistics-square-one).

Once you understand the fundamentals of statistics, it becomes easier to know whether you can trust interpretations of marketing metrics that you use. For instance, if working with a predictive analytics application to determine which customers to target with offers, knowing whether it relies on categorization or regression can help you determine how much to rely on its predictions. Knowing the size of the training dataset can also help you understand how long you will need to use the application before its predictions become even more useful. Knowing statistics can also help you explain data better to stakeholders. For these reasons, a study of statistics is highly recommended to marketers.

Tactical and strategic hard skills

In-demand marketers should be proficient in the standard tools in their area of specialization. At a minimum, marketers should know how to use a CRM system, such as HubSpot, web analytics tools, starting with Google Analytics, and understand some basics of SEO, with the ability to use a keyword planner and SEO auditing tools.

Within marketing, there are many different creative specializations, such as email, direct marketing, content marketing, PR, or social media. A skilled marketing specialist should be able to use the metrics associated with the primary channels they manage. A social media marketer, for instance, should be as well-versed in the metrics tools associated with social media management tools as they are with the social media scheduling features of platforms such as Sprout Social or Hootsuite. Knowing how to measure the impact of their work can demonstrate accountability as well as a strong skillset.

In addition to knowing both general analytics tools as well as the metrics capabilities of their primary channels, marketers should demonstrate a strategic ability to lead with data. Rather than simply reporting the results of their latest campaigns, in-demand marketing specialists communicate to their teams about what those results mean. Taking it a step further, they strive to improve their impact continuously by using results data to point the way toward better marketing programs. Let's go back to our gardening company, Moonstone. Digital Marketing Director Chelsea Omenuko is looking to optimize Moonstone's Instagram reach, using data from their most recent influencer campaign. Once she has synthesized and analyzed the data around the Instagram campaign, she takes a strategic direction by suggesting that the company reach out to home-fashion influencers. She points to the data around engagement from fashion microinfluencers, as well as the sentiment data for consumer comments on home fashion-focused posts. "Whenever we post a home fashion-related story, our sentiment is 97 percent positive and 3 percent neutral, vs when we focus on just the product, it's 78 percent positive, 2 percent negative, and 20 percent neutral. Whenever we post about fashion, we get a great response from our consumer.

More importantly, we have been getting a lot of comments from accounts that have 80,000–250,000 followers, putting them in the important micro-influencer category—that is, influencers with small, dedicated audiences. Over 60 percent of these vital microinfluencers use home fashion-related hashtags and images. I know we think of ourselves as a 'green' brand, but we're really catching on with the interior decor audience. We need to be strategic in pursuing them. I recommend we reach out to 50 of the home fashion microinfluencers who have engaged with us, to do collaborations that will help us broaden our social media reach."

Synthesizing tactical and strategic thinking, using both marketing and quantitative skills, makes Chelsea invaluable to her organization. Interdisciplinary thinking allows her to glean insights that others do not see, building metrics-based insights for her organization. In a few months, she is promoted to Director of Digital Marketing. She grew social media engagement by 230 percent with metrics. Her metrics-focused efforts helped her create marketing strategies that are more than guesswork—they are grounded in science. Doing the same can expand your career, too.

Future-proofing your career with strategic skills

Will your job be replaced by AI? If you are working on the skills in this chapter, likely it will not. Many purely tactical jobs—those where contributors simply perform rote activities—*are* likely to disappear as current advancements in AI become affordable at scale. Calculating figures or testing creative designs developed by others will be taken over by computers. Reasoning with data, making clear recommendations and having the data at hand to illustrate one's reasoning, as Chelsea does in the example above, will be the in-demand skill for marketers.

Visualization with tools

As mentioned in the section on data visualizations, being proficient in presenting data visually is critical to managing marketing. A basic knowledge of spreadsheets can be enough to get you on your way to designing clear, attractive charts. Knowing how to present data using charts requires only basic design skills. Experiment with spreadsheet software and a presentation app such as PowerPoint to create data charts. You can also use tools such as

Photoshop, Canva, and Piktochart to create more compelling charts and infographics.

Learning dashboarding tools is especially important. Free online tutorials abound on YouTube for Google Data Studio, while the proprietary platforms such as Tableau offer their own training modules. It is important to get hands-on with data projects. Look for opportunities to create dashboards at work, getting feedback from stakeholders. Dashboards are as much a communication tool as they are about graphics, so the best bet for learning how to build dashboards is to understand stakeholder needs. That way, you will be able to translate them into powerful data visualizations that are as useful as they are attractive.

Data science skills

You don't need to be a data scientist to be successful as a marketing analyst, let alone as a marketer with an eye toward data. However, it is useful to be able to understand the basics of data science. Knowing the principles of text analytics, statistical modeling, and the capabilities of programming can give a marketer an edge. While you don't have to be able to program, under-standing how programming languages such as R and Python work can help a marketer know what is possible in the world of predictive and descriptive analytics, communicate analytics tasks clearly to data scientists, and effectively interpret data, knowing the power and limitations of technical tools.

Data analytics with programming tools

If you are keen to start delving deeper into data analysis, learning programming is a wise goal. Organizations depend on data analysts with programming skills to process the vast datasets they collect, create predictive analytics models, and manage the increasing velocity of today's data.

A range of programming languages exist for analyzing data. While most marketers don't learn programming, learning Python, R, or SQL can enable analytically minded marketers to expand into data science roles. Being able to understand both marketing and programming can make a marketer highly valuable.

R is a programming language that excels at statistical work, such as machine learning. It has powerful visualization capabilities as well. While it was created two decades ago, its applications are exploding thanks to big data. Developed for academic purposes, it is a bit more challenging to learn than its competitor, Python. However, it is incredibly powerful at performing even complex statistical analyses at scale, quickly. R relies on scripting, which means that analysts write out the directions for the analysis they wish to perform, then run the script to process a dataset, performing that specific analysis. This means that it is easy to streamline repetitive processes with R.

Python, like R, can be used for statistical analysis. It is also useful for creating visualizations, though many argue that R is the stronger candidate in that regard. It is easier to learn than R for many. The language excels especially in text analytics—the use of computer programs and mathematics to discern patterns in written words. Text analytics has many applications in marketing, including sentiment analysis, the practice of analyzing consumers' words to measure their feelings. If you have ever looked at the "positive," "negative," and "neutral" ratings of your followers' social media posts about you in popular tools such as Hootsuite, you have engaged in sentiment analysis. Python is not the only programming language used for such emotional analytics, but it is one of the most popular. Text analytics is also used for predictive modeling; it examines patterns in customers' speech, for instance, in customer service calls to determine whether they are likely to cancel. It is also valuable in translating qualitative data, such as free-response answers in surveys, into statistics.

If you do want to learn programming, there are many free online resources, such as DataCamp (https://www.datacamp.com), Python.org, Swirlstats to learn R (https://swirlstats.com), and CodeAcademy (https://www.codecademy.com). These typically allow you to learn at your own pace using practical, hands-on exercises. Many are free; the others are low cost. It is worth exploring these tools to find out if learning to code is right for you, since there is no risk except a bit of your time. "Coding is a basic literacy in the digital age," according to LearningResources.com, so learning some basic concepts is often useful to your career.

Database management

While often the province of business intelligence or IT, database management is increasingly the responsibility of marketing. While you likely don't have to learn the standard database language, SQL, it is useful to understand some database structure best practices. These include defining the fields, such as names and contact properties, selecting the appropriate tools for managing a database, whether it is the right CRM or another tool. Marketers also need to clean data to eliminate inconsistencies, such as names being entered as one or two fields, or first and last names being in a different order. Good database management can eliminate some of these issues, by ensuring that all the information you need to collect has its own field, and that field is clearly labeled.[2] Understanding how to ensure a clean, efficient database is a welcome skill for many marketers. Taking a basic course on data integrity, listening to stakeholders, and understanding both the data you collect and the capabilities of your data storage systems, such as your CRM, are useful ways to improve your database management skills.

The marketers of the future are metrics-driven— and now, you are one, too

We live in an age of measurement. Organizations expect marketers to create customer insights, demonstrate ROI, optimize digital media, even predict the future—all using metrics. At the same time, counterpressures from privacy advocates ensure that metrics are more regulated than ever. Now is not the time to rely on the methods of the past. Silos, complacency, and an anything-goes attitude have no place in today's marketing organization. Instead, the marketers of the future are systems thinkers, using cross-functional metrics to optimize campaigns. They are also guardians of consumers' privacy, establishing strict guidelines on how data is used in service of stakeholders, never to exploit them.

Whether they can crunch numbers and code alongside the best technical experts, or they use metrics to lift their creativity to new heights, today's marketers are metrics-savvy yet always strategic. Lifelong learners, they know that tools change, while creativity and future-thinking are always critical to success. Whatever the future of marketing metrics, you are now equipped to meet its challenges and take advantage of its opportunities.

Endnotes

[1]   Benes, R (2019) Why are data science and analytics the most in-demand skills at ad agencies? *Insider Intelligence*, https://www.emarketer.com/content/data-science-is-in-demand-at-ad-agencies (archived at https://perma.cc/YC5Y-DKGE)

[2]   Martinez, F (2022) Bad practices in database design: are you making these mistakes? *Toptal Engineering Blog*, https://www.toptal.com/database/database-design-bad-practices (archived at https://perma.cc/8BK7-MFFX)

14

Marketing metrics resources

The world of marketing is dynamic, with new, exciting developments all the time. Technology allows marketers to gather more data, and therefore make better decisions, with new features, data types, and strategies emerging all the time. You need to be constantly up to date, to know what works and what doesn't. This resource guide will provide a good foundation for anyone interested in digital marketing metrics. It is intended for marketers, entrepreneurs, and analysts.

This guide is divided into sections by metrics type and resource type. By no means is it comprehensive; I plan to update it as new resources emerge. Feel free to email me (link at bottom) with suggestions, changes, or feedback. It's a starting point for you to stay on top of the latest developments in the metrics, because things change weekly.

In addition, this guide is meant to be a starting point for you to do your own research and come up with your own strategy and process. The beauty of metrics-driven marketing management is that there are as many unique approaches as there are those of us in the field, and we are all learning from each other. This is a collection of go-to resources, but not the final definition of best practices. That definition is up to you. As you learn and grow in your career, my hope is that this guide will help you on your journey.

Bear in mind that the web changes all the time, so by the time you read this book, links may have changed. A simple Google search should help you find the resources in that case.

Major publications

Whether it is breaking news or practical tips, a wealth of online magazines provide the latest to keep you up to date on all things marketing metrics.

This guide is organized by topic, so you can quickly find the news, tutorials, and information you need.

Web analytics

Keep up to date on the latest thinking in web analytics with resources not only for Google Analytics, but other analytics tools, and more importantly, the strategy behind web analytics.

Google Analytics Products blog

https://www.blog.google/products/marketingplatform/analytics/ (archived at https://perma.cc/3YJT-V4ZV)

This comprehensive blog about all things Google Analytics, Optimize, and related tools keeps you in the know directly from Google.

Adobe Experience blog

https://blog.adobe.com/en/topics/experience-cloud/ (archived at https://perma.cc/Z4LC-8EC2)

Focused on products in the Adobe Experience suite, this blog features case studies, tips and tricks, Adobe news, keynotes from the annual conference, and more. It is especially good reading for creatives looking to understand how to apply analytics in omnichannel marketing.

Optimizely

https://www.optimizely.com/insights/blog/ (archived at https://perma.cc/6U9W-75GG)

This blog offers accessible, practical resources on CRO, multivariate and A/B testing, and general analytics that are beginner friendly.

Market research

Market research publications fall into two categories: methods and research reports. Methods publications are technique-based, focusing on the latest developments in questionnaire design and statistical analysis. Research reports publications offer reports on trends in a range of industries.

Market Research blog

https://blog.marketresearch.com/ (archived at https://perma.cc/E22P-QM82)

Updates on trends in a range of sectors, as well as tips on how to apply market research outside of traditional areas.

Greenbook

https://www.greenbook.org/mr/ (archived at https://perma.cc/F9ZA-DN4W)

A comprehensive site for market researchers, this site provides advice on everything from survey design to recruiting focus group participants.

Decision Analyst

https://www.decisionanalyst.com/blog/ (archived at https://perma.cc/M2XR-W5WW)

Another blog focused on the methods of market research, this publication offers more advice on strategy than on specific techniques.

eMarketer

https://www.emarketer.com/ (archived at https://perma.cc/G2L4-HXS7)

A longstanding source of research reports on the marketing industry, this subscription service offers data on marketing ROI benchmarks, social media platform usage, advertising benchmarks, and more.

Statista

https://www.statista.com/ (archived at https://perma.cc/7X4S-RE8X)

This aggregator of research data on a range of industries, consumer behaviors, and trends is a comprehensive source of reliable consumer information, marketing benchmarks, and sector-related data.

A/B testing, multivariate testing, and heatmapping

A/B and multivariate testing continue to grow in popularity and can be a powerful tool in your marketing arsenal. The blog links below are often publications from testing tools companies, though most of their advice is generally applicable, regardless of the tools you use. Interesting case studies and practical tips are available on each blog.

Unbounce Conversion Intelligence blog

https://unbounce.com/blog/ (archived at https://perma.cc/25PN-UF4E)

Practical guide to A/B and multivariate testing, including test design, what to test, how to test, and interpretation of results. Practical and accessible.

Instapage Resource Library

https://instapage.com/resources (archived at https://perma.cc/6RY9-YUPD)

Guides to A/B and multivariate testing, landing page optimization, and more with templates, strategies, and data analysis.

CrazyEgg blog

https://www.crazyegg.com/blog/ (archived at https://perma.cc/3J5L-9CGE)

Guide to conversion optimization, including testing and data collection, from a leading heatmapping tool. Resource guides and templates for a wide range of digital channels.

Social media

Metrics are a hot topic for many social media publications. The resources below are both well-respected publications that cover social marketing best practices, news, and technical topics.

Buffer blog

https://blog.bufferapp.com (archived at https://perma.cc/KR8D-4RCV)

Focuses on practical advice for social media marketers at all levels. Includes case studies, ebooks, industry information, and more to help you improve your social media skills.

Social Media Today

http://socialmediatoday.com/ (archived at https://perma.cc/XU4G-UKQK)

A UK-based resource that covers all things social media, including interviews with experts, trending news, and best practices.

Social Media Examiner

https://www.socialmediaexaminer.com/ (archived at https://perma.cc/QDQ3-2R55)

Weekly tips on all areas of social media, including Facebook, Twitter, Instagram. Best practices for business with top insights from the best minds in social media marketing.

Mention blog

https://mention.com/en/blog/ (archived at https://perma.cc/ZX4U-NDCY)

The latest facts on measuring what people are saying about you or your brand in the blogosphere. Also contains useful coverage of all facets of digital marketing.

Direct marketing, email, text, and chatbot metrics

Direct marketing metrics are among the most important in the post-cookie world, with the growing need for first-party data. Keep on top of trends with latest insights and best practices to help you measure success.

Conversica blog

https://www.conversica.com/resources/ (archived at https://perma.cc/LL7H-JGSA)

Daily research on strategies for using email, chatbots, and AI for B2B marketing. Guides to news, email marketing best practices, and more. Also includes white papers, guides, and video tutorials.

Litmus blog

https://www.litmus.com/blog/ (archived at https://perma.cc/J29J-YXYS)

Resource guides from a leading email marketing tool, including tips and strategies around personalization, deliverability, and how to meet the challenges presented by GDPR.

MailChimp blog

https://mailchimp.com/blog/ (archived at https://perma.cc/JV38-RFS2)

Comprehensive advice on all aspects of direct marketing via email, with an emphasis on design and copy, but some coverage of metrics. (Full disclosure, the author's agency is a MailChimp partner; however, the author receives no remuneration from this relationship.)

Postalytics blog

https://www.postalytics.com/blog (archived at https://perma.cc/E7P9-LKFF)

The blog of a leading provider of direct marketing metrics tools; provides practical advice on using data to improve marketing initiatives, website performance, and conversions.

Salesforce marketing blog

https://www.salesforce.com/blog/category/marketing/ (archived at https://perma.cc/WD4N-9BL8)

Excellent case studies, strategies, and tactics you can use even if you don't use Salesforce.

Drift blog

https://drift.com/blog/ (archived at https://perma.cc/U73A-5Z9C)

Drift offers live chat software that helps you chat with prospects on your website to answer their questions and ultimately turn them into customers. Their blog is truly helpful for marketers of all experience levels, focusing on how they can help your business by using chat during different stages of the funnel. If chatbot analytics are relevant to you, it is a useful source.

SEO and PPC

SEO is one of the most rapidly changing fields in marketing. These resources keep you up to date.

Search Engine Journal

https://www.searchenginejournal.com/ (archived at https://perma.cc/SJZ2-N85B)

Breaking news and advanced topics on SEO, PPC, and social media algorithms. Strong coverage of search marketing strategy, editorials, and in-depth articles.

Search Engine Land

https://searchengineland.com/ (archived at https://perma.cc/DKE3-M9N4)

News publication with the latest breaking stories on Google search engine algorithms, paid search, and all things digital marketing.

Google Search Central blog

https://developers.google.com/search/blog (archived at https://perma.cc/8HTV-2P4S)

Google's own publication for announcements to the technical SEO community, Google's best practices for search. Highly technical.

Google blog: Search

https://blog.google/products/search/ (archived at https://perma.cc/7PBV-CWV9)

Google's non-technical blog about search marketing. Accessible stories about interesting new trends in search, inspiring creators, and tips and tricks.

Yoast SEO blog

https://yoast.com/seo-blog/ (archived at https://perma.cc/P8WZ-WC6K)

Easy-to-use tips on how to optimize your website, written in an accessible style, based on the latest news and research.

The Moz blog

https://moz.com/blog (archived at https://perma.cc/VA55-CZ8K)

From the developers of one of the leading SEO tools, advanced technical recommendations, high-level strategy, and other professional advice on SEO.

General marketing publications with metrics coverage

Finally, no list would be complete without general publications that cover the entire marketing sector. Here are some of the most popular publications on marketing in general, which often cover metrics in depth.

Marketing Land

https://marketingland.com/ (archived at https://perma.cc/P5PN-VRRM)

Covers all topics related to digital marketing including SEO, paid search advertising, mobile advertising, email marketing, and more.

MediaPost

https://www.mediapost.com/ (archived at https://perma.cc/FKP7-3EKR)

Strongly focused on the advertising industry, this events-driven organization also offers several newsletters dedicated to ad metrics, media ROI, and privacy issues.

Ad Exchanger

https://adexchanger.com/ (archived at https://perma.cc/4NKB-PZ2E)

News, analysis, and data around all things programmatic marketing, including ad buying and selling, creative formats, real-time bidding, display ads, and video advertising.

HubSpot

https://blog.hubspot.com/marketing/ (archived at https://perma.cc/72AA-VEGZ)

Daily blogging on all forms of marketing with an emphasis on the inbound methodology of SEO, social media, content marketing, and landing page best practices.

Personal blogs

While large publications can bring you general information, sometimes, hearing from thought leaders in analytics will give more in-depth, opinion-driven content, along with tales from the trenches. Here are some of the best marketing metrics bloggers in the world, and their blogs.

Occam's Razor by Avinash Kaushik

https://www.kaushik.net/avinash/ (archived at https://perma.cc/4S4Q-5JH3)

The legendary web analyst shares useful strategies in a witty style. Groundbreaking and advanced content.

Neil Patel

https://neilpatel.com/ (archived at https://perma.cc/2PZJ-PYTX)

Named as one of the 100 marketing blogs you must read, Neil Patel's blog is approachable for all levels of digital marketing and analytics experience. Clear and actionable tips and tricks that will help improve your search engine marketing (SEM), SEO, and content marketing.

Beth Kanter

https://bethkanter.org/welcome/ (archived at https://perma.cc/LH9W-UQVJ)

Focused on nonprofit management and marketing, Beth Kanter's blog is equally valuable for marketers and business leaders in any industry. Resources include case studies, how-to guides, and research on content marketing and social media metrics.

Duct Tape Marketing blog by John Jantsch

https://ducttapemarketing.com/blog/ (archived at https://perma.cc/4CPV-AAE9)

Author of the bestselling marketing book *Duct Tape Marketing*, John Jantsch writes a blog that is a must-read for help getting your own creative juices flowing and how to implement your ideas after you have a good idea. His podcast is also a must-listen.

Ann Handley

https://annhandley.com/ (archived at https://perma.cc/EC6Z-7MGH)

Content-marketing maven Ann Handley writes on all things content at MarketingProfs. Focused on giving actionable tips to marketers, Ann's blog is full of smart advice for anyone who wants to write killer content that actually gets read and shared online, including coverage of metrics.

Copyblogger by Brian Clark

http://www.copyblogger.com/ (archived at https://perma.cc/Q9TG-YAQ4)

One of the most popular blogs on content marketing, Copyblogger covers all aspects of producing great writing that will get attention online. Includes resources, tips, and tricks for creating content that is both beneficial to the reader and searchable by Google.

David Meerman Scott

https://www.davidmeermanscott.com/blog/ (archived at https://perma.cc/8C4Y-NM4X)

A must-read for marketing on social media, David Meerman Scott coined the term "newsjacking" and is one of the best inbound marketers ever. His blog offers useful insights into marketing on all types of digital platforms.

CustomerThink

https://www.customerthink.com/ (archived at https://perma.cc/68RR-LNG7)

CustomerThink covers all things marketing research and customer experience. Useful for marketers looking to improve their customer relationships and advocacy, the site also posts valuable content on customer engagement, CRM, and marketing metrics.

Career development and professional associations

For anyone looking to get into marketing metrics, or advance their career, these blogs will help you better understand the jobs picture in the industry, search job listings, and learn about career development in the sector.

Now that you are excited about marketing metrics, joining a professional association will help you stay abreast of the resources and training available for your profession. Additionally, many groups offer certifications or credentials. For many marketers, certification shows you are dedicated and committed to your field.

Marketing Research Association (US)

https://www.mra-net.org/ (archived at https://perma.cc/CSD5-CPQB)

This association has lots of useful information on research techniques, marketing research certifications, and events.

American Marketing Association (US)

https://www.ama.org/ (archived at https://perma.cc/4YXG-HD8V)

The AMA provides a variety of resources for marketers at all levels, including certification tests and conferences. They also provide tons of events both nationally and through active local chapters.

Digital Analytics Association

https://www.digitalanalyticsassociation.org/ (archived at https://perma.cc/Y2EZ-DF3V)

The Digital Analytics Association, or DAA, is a professional association geared toward people who have expertise in using digital analytics to inform business decisions. Membership includes access to events and training opportunities. It also offers certifications, many in technical areas and data science. Its conferences are among the world's largest dedicated to business and marketing metrics.

Association of National Advertisers

https://www.ana.net/ (archived at https://perma.cc/QB4U-ML6Q)

Incorporating the former Direct Marketing Association, the ANA is the primary trade group for large advertisers. On its site you'll find conference information, industry briefs, webcasts on marketing measurement, and more.

Insights Association

https://www.insightsassociation.org/ (archived at https://perma.cc/EZB6-SZD7)

The Insights Association is a nonprofit organization for insights professionals and marketing metric experts. The site provides reports on key industry topics, as well as news from the association, upcoming events, and more.

Marketing Research Association (UK)

https://www.marketingresearchassociation.org/home/ (archived at https://perma.cc/5VTK-8L9V)

This group caters to the United Kingdom and Europe. Its website offers a calendar of events, research briefs, a blog with news from around the world, and more.

Marketing Society (UK)

http://www.marketingsociety.com/ (archived at https://perma.cc/43TH-34K2)

This society is for marketing professionals in both B2B and B2C markets who want to learn more about issues such as consumer behavior and marketing measurement. Membership includes access to training events, networking opportunities, and research reports. Its blog provides insight on the latest industry trends.

Marketing Institute of Singapore

https://www.mis.org.sg/ (archived at https://perma.cc/Y6QD-A99Q)

The Marketing Institute of Singapore is a nonprofit group for marketers and related professionals in Asia. The site offers white papers, research briefs, and updates on industry trends.

Marketing Society (UK)

https://researchsociety.com.au/ (archived at https://perma.cc/543T-E72T)

This association caters to marketers in Australia and New Zealand, who work across a variety of industries including technology, finance, and media. The group's website has information on events, research briefs, and industry trends.

Data Driven Marketing Association

https://www.ddma.nl (archived at https://perma.cc/9L9B-CEES)

The Data Driven Marketing Association (DDMA) is a professional association with industry-specific events and certifications. Membership includes access to the DDMA library, as well as discounts on training and certification exams. While based in the Netherlands, it offers much content in English.

International Association of Privacy Professionals

https://iapp.org/ (archived at https://perma.cc/D8DD-CW9F)

The International Association of Privacy Professionals, or IAPP, is a network for privacy professionals with its own certification program. Membership includes access to the online library and discounts on conferences. It also offers training opportunities on compliance, security, and data governance. The site includes job listings, as well as information about career development. Their newsletter and blog provide in-depth coverage of breaking news in privacy regulation, cybersecurity, and policy advocacy.

Women in Analytics

https://www.womeninanalytics.com/ (archived at https://perma.cc/45VZ-KV4D)

Created by members of the Women in Analytics LinkedIn group, this site offers a job board and other resources for femme-identified professionals. In addition to covering news relevant to analytics professionals, it includes advice columns from experts in the field, as well as opinions on diversity in the profession.

The Marketing Accountability Standards Board (MASB)

https://themasb.org/ (archived at https://perma.cc/A523-GWHD)

The MASB is a nonprofit organization that develops metrics for measuring the value of marketing activities, and works to establish standards for marketing measurement.

Data Science Africa

http://www.datascienceafrica.org/ (archived at https://perma.cc/6QS9-8LUY)

Data Science Africa is a network for data scientists across Africa. Membership includes access to the online community, as well as to recordings from a wide range of conferences from both the continent-wide and national chapters. Chapters in several countries offer local events, trainings, and networking opportunities.

Asia Big Data Association

https://asiabigdata.org/ (archived at https://perma.cc/7NSS-8ST9)

The Asia Big Data Association (ABDA) is an association for professionals who work with data or analytics. It also includes many non-governmental organizations and academic institutions. Membership includes access to the online community and event invitations, and notice of upcoming meetups.

Association of Data Scientists

https://www.adasci.org/ (archived at https://perma.cc/2BNU-KLYJ)

The Association of Data Scientists, or ADaSci, is a professional association with training resources. Membership includes access to the library and discounts on training offered through third parties. It publishes a journal, *Lattice*, dedicated to machine learning. It also has a job-listing portal, and administers the Chartered Data Scientist credential exam.

Data Science Council of America

https://www.dasca.org/ (archived at https://perma.cc/ED9N-AYEE)

The Data Science Council of America (DASCA) is an organization focused on career development for data scientists. Membership includes access to training materials and several certification programs. It hosts conferences, as well as monthly webcasts, and has a newsletter. In addition, it accredits educational institutions offering data science education, though the accreditation is voluntary.

International Institute of Business Analysis

https://www.iiba.org/ (archived at https://perma.cc/Q78U-KPN7)

Focused on business intelligence professionals, this group offers training, certification through their Certified Business Analysis Professional exam and other qualifications, and an online directory of BI professionals. Membership includes access to research publications. It also organizes conferences on topics related to business analysis around the world.

Media Bistro

http://www.mediabistro.com/ (archived at https://perma.cc/37CX-87J6)

Media Bistro bills itself as the premiere online community for media professionals, with specific subsections for marketers and salespeople. Their content includes everything from LinkedIn advice to news on personalized marketing and social selling. It is primarily a job site, so it also has listings for roles across marketing functions and organizations.

Data science

While this book is intended for marketers, if you want to investigate the technical side of metrics, resources abound. For further exploration of data science, check out these accessible resources that give you the background information that will help you speak the language of data analytics.

Data Science Central

http://www.datasciencecentral.com/ (archived at https://perma.cc/3PKA-Y956)

Data Science Central is a community for data scientists, machine learners, and big data aficionados. The site includes an active social community through which members share news and findings. It also features job listings.

Towards Data Science

https://towardsdatascience.com/ (archived at https://perma.cc/Z6GM-4DFP)

This publication has how-to articles, tutorials, case studies, and practical information on all things data science.

DataScience.com

This site offers tutorials on machine learning, data visualization, business intelligence for non-technical users, among others. The blog includes content about the R and Python programming languages, tools for working with large datasets, and applications of AI algorithms in business.

Hackathons and competitions

Feeling ambitious? Check out our list of the top data science hackathons and programming competitions for insight into what's coming next in big data and machine learning! This roundup includes links to registration pages and deadlines, so you know what you are getting yourself into.

Kaggle

https://www.kaggle.com/ (archived at https://perma.cc/G2S5-ULUY)

Kaggle is a platform for data science competitions. Companies with datasets host contests to help them solve important problems, and Kaggle provides prize money when the problem is solved. Members can create profiles, enter contests, and collaborate on code when not competing in contests. Competitions include machine learning and real-world data challenges.

Driven Data

https://www.drivendata.org/ (archived at https://perma.cc/RL42-ATAV)

This platform connects data "hackathons for good" across the globe. It provides a toolkit to host your own community hackathon, as well as a directory of events.

SAS Hackathons

https://www.sas.com/sas/events/hackathon.html   (archived   at   https://perma.cc/4DLZ-EBY7)

SAS runs a series of big-data hackathons to promote their tools and attract new talent. They have events around the world annually, so you can find one in a convenient location. Online global hackathons were organized during the Covid pandemic, and may continue to be held.

DICTIONARY OF MARKETING METRICS AND RELATED TERMS

The dictionary of marketing metrics is a comprehensive list of all the terms and definitions related to marketing. This includes everything from common terms such as return on investment (ROI) to more specialized concepts like market basket analysis.

AARRR: a framework for understanding the customer journey, which stands for acquisition, activation, retention, revenue, and referral.

A/B testing: a method of testing two versions of a web page or email to see which one performs better. This type of testing can be used to determine the best way to present content, the most effective subject lines, and the ideal time to send emails.

Acquisition: in marketing, acquisition refers to the process of getting a new customer.

Acquisition channel: a method by which a company acquires new customers. The most common acquisition channels include paid advertising, organic search engine optimization, and referrals from current customers.

Affiliate marketing: a type of marketing in which companies pay others to refer customers to their products or services.

AIDA: a model that describes the stages that a customer goes through when making a purchase decision. It stands for Attention, Interest, Desire, and Action.

Analytics: the process of gathering and analyzing data in order to understand what it means and how it can be used to improve business results.

Audience: in marketing, the people or businesses who are the target of a marketing campaign.

Awareness: the knowledge that a customer has about a particular product or service.

B2B (business to business): transactions between businesses, rather than between a business and individual consumers.

B2C (business to consumer): transactions between a business and individual consumers.

Banner or display ad: a type of online advertisement that is displayed on a web page. Banner ads are typically rectangular and can be static or animated.

Bounce: in web analytics, a term that refers to when a visitor exits a website after viewing only one page. In email marketing, a bounce is when an email is not delivered to the recipient's inbox.

Bounce rate: the percentage of website visitors who leave the site after viewing only one page.

Brand: the name, term, design, symbol, or other feature that identifies one seller's product or service as different from those of other sellers. Also the emotional, cognitive, and social associations that a customer has with a given brand.

Brand awareness: the degree to which a customer is aware of a particular brand and its products or services.

Branding: the process of creating a unique identity for a product or company.

Brand loyalty: the degree to which a customer is loyal to a particular brand and its products or services.

CAC (customer acquisition cost): the total cost of acquiring a new customer.

Campaign: in marketing, a specific effort to achieve a particular goal, such as increasing sales or raising awareness about a product or service.

Churn: the percentage of customers who discontinue using a product or service.

CMO (Chief Marketing Officer): the executive responsible for overseeing all marketing activities within a company.

Competitive analysis: the process of studying the strategies and tactics used by one's competitors in order to identify potential areas of opportunity.

Competitor analysis: the study of a company's competitors in order to understand their strengths and weaknesses.

Consideration: the point at which a customer begins to think seriously about purchasing a product or service.

Content calendar: a planning document that outlines all the content that will be published on a website or blog over a given period of time. A content calendar can help to ensure that there is sufficient variety and volume of content, as well as track deadlines and publish dates.

Content marketing: a type of marketing that focuses on creating and sharing valuable content with the goal of attracting and retaining customers.

Conversion: when site visitors or other prospects complete a desired action, such as filling out a form or making a purchase.

Conversion funnel: a diagram that illustrates the steps a customer takes to complete a desired action, such as making a purchase.

Conversion rate: the percentage of site visitors or other prospects who complete the desired action.

Cookies: small files that are placed on a customer's computer by websites in order to track their behavior and preferences.

CPA (cost per acquisition): how much it costs to acquire a new customer, typically calculated by dividing marketing expenses by the number of new customers acquired in a given period.

CPC (cost per click): how much an advertiser pays each time someone clicks on one of its ads.

CPL (cost per lead): how much it costs to generate a new lead, typically calculated by dividing marketing expenses by the number of leads generated in a given period.

CPM (cost per thousand impressions): how much an advertiser pays each time its ad is shown 1,000 times.

Creative: in marketing, a creative is a piece of content such as a blog post, video, or email that is designed to generate interest in a product or service.

CTA (call to action): a text or graphic that encourages site visitors to take a specific action, such as making a purchase or subscribing to a newsletter.

Customer experience (CX): the sum total of all the interactions that a customer has with a company and its products or services. These interactions can take place in person, online, or via other channels. Also, the art and science of optimizing this experience.

Customer journey: the path that a customer takes from first hearing about a product or service to becoming a paying customer.

Customer journey map: a visual representation of the steps a customer takes from their first interaction with your company to becoming a loyal customer.

Customer lifetime value (CLV): a measure of the total value a customer brings to a company over the course of their relationship with the business. This metric can be used to determine how much money a company should spend on marketing in order to acquire new customers.

Customer loyalty: a measure of how likely customers are to continue doing business with a company. Customer loyalty can be measured by surveys, customer retention rates, and the amount of money customers spend on products and services.

Customer relationship management: (CRM) the process of managing customer interactions and data in order to improve business results.

Demographics: the study of population characteristics, including age, sex, income, and education level. Demographic information can be used to target marketing campaigns.

Direct marketing: a type of marketing that involves sending individualized messages directly to potential customers.

Drip campaign: a series of automated emails that are sent to a prospect over a period of time.

Email marketing: the process of sending emails to a list of subscribers in order to promote a product or service. Email marketing can be used to build relationships with customers, increase brand awareness, and generate sales leads.

Engagement: a measure of how involved people are with a piece of content. Engagement can be measured by looking at factors such as the number of comments, shares, and likes that a post receives.

Flywheel: in inbound marketing, the process of attracting, engaging, and delighting customers. Once a customer is delighted, they will become a promoter of your company and will recommend your products or services to others.

4Cs: the 4Cs of marketing are a framework for understanding how to create value for customers and promote it through the marketplace. They stand for Customer Value, Cost, Convenience, and Communication.

- o Customer value: the degree to which a customer perceives that a product or service is worth the price.
- o Cost: the amount of money that is spent to produce or obtain the product.
- o Convenience: the ease with which a customer can obtain or use the product.
- o Communication: the methods by which a company communicates the value of its product to customers.

4Ps: the 4Ps of marketing are a framework for understanding how to create value for customers and promote it through the marketplace. They stand for Product, Price, Place, and Promotion.

- o Product: the good or service that is being offered to customers.
- o Price: the cost to purchase or use the product.
- o Place: the location where the product can be found or used.
- o Promotion: the methods by which a company communicates the value of its product to customers.

Gated content: content that is available only to people who complete a specific action, such as registering for a website or downloading a white paper.

Generating leads: getting potential customers to provide their contact information so that they can be contacted by a sales representative.

Google Ads: a service offered by Google that allows businesses to place ads on Google.com and millions of other websites across the web.

Google Analytics: a free analytics tool offered by Google that helps businesses track website traffic and measure the effectiveness of their marketing efforts.

Inbound marketing: a type of marketing that focuses on attracting customers through content such as blogs, podcasts, and social media posts.

IP address: a unique identifier assigned to devices that connect to the internet. IP addresses can be used to track website traffic and measure the effectiveness of marketing campaigns.

Kano model: a framework for understanding how customers perceive the quality of a product. It breaks down quality into three categories: basic needs, performance, and excitement.

Key performance indicator (KPI): a metric that is used to measure the success of a marketing campaign or initiative. KPIs can vary depending on the goals of a given campaign.

Keyword: in search marketing, a keyword is a word or phrase that people type into a search engine to find information.

Lead: the name and contact information of an individual who has indicated an interest in your product or service.

Lead generation: the process of obtaining leads from potential customers. This can be done through various methods, such as online surveys or email lists.

Lead nurturing: the process of developing relationships with potential customers who have inquired about a product or service. This can involve providing them with additional information or trying to persuade them to make a purchase.

Market basket analysis: a technique used to study the items that are purchased together. This information can be used to identify potential customer segments and create marketing messages that appeal to them.

Marketing automation: the use of software to automate certain marketing tasks, such as email marketing or social media campaigns.

Marketing channel: a method of reaching potential customers, such as television advertising, online advertising, or social media marketing.

Marketing funnel: a diagram that illustrates the customer journey, from awareness to purchase and beyond.

Marketing mix: the combination of marketing tools used to achieve a company's marketing goals. The four main components of the marketing mix are product, price, place, and promotion.

Marketing plan: a document that outlines a company's marketing goals and strategies for achieving them.

Marketing research: the process of gathering information about a target market and using that information to create a marketing strategy.

Media buying: the process of purchasing advertising space or time from TV, radio, print, or online outlets.

Media efficiency ratio: the ratio of marketing expenses to the number of leads or customers generated.

Medium: the means by which a message is delivered, such as television, radio, print, or online.

Metrics: in marketing, metrics are quantitative measurements used to track the performance of marketing campaigns and activities. Examples of marketing metrics include website traffic, conversion rates, and email open rates.

Microconversion: a conversion that takes place on a small scale, such as subscribing to a blog or downloading a white paper.

Microsite: a website that is dedicated to a single topic or product.

Mindshare: the percentage of a market's attention that is focused on a particular brand or product.

Multi-touch attribution: attributing marketing ROI to the range of engagements, or "touches" from a brand that a customer encounters during the customer journey.

Multivariate testing: a type of testing in which multiple versions of a website or email are tested at the same time. This type of testing can be used to determine which version of a website or email is most effective.

Open rate: the percentage of people who open an email that was sent to them.

Optimization: the process of making changes to a website or other marketing campaign in order to improve its performance.

Opt-in: the act of voluntarily providing one's contact information, such as an email address or phone number, to a company in order to receive future communications from it.

Opt-out: the act of refusing to provide one's contact information to a company, either by not providing it when asked or by unsubscribing.

Organic keywords: keywords that are not paid for, but their appearance in search is instead earned through good SEO practices.

Organic search: the unpaid results that are displayed in a search engine in response to a query. These results are generated by algorithms that consider the relevance of a website to the keywords used in the search.

Organic social media: social media posts that are not paid for, but instead are generated by the company's social media team or by customers who mention the company on their own profiles.

Outbound marketing: a type of marketing that involves reaching out to potential customers through methods such as telemarketing, direct mail, and non-targeted advertising.

Pageviews: the number of times a web page is loaded in a browser. Pageviews can be used to measure the popularity of a website or the effectiveness of online marketing campaigns.

Paid search: a form of online advertising that involves paying a search engine to display your company's ads when people search for specific keywords.

Paid social media: advertising that is purchased on social media platforms such as Facebook, Twitter, and LinkedIn. It can be used to drive traffic to a website, increase brand awareness, or generate leads.

Pay per click (PPC): a type of online advertising in which companies pay a fee each time someone clicks on their ad. PPC is often used to target potential customers who are already interested in the product or service being offered.

Persona: a fictional character who represents a segment of the target audience.

PESO: a marketing model that uses four channels to reach customers: Paid, Earned, Shared, and Owned media.

Pillar page: a type of content that provides an overview of a topic and is designed to rank high in search engine results. A pillar page typically provides a summary of a topic, and contains links to other pages on the same topic.

Point-of-sale (POS): systems used by retail businesses to track sales and inventory. A point-of-sale system typically consists of a cash register, a computer, touch screen, barcode scanner, and printer. Modern POS systems can also include features such as a customer loyalty program, credit card processing, and digital receipts.

Positioning: the process of defining how a company or product is perceived by the public. This can involve creating a unique selling proposition or targeting a specific audience.

Pricing strategy: the decision-making process involved in setting prices for a company's products or services.

Product management: the process of overseeing the development and marketing of a product from conception to release.

Product marketing: the process of creating and implementing plans to market specific products or product lines.

Psychographics: the study of people's lifestyles, values, and interests. Psychographic information can be used to create targeted marketing campaigns.

Public relations (PR): the practice of building positive relationships with the media and other public outlets in order to promote a company or product.

Referral: in marketing, referral refers to the process of getting customers to refer other people to a company or product.

Retargeting: the practice of targeting ads to individuals who have visited your website or clicked on one of your ads in the past. This type of advertising can be used to increase the likelihood that a visitor will convert into a customer.

Retention: in marketing, retention refers to the process of keeping current customers.

Retention rate: the percentage of customers who remain loyal to a company over a given period of time.

ROAS (return on ad spend): a measure of how effective a given marketing campaign is in terms of generating revenue.

ROI (return on investment): the ratio of profits generated to the amount of money invested in a given venture or campaign, typically expressed as a percentage.

Segmentation: the process of dividing a population into smaller groups, or segments, based on shared characteristics.

Sentiment analysis: a technique used to determine the tone of online conversations about a company or product. This information can be used to identify potential areas of concern or opportunity.

SEO (search engine optimization): the process of improving the ranking of a website on search engines such as Google and Bing through the use of keyword usage, backlinks, and other tactics. Also can be defined as the process of improving a website's visibility and ranking in search engine results pages.

SERP (search engine results page): the page displayed by a search engine in response to a query, containing a list of the websites that were found to be the most relevant.

Sessions: in web analytics, a session is defined as a group of interactions that take place on a website within a given time period. A session ends when there is no activity on the website for a set amount of time. A session can include multiple pageviews, events, and transactions.

Share of voice: a metric that measures a company's share of the total conversation about its products or services online.

Social CRM (social customer relationship management): the process of managing customer interactions and data across social media channels.

Social listening: the process of tracking and analyzing conversations about a company or product on social media. Social listening can be used to identify customer complaints, understand customer sentiment, and track the effectiveness of marketing campaigns.

Social media marketing: the use of social media platforms to promote a company or product. This can involve creating and publishing content, running ads, or engaging with customers on social media.

Tagline: a short phrase that encapsulates the essence of a company or product.

Target market: the specific group of people or businesses that a company is trying to reach with its marketing efforts.

Testing: in marketing, the process of experimenting with different variables in order to determine which ones produce the desired results.

Unique selling proposition: a statement that describes what makes a company or product different from its competitors.

URL (uniform resource locator): the address of a specific web page or file on the internet.

User experience (UX): the overall experience a customer has when interacting with a company's products or services. Good UX is essential for keeping customers engaged and encouraging them to return.

Web analytics: the collection and analysis of data about how people use websites. This information can be used to improve website design, understand customer behavior, and measure the effectiveness of online marketing campaigns.

Word-of-mouth marketing: the process of marketing a product or service through word-of-mouth referrals from current customers. Word-of-mouth marketing is typically the most effective type of marketing.

YMOYL (your money or your life data): a term used in data analytics to describe the most sensitive data for consumers. YMOYL data includes information about customer finances and health.

INDEX

Printed in the USA
CPSIA information can be obtained
at www.ICGtesting.com
JSHW071546300823
47570JS00011B/221